American River College Library
4700 College Oak Drive
Sacramento, CA 95841

The Great American
Crime Decline

Franklin E. Zimring

The Great American Crime Decline

OXFORD
UNIVERSITY PRESS

2007

OXFORD
UNIVERSITY PRESS

Oxford University Press, Inc., publishes works that further
Oxford University's objective of excellence
in research, scholarship, and education.

Oxford New York
Auckland   Cape Town   Dar es Salaam   Hong Kong   Karachi
Kuala Lumpur   Madrid   Melbourne   Mexico City   Nairobi
New Delhi   Shanghai   Taipei   Toronto

With offices in
Argentina   Austria   Brazil   Chile   Czech Republic   France   Greece
Guatemala   Hungary   Italy   Japan   Poland   Portugal   Singapore
South Korea   Switzerland   Thailand   Turkey   Ukraine   Vietnam

Copyright © 2007 by Oxford University Press, Inc.

Published by Oxford University Press, Inc.
198 Madison Avenue, New York, New York 10016

www.oup.com

Oxford is a registered trademark of Oxford University Press

All rights reserved. No part of this publication may be reproduced,
stored in a retrieval system, or transmitted, in any form or by any means,
electronic, mechanical, photocopying, recording, or otherwise,
without the prior permission of Oxford University Press.

Library of Congress Cataloging-in-Publication Data
Zimring, Franklin E.
The great American crime decline / Franklin E. Zimring.
p. cm.— (Studies in crime and public policy)
Includes bibliographical references and index.
ISBN-13 978-0-19-518115-9
1. Crime— United States— History— 20th century.   2. United
States— Economic conditions— 1981–2001.   3. United
States— Social conditions— 1980–   I. Title.   II. Series.
HV6783.Z56 2007
364.97309′049—dc22   2006012374

3 5 7 9 8 6 4 2
Printed in the United States of America
on acid-free paper

Preface

The crime decline that is the subject of this book started quietly. The rate of reported crimes in the United States dropped each year after 1991 for nine years in a row, the longest decline ever recorded. This was a big drop in two other respects. The rates of every serious offense dropped in the United States, even though there are no close or obvious connections between violent offenses, such as homicide and rape, and common theft. And crime dropped all over the United States—in every region, in the country as well as the city, in poor neighborhoods as well as rich neighborhoods. By the start of the twenty-first century, most serious crime rates had dropped by more than 35%.

The great American crime decline was a surprise when it began and is a mystery to this day. No experts were predicting declining crime for the 1990s, and few observers paid much attention to the accumulating good news even during the first four years of the drop. Fifteen years after the decline began, there is little consensus among experts about what changes in circumstances produced the crime decline or what is likely to happen next. Sadly, this lack of consensus has not inspired extraordinary efforts by government or social science to focus scientific resources and attention on study of this remarkable chapter of American history.

This book is my attempt to understand the mysterious good news from the 1990s. The major subjects of my study were the character, the causes, and the consequences of the crime decline, but my research then led to broader conclusions about the nature of crime in America. For the long run, these broader conclusions may be of more importance to criminology and to public policy.

With respect to the causes of the crime decline, there are plenty of plausible candidates to take some credit for the 1990s, including a decline in the proportion of the population in its high-risk younger years, a substantial expansion of the population incarcerated, and the longest economic boom of the past half-century. But even with this bumper crop of likely causes, my analysis of crime cycles in Canada suggests that cyclical forces that are not the result of crime policy changes, population trends, or the economy could be responsible for almost half of the U.S. decline.

The consequences of sharply lower crime rates deserve much more attention than they have received. The crime decline was the only public benefit of the 1990s whereby the poor and disadvantaged received more direct benefits than those with wealth. Because violent crime is a tax of which the poor pay much more, general crime declines also benefit the poor, as likely victims, most intensely. And impoverished minority males in big cities also benefited from less risk of both victimization and offense. The crime decline among younger persons not yet committed to criminal careers was greater than the aggregate crime drop, because those in the middle of active criminal careers do not alter their personal behavior as quickly as the general rates drop.

The two most important lessons from the 1990s are the room for further crime decline that most communities have even now, and the loose linkage between the demographic and social structures of American urban life and any particular level of crime. Relatively small changes in urban environments can produce 75% reductions in crime. The sharpest declines that big cities experienced in the 1990s could not have happened if crime was an inherent byproduct of urban disadvantage. That is the biggest story from the 1990s and an important lesson for the American future.

The book is divided into four two-chapter installments. Part I provides the vital statistics on the national crime decline and shows how crime trends can bias public and expert assumptions about the power of government to control crime. Part II is a critical survey of published explanations of the causes of the 1990s decline. The third part of the book presents two new perspectives on U.S. crime trends, based on studies of Canada and New York City. The last part applies the lessons of this study to the current and future circumstances of crime in the United States.

Acknowledgments

The events, institutions, and people who conspired to help me produce this study in 25 months deserve much more than my brief thanks. My first effort to collect and evaluate materials on the 1990s crime decline was to prepare a six-hour review for a seminar on empirical research on crime and criminal justice that Joan Petersilia, Simon Cole, and I offered at the Department of Criminology, Law and Society at the University of California, Irvine, in the winter of 2004. That experience was the sine qua non for this book, the jump start without which the project would not have been launched.

My return to Berkeley in June 2004 was well timed to continue a major research project. A new dean at Boalt Hall, Christopher Edley, Jr., provided expanded support to the program in criminal justice studies and created, with Werner and Mimi Wolfen, the Wolfen Research Scholar designation, which supported the writing and rewriting of the volume. I hope that I have provided a good start to the Wolfen program; it has certainly provided a terrific boost to the completion of this venture.

The special studies reported in chapters 5 and 6 required and received help from research fellows of the Boalt Hall Criminal Justice Research Program in far-flung outposts. Professor Anthony Doob of the University of

Toronto facilitated a study of Canadian crime patterns and hosted my presentation to the Institute of Criminology in March of 2005. Carolyn Greene, a doctoral student at Toronto, became a careful and creative student of Canadian crime and criminal justice. Without her efforts, chapter 5 could not have happened. Jeffrey Fagan of Columbia University has been helping me study crime and violence in New York City for a decade. His fingerprints are all over chapter 6 of this book.

The materials in chapter 4 on fertility, abortion, and crime in the United States and several other developed nations required help from a demographer and data from many different nations. It was my good luck to find and employ Bryan Lamont Sykes, a doctoral student in demography at Berkeley, and then to interest him in conducting independent research on the issue of fertility control and its eventual impact on crime rates.

I was also ruthless in seeking help from friends and colleagues to obtain data on the age distribution of criminal populations in Europe and Australia. Pat Mayhew, now at Victoria University in Wellington, New Zealand, helped me locate data sources in Great Britain and Australia. I only hope her sterling reputation in both nations has survived association with the project. Cristina de Maglie at the University of Pavia found the national statistics for Italy. My colleague Loic Wacquant at Berkeley led me to French data. Jenny Mouzos of the Australian Institute of Criminology, Suzanne Poynton and Sarah Williams of the New South Wales Bureau of Crime Statistics and Research, Laurent Mucchielli of the Centre de Recherches Sociologiques sur le Droit et les Institutions Péénales (CNRS/Ministèère de la Justice), and Chris Kershaw and Kathryn Coleman of the British Home Office provided statistical access and data. This project is further evidence that on the smaller planet we now inhabit, all studies of crime and criminal justice must have a comparative dimension.

I have already mentioned two research assistants (Greene and Sykes) who made the staff of this project both international and interdisciplinary. But the home team of Boalt Hall research help was also creative and multifunctional to an extraordinary extent. Munir Zilanawala, J.D. 2006, Tom Fletcher, J.D. 2007, and Richard M. Oberto, J.D. 2006, were primarily assigned to the project, and Scotia J. Hicks, J.D. 2007, helped with crime data collection.

A medium-sized collection of the usual suspects helps me write, prepare, and revise large lumps of prose, including this one. Dedi Felman of

Oxford University Press was her standard indispensable self in shaping this book. James Cook of Oxford joined the party in 2005 and pushed the project over the finish line. Toni Mendicino of Berkeley's Institute for Legal Research created the manuscript and graphics and maintained many of the electronic data elements of the research project and the book.

Two colleagues, David Johnson and David Sklansky, read the entire manuscript and provided helpful suggestions. Tony Doob and Rosemary Gartner of Toronto provided analysis and suggestions for chapter 5; Jeffrey Fagan, James Jacobs, and Jan Vetter were reader/critics of chapter 6; Richard Rosenthal helped with chapters 3 and 4. Richard A. Berk of the University of California, Los Angeles, provided helpful comments on a late draft of the manuscript.

One other group of scholars provided important help to this venture and should be recognized here, as well as in my frequently acerbic prose in chapters 3–6. The brave and creative criminologists and economists who published accounts of the causes of crime decline are extensively mentioned in this text, but the tone is often critical. In fact, we are all in the debt of Al Blumstein, Rich Rosenfeld, John Donohue, Steve Levitt, and others who took notice of the important events of the 1990s and frequently took risks on paper in exploring the decline. I gratefully salute them, even as I join the ranks of visible scholarly targets for future students of this remarkable chapter in the story of crime in America.

Contents

Part I

What Happened in the 1990s?

Introduction to Part I

These introductory chapters provide a two-part profile of the national crime decline. Chapter 1 concerns the vital statistics of changing patterns of crime in the United States, placing the crime drop of the 1990s in historical and statistical context. The statistics in chapter 1 produce a much clearer picture of the central questions considered in the rest of the book. Chapter 2 explores the impact of crime trends on the attitudes of policy actors and experts about whether government policy can reduce crime. I show that sustained crime increases invite observers to conclude that "nothing works," while cascades of good news encourage optimistic assessments about the ability of governments to control crime and the capacity of experts to understand crime trends. This is one reason that many observers express confidence in their ability to understand the crime declines of the 1990s, despite the fact that nobody had predicted that a major crime drop was on the horizon.

The Size and Character
of the Crime Decline

1

This chapter aims to be more than a statistical profile of how crime dropped in the 1990s, although there will be plenty of statistics used in the analysis. What I hope to describe is the character of the crime decline, and to do this I present statistics that illustrate the size, the range of offenses, and the length of the decline and how those features set what happened between 1991 and 2000 apart from other eras in modern American history. What the chapter examines is not simply the numbers but how the peculiar facts of the 1990s can help us understand the nature of the crime decline.

The chapter begins with a series of statistical accounts of the 1990s, showing the patterns revealed by each of the vital statistics in the survey. A second section steps back from the individual statistical analysis to suggest three broader lessons to be drawn from the collective impact of several different analyses. While the numbers in this first chapter are by no means the end of the story about causes or consequences, they provide a clear picture of the phenomenon at the center of this study, and frame the much more specific questions that the rest of the book will address. The data show a very substantial and nationwide drop, across all categories of serious crimes, steadily progressing through the decade. It is also a decline that came as a total surprise to all the professional observers of crime and criminal justice in the United States.

Some Statistical Background

For most of American history, the measurement of crime and violence was not possible with any precision at the local level, and meaningful national statistics on crime and violence have been created only in the last generation. The two centuries without significant American crime statistics were a product of both political and methodological problems. The only agencies that receive regular reports of most criminal events are local police departments, where the measurement of crime trends is a low priority, and conflicts of interest may exist because trends in crime can be used to evaluate police performance; and police are not well-trained statisticians. The local nature of crime data means that different places will often use different criteria of crime classification, and aggregating local statistics into state and national totals was therefore a high-risk venture even after the Federal Bureau of Investigation (FBI) tried to impose common standards and definitions. The FBI Uniform Crime Reporting program started in the 1930s but acquired credibility only much later for most offenses.

For one crime, however, good reports can be found outside the police. Because criminal homicides also generate death statistics, the national health statistics vital statistics program created a separate system of death reporting and classification for them at the county level and reported them nationally. After 1933, this information was reported for all states.

The local nature of government responsibility for crime reporting was paralleled by a tradition that crime policy was considered a local concern. One reason that little attention was paid to national-level crime measurement until the middle of the twentieth century was the absence of concern about crime as a national problem. Only in the 1920s and 1930s did crime emerge as a national political issue.

Among the range of offenses for which the FBI attempts to compute a crime rate by adding up crimes reported to the police, the two offenses with the best reputation for accuracy are homicide (because of its importance and the presence in most cases of a body) and auto theft (because of widespread insurance). At the other end of the scale are rape (because of victim reluctance to report) and larceny (not important to most victims and easy to manipulate). Of course, this statistical report card excludes the incidence of crimes without victims willing to report them, such as drugs and prostitution. These simply cannot be measured by police statistics.

Homicide Trends

I start this inquiry about crime in the 1990s with the best reported data set, the vital statistics data on homicide. Figure 1.1 shows trends in homicide for all the years after 1950, which was 17 years after the national death registry was reported to be complete.

In an abbreviated telling of the story, the half-century divides into two trendless periods—one prior to 1964 and another between 1974 and 1993—and two clear trends: one a decade after 1964, when the homicide rate more than doubled, and the period after 1991, when it dropped consistently. Even with more than 2,800 killings from the attack on September 11, 2001, the homicide rate that year was more than 30% lower than the periodic peak rates that were the top portions of the 20-year cycle that began in the mid-1970s.

There is in the entire post-1950s period only one other time period that might qualify as a downward crime trend, the four years after 1980; but that decline lasted only half as long. Further, the next upturn in the late 1980s brought homicide quickly up to almost the same peak rate area in 1991 as 1980 and 1974.

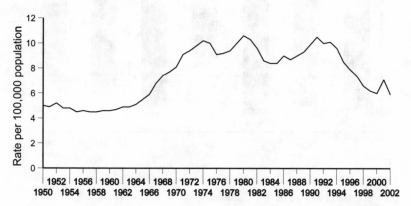

Figure 1.1. Homicide rate (NVSS), United States, 1950–2002. Source: National Center for Health Statistics. 2005. *Health, United States, 2005.* Hyattsville, Md.

How Big a Decline?

The scale of figure 1.1 provides a useful context for estimating the size of the decline in homicide after 1991. The increase in homicides in the decade after 1964 was just over 100%. The magnitude of the decline after 1992 was more than 70% as large as that increase—by 2002, the homicide rate in the United States was only 15–20% higher than in the early 1960s.

How Broad a Decline?

While homicides are the most serious crimes in the United States, they are a tiny part of the statistical tapestry of crime in America. One obvious question in measuring the crime trends of the 1990s is to determine how broadly the downward trend ranged across the spectrum of well-reported crimes. This type of investigation must leave behind the vital statistics, which only report deaths, in favor of police statistics and a national program of surveys of households that measures crime victimization for persons over 12 years of age.

The official crime reporting system for most offenses in the United States is the FBI's Uniform Crime Reports (UCRs), which focus on a category of eight "index" crimes. Not all the "index" crimes are serious (any theft offense is included in larceny), but all of the most serious ordinary crimes are included in the index category. Figure 1.2 launches the inquiry by

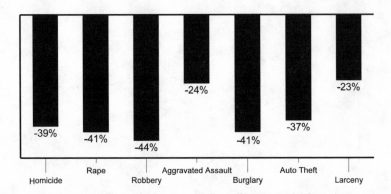

Figure 1.2. Everything goes down in the 1990s. Source: U.S. Department of Justice. Federal Bureau of Investigation. 1990, 2000. *Uniform Crime Report.* Washington, D.C.

comparing trends in all seven of the traditional FBI crime index offenses, comparing the census years 1990 and 2000. An eighth offense, arson, new to the FBI index, is excluded from the comparison.

The rate of all seven offenses reported in figure 1.3 declined significantly over the 1990s, with the aggregate declines ranging from 23% to 44%. For five of the seven offenses, the declines are of similar magnitudes— homicide, rape, robbery, burglary, and auto theft all report declines quite close to 40%. This group includes the two offenses with the best reputations for accuracy—the violent offense of homicide and the oft-reported property offense of auto theft.

The two crimes with markedly smaller declines were aggravated assault (down 24%) and larceny (down 23%). Aggravated assault is the most frequent of the violent crimes used in the crime index. Attacks where the use of a deadly weapon is threatened or occurs or where serious injury is intended or inflicted are the bulk of aggravated assaults reported in the United States. The border between simple and aggravated assault is difficult to determine, and trends in aggravated assault are frequently a puzzle (Zimring 1998, p. 93).

Larceny is by far the most common crime reported to the police everywhere and is also the least harmful of the crimes with definite victims. By itself, the number of larcenies reported to police in the United States forms the bulk of all index crime, about 60% of reported index felonies in 2000. The reason for this huge statistical impact is that larcenies of all sizes are counted into the crime index, in contrast to the treatment of the assault offense, which police exclude from the crime index if they classify an attack as a simple rather than "aggravated" assault.

The rationale for this inclusive approach for larceny is a cautionary tale about reforms in crime statistical reporting. The reason even small thefts have been counted in the index total since 1973 is that in prior years, when the FBI only counted larceny in the serious index category if the value of the properly taken was over $50, police departments could keep their reported offense rates low by underestimating the values of stolen properties (Seideman and Couzens 1974). To get around this problem, since 1973 the FBI has included in the index of all serious crimes a mass of thefts far more frequently petty than grand.

The smaller decline in larceny does mean that the aggregate number of offenses known to the police has not dropped as fast as the rates of offenses like robbery and burglary, but most serious crimes feared by the public ("fear" crimes) dropped by 40% during the 1990s, and in that sense, the larger declines are clustered just where most citizens would want them to occur (Zimring and Hawkins 1997, ch. 1).

Victim Surveys

When the focus shifts from crimes known to the police to the estimates from household surveys, the trends are substantially confirmed. Figure 1.3 compares the trends over the period 1990–2000 for the police data reported in the UCRs and the household survey data reported by the Bureau of Justice Statistics (BJS).

The crime declines estimated from the household survey are equal to or greater than the police statistics in all six crime categories, with the survey showing much larger declines in larceny, assault, and rape. The victim surveys not only confirm the trends found in the police data but also move the larceny and assault declines much closer to the average declines for other index crimes than do the police statistics. If we regard the National Survey data as a test of the size and breadth of the decline shown by police reports, it is a test that the crime decline passes with flying colors. If police statistics are to be faulted, it is that they underestimate the downtrend in assault, rape, and larceny.

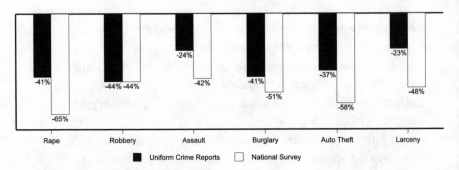

Figure 1.3. Official versus victim survey estimates of crime decline, United States, 1990–2000. Sources: U.S. Department of Justice. Federal Bureau of Investigation. 1990, 2000. *Uniform Crime Report.* Washington, D.C. U.S. Department of Justice. Bureau of Justice Statistics. 1990, 2000. *National Crime Victimization Survey.* Washington, D.C.

What Happened in the 1990s?

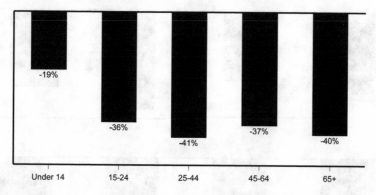

Figure 1.4. Trends of homicide victimization by age of victim, United States, 1990–2000. Source: National Center for Health Statistics. 2005. *Health, United States, 2005.* Hyattsville, Md.

The Demography of Decline

There are also encouraging signs that the benefits of lower crime rates have been spread widely across the social and demographic categories of the American nation. My focus in reporting on these matters will be on homicide, both because it is the ultimate fear crime and also because homicide statistics include many killings of victims of other offenses, most often robbery and assault but also sex offenses. In this sense, homicide trends also measure variations in other violent crimes.

Figure 1.4 shows 10-year trends of homicide victimization by age of victim.

With the exception of children under 14, where the rate decline was 19%, the relative declines in homicide victimization are extraordinarily flat, ranging only between 36 and 41%. This does not mean that homicide risks are spread evenly across age groups—rates of youth and young adults are much higher at both the beginning and the end of the 1990s—but the evenness of the decline over time of relative risk is impressive.

The pattern over time is slightly different when the declines in homicide victimizations are disaggregated by gender, by race and by city size (fig. 1.5).

The decrease in homicide for men is 42%, one-third more than for women. The decrease for nonwhites is 46%, again one-third more than the decline for whites, and the decline in big cities is 49%, much more than the drop in other cities, in suburbs, or in rural areas. The higher the rate

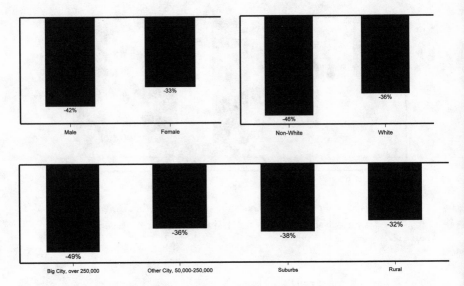

Figure 1.5. Homicide declines by demographic detail, United States, 1990–2000. Source: National Center for Health Statistics. 2005. *Health, United States, 2005.* Hyattsville, Md.

of homicide in 1990, the bigger the drop in the rate over the next 10 years. This is of critical importance, because it suggests that the benefits of the crime decline are concentrated in those groups with the highest exposure to crime.

Regional and City-Level Trends

The 10-year trends for the six index crimes other than larceny are shown by region in figure 1.6.

The pattern of decline by region is even, with one exception: the Northeast shows higher than usual declines for homicide, auto theft, and burglary. Only the UCRs statistics can be broken down by region, so that there is no independent measure to test against variations produced by the police statistics.

With respect to auto theft, the decline in the northeastern region is twice that of other regions, while the Northeast shows a 20–30% advantage for homicide and burglary. Except for this northeastern edge, there are no consistent regional patterns. Because very large cities have a substantial impact on the UCRs crime categories, it is prudent to defer discussion of the Northeast until I have identified and discussed the New York City pattern.

What Happened in the 1990s?

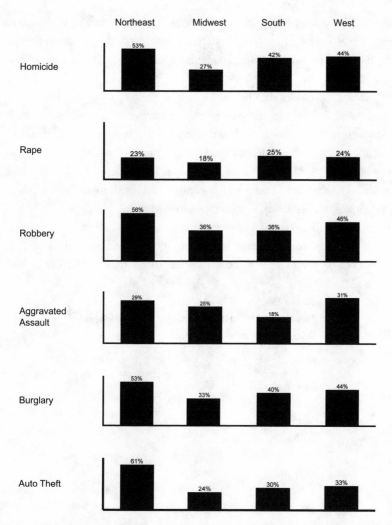

Figure 1.6. Regional trends in Uniform Crime Report crime, 1990–2000. Source: U.S. Department of Justice. Federal Bureau of Investigation. 1990, 2000. *Uniform Crime Report.* Washington, D.C.

Crime Trends in Big Cities

The crime trends in big cities are an important element of the national crime picture in eras of good and bad news. When high crime rates are a focus of public concern, media pay particular attention to which large American city is described as the nation's "murder capital." When crime rates fall, the experiences of particular cities may again play an important role in public discussion. In the late 1990s, the experience of the nation's largest city—New York—was of particular interest to those tracking crime trends. As I will show, this special attention was appropriate, given the singular performance of New York City crime.

Table 1.1 provides data on the average ranking of each of 15 large cities for the decline in seven crime categories. (Data were not available for both comparison years for the fifteenth largest city, Jacksonville, Florida; so Columbus, Ohio, the sixteenth largest city in 1990, is substituted for Jacksonville in table 1.1.) The ranks I use in table 1.1 test each of these cities against the other 14 to find out how evenly distributed the drop was in big-city crime. If all the nation's large cities averaged a rank of between 6 and 8 in the table, no cities stand out as either leaders or laggards in the comparison.

If we search for large cities with the best crime decline records, we find table 1.1 to be one of several indicators that shows the city of New York to

Table 1.1
Average rank of crime decline for seven offenses, 15 largest U.S. cities, 1990–2000.

	Average rank
New York City	1.6
San Diego	4.4
San Francisco	5.4
Dallas	5.6
Los Angeles	6.0
Houston	6.3
San Antonio	6.8
San Jose	6.9
Chicago	8.8
Indianapolis	9.9
Phoenix	9.9
Detroit	11.3
Columbus	11.6
Philadelphia	12.3
Baltimore	12.7

Source: U.S. Department of Justice. *Uniform Crime Report* 1990 and 2000. Washington, D.C.: U.S. Government Printing Office.

Ranks derived from index crime rate declines for seven offenses (excludes arson).

What Happened in the 1990s?

be literally in a class by itself. Across the seven FBI index crimes, the average rank for New York City was 1.6 out of 15, showing that this city was almost uniform in reporting the largest or second largest decline among the 15 biggest cities in the nation for a variety of different crimes. The next best performance by a major city was that of San Diego, but the distance between the average rank of New York and San Diego was almost three full ranks. San Diego's rank (and San Francisco's) shows that these cities consistently scored in the top third in crime reduction among major American cities over the 1990s. New York is consistently at the very top, recording the highest level of crime decline in four of the seven categories (homicide, robbery, auto theft, and burglary), recording the second highest in two (rape and assault), and falling to third only once (for larceny). While Baltimore scores the lowest of the 15 cities, we don't observe the same extreme values at the bottom of the distribution as there are at the top.

Figure 1.7 shows the relative magnitude of the official records of crime decline in New York City by comparing the percentage decline in New York police statistics with the decline noted in the rest of the United States over the period 1990–2000.

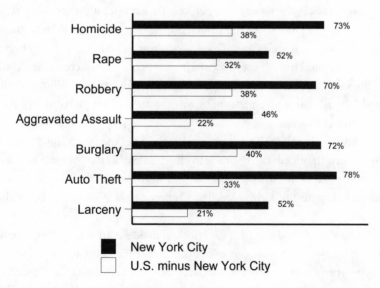

Figure 1.7. Percentage declines in New York City and the rest of the reporting areas in the United States, 1990–2000. Source: U.S. Department of Justice. Federal Bureau of Investigation. 1990, 2000. *Uniform Crime Report.* Washington, D.C.

While there is some variance by type of crime, the best rule of thumb for comparing the magnitude of New York City's crime decline to that of the rest of the United States is that any crime drop for the rest of the United States is doubled in New York City. While homicide is down 38% in the rest of the nation, it drops 73% in the nation's largest city. And the highest magnitudes of decline are found in traditionally well-reported categories with independent data sources for confirmation, such as auto theft (−78%) and homicide (−73%).

There are two further indications of the special nature of New York City's performance in the 15-city comparison. First, a review of the rest of the large city records provides reasons to doubt that New York was helped in its exceptional record by strong regional trends. Philadelphia, the closest big city to New York, had a relatively poor performance over the 1990s. Baltimore, much further south, did not fare better. Boston was the one other large northeastern city with a strong relative decline (see appendix 4).

By contrast with New York's isolation at the top of the charts, the second, third, and fifth best records in the 1990s belong to West Coast cities, leaving more than a hint that their regional position was related to the relative place of these cities in the crime decline comparison.

A final factor that underscores New York's exceptional status among the large cities in the 1990s is its size. New York is not only a very big city, it is by far the largest city in the United States, larger by itself than the next two cities—Los Angeles and Chicago—combined. All other things being equal, we would not expect to see the largest proportional change in crime in the very largest city. The scale and diversity of a city of 8 million would tend to push the entire metropolis toward an average performance and away from extremes.

But all other things were not equal in the cities during the 1990s. In the same spirit that media were prone to choose a city as the "murder capital" of the United States when crime statistics were issued, New York City was beyond dispute the Crime Decline Capital of the United States in the 1990s.

The size of the New York City decline makes it an important place to search for clues about the causes of declining crime in the 1990s and to examine when trying to observe the effects of lower crime rates on the distribution of crime, on social relations, and on government. Because the declines in New York City were the chief cause of the high declines in auto theft and homicide in the Northeast, the regional patterns observed in the previous section are better understood as a New York City effect. Chapter 6 of this book will examine the New York City experience in detail.

Some International Comparisons

One natural question to consider is whether the declines noted during the 1990s have any parallels in other developed nations. Table 1.2 approaches this question by profiling trends in reported crime for five of the six nations other than the United States that are included in the "G-7" group of economic powers. Only Germany is absent from the table, because the re-unification of Germany at the start of the 1990s made a valid statistical portrait of crime trends in Germany over the 1990s all but impossible. I use the G-7 nations here because of a focus on this group in some of my earlier comparative work (Zimring and Hawkins 1997) and because nations with similar degrees of economic development appear to be more appropriate for comparative purposes.

Three patterns in table 1.2 deserve mention. The first is that there is no single trend that spans all these developed nations over the 1990s. Homicide rates drop significantly in three of the five nations, but range in the five nations from Italy's drop of 59% to a 34% increase in the United Kingdom. Robbery rates declined by more than half in France during the 1990s, while they more than doubled in the United Kingdom, just across the English Channel. There is no typical pattern.

A second contrast with the American pattern is that most developed nations exhibited much more variation in their trends for different types of crime than did the United States in the 1990s; the United Kingdom was up

Table 1.2

Changes in reported crime in five European countries, 1990–2000.

	Homicide	Robbery	Burglary	Auto theft	Theft
Canada	−34%	−13%	−30%	+26%	−39%
France	−25%	−61%	−11%	n/a	−3%
Italy	−59%	+29%	n/a	n/a	−16%
Japan	+9%	+204%	+26%	n/a	+44%
United Kingdom	+34%	+151%	−21%	−26%	−23%

Source: United Nations Office on Drugs and Crime. 2000. *The Seventh United Nations Survey on Crime Trends and the Operations of Criminal Justice Systems (1998–2000).* Vienna: United Nations Office on Drugs and Crime.

in two crime categories but down in three. Italy had the largest homicide rate decline in the G-7 but a 29% increase in robbery. Japan showed increases in the four crime categories with reporting, but its homicide rate change was slight, while the percentage changes for property crimes were substantial. France had significant declines in homicide and robbery but slight movement in theft and burglary. This pattern in the 1990s parallels an earlier contrast I noted between crime statistics in the United States and other nations. Rates for different types of crime ebb and flow together more often in the United States than in other nations (Zimring and Hawkins 1997, ch. 2). The third pattern worthy of note is the similarity between the United States and Canada. Only the Canadian pattern approached the uniformity and magnitude of the United States declines in the 1990s.

Perhaps it is just a coincidence that the closest nation to the United States pattern of crime decline is our neighbor to the north, but the parallels between these two contiguous nations require scrutiny. Table 1.3 provides a comparison between Canada and the United States for offenses that parallel all seven of the "index offenses" in the United States.

For five of the seven offenses reported in table 1.3, the magnitude of the declines in Canada were quite close to those in United States. For robbery, the Canadian decline was only one-third the size of the U.S. decline, while the Canadian auto theft rates increased in the 1990s. Chapter 5 will provide a detailed comparison of the United States and Canada.

Table 1.3
Aggregate crime trends in the 1990s, United States and Canada.

	United States	Canada
Homicide	−39%	−34%
Rape	−22%	−22%[a]
Aggravated assault	−24%	−62%
Robbery	−44%	−13%
Burglary	−41%	−30%
Auto theft	−37%	+26%
Larceny	−23%	−39%

Source: U.S. Department of Justice. Federal Bureau of Investigation. (1990–2000) Uniform Crime Report. Washington, D.C.: U.S. Government Printing Office. Statistics Canada IMDB (Integrated Meta Database), Ottawa.
[a]Sexual assault in the Canadian statistic.

What Kind of Decline?

The aim of this concluding section is to step back from the specific findings just examined to frame a broader set of questions that later chapters will address. What are some of the important unanswered questions to be confronted when the known facts of the 1990s decline are considered collectively? What is the value of knowing the particular way crime declined in the 1990s when considering possible causes? Why was the decline so totally unexpected?

Open Questions

Now that longer term trends have been examined, it is prudent to reopen three questions: (1) how substantial the drop in crime was during the 1990s, (2) when it began, and (3) when and how the downtrend in crime ended. There is also an open question about the geographical reach of the decline—whether it involved a single country or both the United States and Canada.

One illustration of some of these issues will come from the homicide data included in figure 1.1, although any of the crime trend analyses could be used to the same effect. Homicide had the same size decline as most other index offenses and the same pattern over time.

When the different cyclical ups and downs of homicide rates are taken into account, there are three different plausible starting points in figure 1.8 that could be selected for the homicide decline in the 1990s, and three different magnitudes of decline that match these alternative points of beginning.

The first possible starting date for homicide decline is 1992, the first year that homicide rates were lower than the previous annual total. The obvious advantage of 1992 as a beginning of the decline is the ease of identifying it. The obvious problem is that we might be confusing ordinary cyclical variations without any special causes or substantive implications with the beginning of a decline with discrete causes. If we use total drop after 1991 as the measure of decline, the total drop by 2002 is 41%.

One way to correct for cyclical phenomena is to regard the "real" decline as starting when homicide rates fall below a long-term average for homicide in the United States. If the decline's size and start is estimated from when the rate first dropped under the previous 18-year average for homicide, there is 32% decline that begins in 1995. The justification for

using the 18-year average as a starting point is minimizing cyclical variations. A still more cautious estimate would be to find the point at which the
previous low rate in the 1980s was crossed; in this case, the start year would
be 1996 and the total drop estimated as caused by noncyclical factors would
be 27% rather than 41%. The risk one runs by waiting until homicide
breaks through its previous 25-year low is underestimating both the size
and duration of the noncyclical decline. The risk of assuming that a major
substantive change in U.S. homicide started the first year homicides did not
go up is that we probably overestimate both the size and length of a decline.

Is all this concern about when a "real" decline starts of any importance?
Yes. Ambiguity about when a downtrend that is independent of ordinary
temporal cycles starts is of particular concern in testing theories of the cause
for the decline. If we are testing the impact of job market conditions or punishment trends on homicide, is 1992 the year to expect substantive changes
that have discrete effects, or is it 1995 or 1996, when it is more likely that noncyclical phenomena will be necessary to explain nonusual changes? There is
certainly no reason to suppose that we should ever attribute all of the reduction from any cyclical high point in a crime rate to noncyclical causes.

The Value of Hindsight

To some extent, we can use hindsight to gain confidence that most of the
decline that starts in the early 1990s is noncyclical. Every additional year of
decline, and each increment in total reduction, makes it more likely that
the 1990s are a special period. But can we conclude retrospectively that because so much of the decline is noncyclical, all of it should be regarded as
noncyclical? Probably not. It is likely that cyclical and noncyclical variations overlap in the 1990s, particularly in the early years of the decline. It is
likely that we cannot ever decide with full confidence on a single year or
beginning rate for the starting point of the noncyclical declines that are
launched during the 1990s.

Has the Downturn Ended?

Yet another ambiguity about the crime decline at the center of this study
is when and how it has ended or will end. Putting aside the sharp increase
in homicide rate that was produced when the death toll from homicide

included all the 2001 World Trade Center and Pentagon victims, the first years of the twenty-first century have produced a flat trend line for most national-level crime aggregates. It is difficult to determine whether this level performance is very good news or not. It tells us that crime in the nation remains as low as it has been for a generation, but does it also signal that the era of consecutive declines has ended? I consider this question in detail in chapter 7, and I argue that the national decline did end at the turn of the century.

But if the first years of the new century are in fact the aftermath of the downward trend, they are a very different pattern than the one that followed the steep decline in the 1980s, when crime rates headed up almost as soon as they stopped falling. A flat crime performance would recall the 1950s more than the ups and downs of the two decades after 1974. So one possibility is that the downtrend has already ended in the United States but has been replaced by a trendless "soft landing." The other possibility is that downward momentum might continue later. There is certainly no law of physics that would be violated by further declines in crime in the United States. And the very fact that the terminal phase of a major crime decline is hard to identify with precision is cheerful news: more discrete end stages are easy to identify but generate a larger body count.

The Puzzle of Canada

One final open question about the 1990s concerns the geography of the crime decline. The statistical career of the United States in the 1990s was distinct from the pattern of other developed nations in Europe and from Japan, but Canada experienced a crime decline during the decade that involved both a large number of offenses and a magnitude of decline not far removed from the aggregate U.S. rate. There is more than a possibility that the crime drop during the 1990s was a North American phenomenon that was not confined to the United States, although why contiguous geography might produce similar crime trends is not an easy question to answer. While it seems quite clear that the crime decline involved the whole of the United States, it may have been broader than that. Chapter 5 will explore this two-nation trend, and show its importance to determining what caused the drop in the United States.

A Process, Not an Event

Even if we cannot fix on a single time that the noncyclical decline in crime started or measure with precision the extent to which crime and violence decreased when cyclical change is discounted, there is one very important clue on the face of the 1990s decline that requires emphasis. When the years that make up the most recent decline are compared to earlier fluctuations in crime, what distinguishes the pattern in the 1990s is the length of the decline rather than the rate at which crime went down in one short period of time.

The best comparison for this purpose is with the declines noted in the early years of the 1980s, and the important difference between the two periods is almost always in the length of the decline in crime. Examining the homicide trends in figure 1.8 shows that the 1990s decline in crime was twice as large as the 1980s decline because it was twice as long. The average annual decline noted in the 1990s was, for most offenses, similar to the size of earlier downturns. It was the cumulative impact of a large number of consecutive declines that produced the large aggregate total declines that set the decade apart from every earlier interval of declining crime in the post–World War II era.

So the big crime drop of the 1990s was a gradual and cumulative process rather than a sharp turn that could be clearly associated with a particular

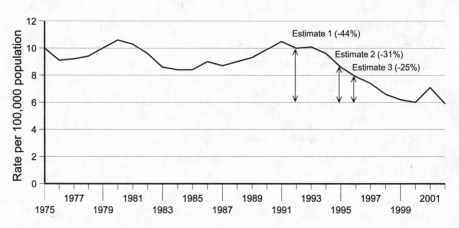

Figure 1.8. Three ways to measure the crime decline. Source: U.S. Department of Justice. Federal Bureau of Investigation. 1975–2002. *Uniform Crime Report.* Washington, D.C.

What Happened in the 1990s?

year or event. This gradual onset and sustained duration is an important defining element of the trend. In searching for causes, we should focus on processes that seem to fit the pattern of the decline. In one sense, the cumulative and gradual nature of the decline makes the search for its antecedents more difficult—we cannot concentrate attention on a single year, and we must look for potential causes that are themselves continuous processes rather than discrete events.

The gradual and continuous character of the changes in crime rate provides, as well, additional evidence against searching for a single cause of the crime decline of the 1990s. Academic experts on crime are rarely unanimous about anything, so that the consensus one finds in the academy against any single-cause explanation of the almost decade-long crime decline is worth close attention. As later chapters will show, different types of social scientists have very different short lists of causes they favor in explaining the crime decline. But there is no plausible single-cause theory found among the analysts who participate in discourse on causes. One reason for the lack of single-cause theories is the incremental pattern that characterized the decline.

Anatomy of a Surprise

One important element of the crime decline documented in this chapter was its singular status as a surprise to criminologists, demographers, policy analysts, and criminal justice planners. None of the talking heads in the crime business saw the crime declines of the 1990s on the horizon. Even more remarkable, the early years of declining crime rates were among the most pessimistic periods about crime in American history. By 1995, when homicide rates had been declining for three years, James Q. Wilson ended his essay "Crime and Public Policy" with the following warning.

> Meanwhile, just beyond the horizon, there lurks a cloud that the winds will soon bring over us. The population will start getting younger again. By the end of this decade there will be a million more people between the ages of fourteen and seventeen than there are now. This extra million will be half male. Six percent of them will become high-rate, repeat offenders—30,000 more young muggers, killers and thieves than we have now. Get ready. (1995, p. 507)

And Professor Wilson was by no means the most pessimistic of his peers. One year later, John DiIulio, then of Princeton University, pushed the horizon forward 10 more years and upped the ante: "By the year 2010, there will be approximately 270,000 more juvenile super-predators on the streets than there were in 1990" (1996, p. 4). James Fox (1996) of Northeastern University projected forward from high rates of youth homicide arrests in the early 1990s to predict "a blood bath" by 2005. The National Center for Juvenile Courts projected a doubling of juvenile arrests by 2010 (Snyder and Sickmund 1995), and the Council on Crime in America, a conservative lobbying group, warned of "a coming storm of juvenile violence" (1996).

Nor were juveniles the only source of public pessimism. The middle 1990s were one of the angriest and most fearful periods in the modern politics of criminal justice—an era of three "strikes and you're out" laws and truth-in-sentencing crusades (Zimring, Hawkins, and Kamin 2001). The United States was well into the 1990s crime decline before anybody noticed.

Only part of the pessimism of the mid-1990s was a result of extrapolation from demographic trends. And the demographic news of the 1990s was not, in hindsight, really bad news at all, as will be shown in chapter 3. The 1990s expansion of the youth population was gradual, with 13- to 17-year-olds projected to grow from 6.7% of the population in 1990 to 7.2% of the population in 2010. Meanwhile, the proportion of the U.S. population aged in the relatively high-crime early twenties fell in the 1990s, because the smaller cohort of those who went through their teens in the 1980s grew into the young adults of the 1990s.

By no means all the criminologists writing about trends in crime and violence in the 1990s were predicting a "coming storm" of violence. At least as many professionals responded to the predictions of superpredators and blood baths with an agnosticism best summed up in a rhyme coined by Norval Morris: "I don't know, and you don't know, and neither does DiIulio!" But even this agnosticism was a far cry from actually predicting a sustained crime decline. Why did nobody see the great crime decline of the 1990s coming?

Three aspects of our attitudes and knowledge about crime conspired to keep the crime decline off the nation's radar screens until five or six years into the decline. The first problem is that we draw our attitudes and expectations about crime from the recent past, and that always produces delay in attitudes catching up with current events. The crime trends that had the greatest impact when Wilson and DiIulio were worrying in the mid-1990s were statistics from the late 1980s and very early 1990s, when youth violence was on the increase. Just as it takes three or four years to notice trends, public perception about crime probably relies on events that have taken the media and opinion leaders years to digest. In this sense, the attitudes, even of experts, are what economists call a "lagging indicator" of crime trends, in that this year's beliefs are most closely tied to the crime events of three or four years ago. That expert opinion lagged behind the downturn in crime is, in this respect, unremarkable.

Second, a long and deep crime decline was unprecedented in the post–World War II history of the United States. The trendless homicide experience of the early 1950s and early 1960s had been followed by a decade of growth and two decades of fluctuation, down from a homicide rate of about 10 per 100,000 per year and then back up.

Prior to 1991, the largest decline of the post-1950 era was four years of dropping crime after 1980, followed by a reversal of direction after 1985 and an increase back to the neighborhood of the 1974 and 1980 highs. If the experience of the 1980s was the applicable precedent, even a sharp decline for four years might prove to be the prologue to another cycle of sharp increases, so the experience of the 1980s may have invited crime experts to discount the significance of the first years of decline in the 1990s. It was only after the crime numbers began to break new ground in 1996 and 1997 that evidence began to accumulate that suggested a nonstandard decline. To the extent that expectations are based on experience, the post–World War II experience of the United States did not include any suggestion that protracted crime declines were a contingency worth considering. The unprecedented crime decline of the 1990s only seemed plausible after it happened.

The third reason that professionals did not see the 1990s decline coming is the absence of good predictive tools for crime forecasting. The list of plausible "leading indicators" of movements in crime rates is short or nonexistent. And one interesting confirmation of the absence of good models for projecting crime rates is the lack of professional chagrin about the failure to predict the protracted 1990s decline. That there is no sign of fault-finding in the professional literature on criminology and crime policy when almost a decade of crime reductions were not anticipated is good evidence that powerful tools for predicting future crime rates did not exist in the early 1990s. Just imagine the professional soul-searching if economic indicators failed to signal a major boom or recession. We do not blame the crime experts for failing to predict the 1990s, because the lack of good leading indicators is an open secret.

The next chapter will show that the long crime declines of the 1990s have made some analysts much more confident in their abilities to predict and influence events but that this kind of optimism may not be warranted. Once we acknowledge how little we knew about future crime rates in the early 1990s, the next obvious question is whether we know a great deal more in 2006. If so, where, when, and how did we learn these new lessons?

The 1990s witnessed the longest and deepest decline in crime by far in the United States since World War II. Because it is difficult to separate cyclical fluctuations from noncyclical declines, both the starting date and magnitude of the noncyclical decline in crime in the 1990s are uncertain, but the decline was distributed widely across different types of crime, different regions, and different demographic groups. While most of the nation experienced 20–40% crime drops, New York City had crime declines about double the national average and greater than any other large city in America.

What set the crime decline of the 1990s apart from other downturns was its length rather than its precipitous magnitude. It was a cumulative decline that was a complete surprise to those regarded as experts in the field.

The Environment for Optimism

Crime Trends and Attitudes about the Effectiveness of Crime Policies

2

This chapter is about a second "great divide" in attitudes about government and appropriate crime policy. A first great divide about crime policy is associated with the split in most developed nations between left-wing and right-wing political ideologies. While crime control has not traditionally been a major arena of left-versus-right political conflict in most nations, the contrast in policy preferences on crime between left and right is usually clear. Severity of punishment and support for strict law enforcement have been the consistent preferences of the right wing of the political spectrum in developed nations, while the left usually puts more emphasis on the structural and social conditions associated with crime as proper targets for government programs. In the recent past, for example, hardline policies on crime have emphasized prison construction and long sentences in the United States, while the responses from left and center have shifted. In the federal crime-control debates of 1993 and 1994, conservatives pushed policies that encouraged imprisonment while liberals supported gun control and prevention programs, but a centrist Democratic president also famously pushed for federal money to support the hiring of 100,000 more local police (Windesham 1998).

The focus of this chapter is not on the well-known ideological battle between left and right about crime policy but on a more subtle contrast between optimism and pessimism about the effectiveness of governmental policies to control crime. As I will use the terms, crime-control optimists are persons who think that what they regard as appropriate government efforts can dramatically reduce crime. A pessimist thinks that even the best tools available to government will have a minor impact on crime rates. The optimist-versus-pessimist contrast can easily be confused with the clash of conservative and liberal ideologies but is better regarded as distinct from general ideology, a schematic depicted in table 2.1.

Those who believe that harsh punishment and strict law enforcement are the correct policies for government to pursue do not necessarily also believe that crime is easy or even possible to control. There are hard-line pessimists as well as hard-line optimists on the right-hand side of the political spectrum. Many favor harsh punishment because they believe it is deserved, whether or not it also functions to reduce crime. One need look no further than the Calvinist tradition in Europe and America for the combination of a hard line and pessimism as a worldview of sin and presumably also of crime.

On the left-hand side of the ledger, soft-line programs like midnight basketball or tutoring are frequently supported as the lesser of evils in crime policies, even by citizens without firm convictions that this year's policy will have a substantial impact on next year's crime rate. I categorize these citizens as soft-line pessimists on policy. Particularly when crime policy choices are largely symbolic (e.g., "drug-free school zones") and

Table 2.1
Four differing views of appropriate crime policies.

	Hard-line	Soft-line
Optimist	Strict law enforcement and punishment will reduce crime substantially.	Social programs will cut crime substantially.
Pessimist	Strict law enforcement and punishment is appropriate but will not reduce crime much.	Social programs are worth support but will not reduce crime much.

low cost, people will frequently support gestures as policy without great faith that they will produce dramatic results.

This chapter is about some of the factors that influence how strongly experts, as well as citizens, believe that governmental actions can significantly influence crime rates. My main thesis—reflected in the title of the chapter—is that a long period of declining crime provides an environment where those concerned about crime policy tend to believe that this year's actions by government can have substantial impact on next year's crime rate. If I am correct in supposing that declining crime rates are an environment for optimism, then it is also likely that substantial increases in crime should push attitudes toward pessimism. A long period where nothing that the government is doing seems to work will bias observers toward the view that the potential impact of government is quite slight. If nothing is working, isn't that evidence that nothing can work?

I argue here that sustained eras of good or bad news push moods about effectiveness further than the facts warrant—that what tends to happen is an overreaction rather than merely an empirically based set of changed perceptions. Of necessity, this chapter's exploration must stop short of a systematic study of the relationship between attitudes toward crime and the environment of events—for the postwar era, there is no scholarly foundation to build on, and there are not many clear trend periods to examine. Instead, I will first profile some of the predominant attitudes in criminal justice writings of the 1970s and then contrast the tone of that decade with the writings about the effectiveness of crime-control strategies in the late 1990s. The predominant mood in the earlier era is gloomy, while the later era exudes confident optimism.

My analysis of the 1990s will show some changes in attitude over time about the crime-reduction impact of specific programs that were discussed before and after the recent crime decline, documenting the growth of positive expectations as the 1990s trends developed. The advantage of listening to changes of attitudes about the same strategies in different eras is the opportunity to document how much difference mood swings can make. A third section will speculate on what psychological and statistical features of crime declines foster optimistic views of policy effectiveness.

But why is an analysis of the mood changes produced by crime trends an early chapter in a book about the crime decline of the 1990s? I think that the optimism produced by declining crime in the 1990s produced confidence in both the ability of crime policy to change crime rates and assumptions that crime declines can be fully explained. By the end of the 1990s, social scientists and policy advocates were confidently explaining the factors that had produced a crime decline that none of them had predicted in advance. I believe that a big part of what they call in Hollywood the "backstory" to many claims about what explains crime declines was a product of the era of good feelings produced by nine consecutive years of crime drops. But just as the pessimism of the 1970s seems overstated in historical perspective, the optimism of the late 1990s is vulnerable to overstatement if it is more a result of elevated mood than of scientific advance. So this chapter will serve as a cautionary tale that is the justification for both the tone and the organization of part II.

Tales from the 1970s

Very few publications in the history of criminological research become as famous in their era or as notable in the telling of that era's history as Robert Martinson's article entitled "What Works? Questions and Answers about Prison Reform," published in *Public Interest* in 1974. The article reported on a review Martinson and two colleagues had conducted of the research studies evaluating interventions designed to improve the behavior of criminal offenders. Summarizing the results, Martinson concluded that "with few isolated exceptions, the rehabilitative efforts that have been reported so far have had no appreciable effect on recidivism" (p. 25). Martinson's message caused a sensation, inspiring critics on the left and right to attack regimes of parole release and sentencing systems committed to using prisoner responses to treatment programs as a basis for committing offenders to prison as well as releasing them.

The slogan that summarized the popular understanding of Dr. Martinson's message, "Nothing Works," became not simply a description of the impacts of correctional programing but a default characterization of most governmental efforts to cope with the crime problem. As I shall soon show, rehabilitative programers were not alone in feeling the disdain of program evaluators in the 1970s. Standard features of policing such as preventive patrol and quick responses came under intense scrutiny. And there was little in the way of hopeful innovations to counterbalance the negative findings during the 1970s. When Spiro Agnew a few years earlier complained about "nattering nabobs of negativism," he could well have been describing a criminological research summary of the 1970s.

But the sensation generated by Martinson's announcement that most correctional programs did not have a significant impact on recidivism was also a puzzle to well-informed observers. Francis Allen, delivering the Stores Lecture at Yale in 1980, posed the mystery of the Martinson phenomenon with elegant economy:

> It can be said without derogatory intent, that in many respects the [Martinson] statement is more interesting in its history than its content. For although the evaluation of rehabilitation research conducted by Martinson and his colleagues was no doubt more extensive than studies undertaken earlier, there was, in fact, little new about the skepticism expressed in the Martinson study of the rehabilitative capabilities of correctional programs or the existence of validated knowledge relevant to the avoidance of criminal recidivism. At least since World War II expressions of such skepticism have abounded in penological literature, as have criticisms of correctional entrepreneurs whose claims of significant reformative achievements were unsupported by scientific demonstration. There is little to indicate, however, that public attitudes toward correctional policy were greatly affected by the earlier doubts and protest. One of the most important aspects of the Martinson study may well be that its immediate and widespread impact constitutes a demonstration of public attitudes in the 1970s receptive to the conclusions stated. (1981, p. 57)

One element of the 1970s that rendered the public ready to conclude that "nothing works" in penal rehabilitation may well have been a more general pessimism about the capacity of government efforts to control crime that was incubated by the growth of public fear and of crime rates throughout the 1960s and early 1970s.

By 1974, homicide rates had more than doubled in a decade, and every street crime of significance to public fear had increased by similar magnitudes. Much has been made of this crime increase producing a public backlash toward punitive crime-control policies, but there is also a substantial basis for seeing unchecked crime as a reason for doubting not only the good intentions of government or the ideological correctness of current policy but also the capacity of government actions to make a significant dent in street crime. In this sense, the expression "Nothing works" captured the appetite of many to recognize in the events of the late 1960s and early 1970s evidence of governmental incapacity. Certainly, viewing this as a pessimistic rather than a conservative reading of "Nothing works" explains why this sentiment was welcomed across the political spectrum during the mid-1970s when efforts were being made to deconstruct indeterminate sentencing, most notably in California (Messinger and Johnson 1977). That all this occurred with a backdrop of governmental infelicities in other domains such as Watergate and Vietnam certainly would help explain the cachet of pessimism in the relations of citizens to their government. What better time for the distrust of government to be in fashion? And there is little evidence in the 1970s that either elites or average citizens believed that simply shifting strategies would yield dramatic progress in combating crime.

A Kansas City Bombshell

If the assessment exercise that produced Robert Martinson's "What Works?" report was old wine in new bottles, the second landmark adventure in criminal justice evaluation during the "nothing works" era—the Kansas City Preventative Patrol experiment—was a revolutionary collaboration between independent researchers and a major police department to use powerful methods to assess the impact of conventional police tactics on crime rates. While the systematic assessment of offender treatment programs had a 50-year history of implementation by 1970, the systematic evaluation of police tactics had no history in the major police departments of the United States. The methodology of correctional program evaluation was uneven at best and more often weak, but testing by independent experts of the tenets of police strategy in city streets was nonexistent. A very few police administrators had ties to academic criminology after the 1920s—August Volmer, O. W. Wilson, and Joseph Lowman—but the gulf between police administration and evaluation research was generally enormous. In 1969, the Ford Foundation, under some pressure from Congress to find philanthropic targets of resonance to middle America, funded the creation of the Police Foundation, based in Washington, D.C., with extensive material resources to support the evaluation and improvement of police activities in the United States. In the automobile-based cities of the midwestern and western United States, the orthodox method of street-level policing had by midcentury become routine preventive car patrol by uniformed officers. The presence of police cars patrolling through the community was believed to deter potential criminals and reassure citizens, who would observe the patrol cars. But the efficacy of preventive patrol was an article of faith in professional police circles rather than an empirical fact. As Clarence Kelley—then the police chief in Kansas City and soon to be the director of the FBI—put it, "many of us in the department had the feeling we were training, equipping and deploying men to do a job neither we, nor anybody else, knew much about" (Kelling et al., 1974, p. v).

The mix of progressive police administrators (Patrick Murphy, Clarence Kelley, Joseph McNamara), defense and counterinsurgency analysts (Joseph Lewis, the Police Foundation's research director), and social scientists that mounted the patrol experiment were not believers in the orthodoxy of preventive patrol, so in that sense it is fair to suppose that testing the null hypothesis was not only the technical objective of the research but its desired outcome as well. The year the research was reported, 1974, was a vintage year for the null hypothesis, as I have already noted.

Here is the description Joseph McNamara, the police chief in Kansas City in 1974, gave of the research and its results:

> Three controlled levels of routine preventive patrol were used in
> the experimental areas. One area, termed "reactive," received no
> preventive patrol. Officers entered the area only in response to
> citizen calls for assistance. This in effect substantially reduced
> police visibility in that area. In the second area, called "proac-
> tive," police visibility was increased two to three times its usual
> level. In the third area, termed "control," the normal level of pa-
> trol was maintained. Analysis of the data gathered revealed that
> the three areas experienced no significant differences in the level
> of crime, citizens' attitudes toward police service, citizens' fear of
> crime, police response time, or citizens' satisfaction with police
> response time. (Kelling et al., 1974, p. vii)

The chief then put the following positive spin on this example of the "nothing works" vintage of 1974:

> The results of the preventive patrol experiment described in this
> report repudiated a tradition prevailing in police work for almost
> 150 years. The toppling of traditions brings forth uneasiness inher-
> ent in the process of great change. Yet, the experiment

demonstrated something that should make the great changes we face less disturbing. The project was conceived by patrol personnel and executed by them with technical assistance from researchers. Thus, it is apparent that with the right kind of leadership and assistance, urban police departments have the capability to mount successful controlled experiments necessary to develop viable alternatives to the obsolescent concept of preventive patrol. (p. viii)

While exercises like the preventive patrol evaluation provided a foundation for later development and testing of promising new techniques of policing, in the short term there was far more than "the process of great change" that provoked feelings of uneasiness. The structure of the experiment and its results produced no positive findings of differential effectiveness in police patrol. Proactive patrol, regular levels of patrol, and solely reactive police car service produced the same results in crime levels and citizen satisfaction. The scientific finding was, in this sense, totally destructive—a tradition was repudiated, and nothing was put in its place. Whatever the longer term value of reducing faith in car patrol, the short-term impact of the experiment was an undiluted dose of "nothing works"!

And the police literature in the mid-1970s was not alone in containing a shortage of promising new techniques for control of crime. It was an era in which policy changes were frequently on the horizon but the sort of optimistic expectations that often accompany change were not apparent in discourse on urban conditions, on crime, on police, on prisons, or on criminal justice reform.

In the middle of this pessimistic deconstruction of orthodox theories of rehabilitation and policing, Charles Silberman published his long-awaited study *Criminal Violence, Criminal Justice*, a well-informed and mildly left-of-center journalistic review of the functions and prospects of criminal justice in 1978. The six-year Silberman project had been funded by the Ford Foundation and coordinated with the work of the Police Foundation not only in Kansas City but in its attempt to implement an early version of "team policing" in Cincinnati. From beginning to end, Silberman's chapter on the police was a testament of progressive pessimism. The title itself, "What the Police Do—and Don't Do," announced deflated expectations, and while the conclusion attempted to adopt a positive tone, it reads now like the valedictory summary of a pessimistic era:

Serious research and experimentation on policing are barely
15 years old; their main contribution has been to destroy the
assumption on which most police activity has been based—to
demonstrate the extent of our ignorance about what the police
can, and cannot, do to reduce crime and improve domestic tran-
quility. What is needed is not more hardware, communications
equipment, or personnel, but more research and experimentation. In the meantime, we—police officials, government leaders,
citizens, all of us—would do well to abandon our quixotic faith
that there is a police solution to the problem of criminal violence. (Silberman 1978, p. 252)

In retrospect, it seems obvious that the discouraging crime news of
the 1960s and 1970s fed into pessimistic assumptions about the effectiveness of governmental efforts and that both liberals and conservatives were
vulnerable to this type of discouragement. Combining the values of hindsight with the classification scheme set out in table 2.1, the entire Silberman volume could be classified as an encyclopedia of soft-line pessimism
about crime and criminal justice.

But was this attitude anything more than a realistic view of crime
and justice in the real world? I think so. The atmosphere of discouragement that is produced by steadily rising crime provokes an overreaction,
not merely absorbing the lessons of experience but also inducing a bias
that goes beyond the weight of current evidence, a willingness to assume
that government efforts are bound to fail that is broader than the facts
suggest.

To explore this dimension of the psychology of rising crime, we need
go no further than Charles Silberman's end-of-chapter injunction to
"abandon the quixotic faith that there is a police solution to the problem
of criminal violence." The evidence against police capacity to control
homicide that the Silberman chapter surveyed included the preventive
patrol experiment in Kansas City and a "team policing" regime in Cincinnati that failed to produce lower crime rates in test versus comparison
areas. As Silberman acknowledged, his book was written when the field
of evaluating police countermeasures was in its infancy. But why, then,
impose the view that it was "quixotic" to expect police to reduce homicide? That such broad statements emanated from a pessimistic mood as

much as from then current data seems, in retrospect, both obvious and easy to understand.

Effects in Search of Causes

The tendency for crime declines to push observers to unjustified belief that government policies work is more powerful than the pessimistic bias that is produced by crime increases, because there are strong institutional pressures that compound the psychological powers of good news. To be sure, the fact that crime rates do go down suggests that variability in the desired direction exists. This alone can produce optimism because, to appropriate the only hopeful chapter title in Charles Silberman's book, "Whatever Is, Is Possible" (1978, p. 424). But simply because crime rates can decline does not imply that government actions can create significant crime reductions, so why does a crime drop produce assumptions that declining crime is the effect of manmade causes?

Responding to crime is the principal occupation of several agencies of government, including police, courts, public prosecutors, and public institutions of incarceration. All of these activities have the reduction of crime as a primary purpose, so that the capacity of government to reduce crime is an article of faith that is hardwired into the mission and organization of many government operations.

When the crime news is discouraging, the agencies of criminal justice heed the warnings of social scientists and take public relations refuge in their limited capacities. The FBI's *Uniform Crime Reports* of the 1960s and 1970s tempered each year's bad news about homicide with the observation that "criminal homicide is largely a societal problem which is beyond the control of the police" (see, e.g., *Crime in the United States* 1973, p. 9 [U.S. Department of Justice, Federal Bureau of Investigation]; this standard warning disappeared in 1988). But this disassociation goes against the grain of law enforcement and prosecution. If the work of police and prosecutors and prison guards is not effective in preventing crime, what is the social importance of their jobs?

So the first sign of declining crime revives the faith in effectiveness that is latent in the political and administrative framework of criminal justice at all times. If an assumption of causality is always present at some level, the assumption will always be ready to spring to the surface to greet good tidings on the crime front. "What did we try last year?" will be the question the mayor or the police commissioner ask when the news is released, followed by the statement: "It worked." The pervasiveness of an assumption that declining crime is a policy effect of governmental activity is not hard to document from media coverage.

Only Yesterday

The most concrete demonstrations of how a sustained crime decline influences attitudes about the efficacy of police comes from watching the change in how those who support a particular policy describe its benefits as times change. The two exhibits I will offer on this account concern "broken windows" policing, the zero-tolerance theory of law enforcement now widely regarded as the cause of New York City's huge crime decline, and the "three strikes and you're out" package of mandatory prison sentences that California adopted in 1994. In each instance, it appears that a decline in crime has changed the nature of what advocates of crime policies expect from policy changes.

Broken Windows

In my view, Robert Martinson's article "What Works?" was only the second most influential media article on crime policy of its era. For all the attention it commanded, the Martinson article probably confirmed more opinions than it changed. An article published in the Atlantic Monthly in 1982 by James Q. Wilson and George Kelling probably had even more impact on policy thinking. That article, entitled "Broken Windows," provided the rationale for a new strategic emphasis on maintenance of order as a police objective.

As described by Wilson and Kelling, the empirical case for "order maintenance" policing can be traced to the evaluation of a New Jersey State Police "foot patrol" experiment that was financed by the Police Foundation in the late 1970s, in Newark. This was the foundation's effort to replace the presumed effectiveness of the car patrols that the Kansas City experiment had discredited with scientifically established steps to neighborhood safety. While Wilson and Kelling were enthusiastic when advocating the virtues of foot patrol as an instrument of "order maintenance" policing, one claim was notably missing from the 1982 brief for "broken windows" policing: any claim or indication that this approach would reduce the incidence or severity of crime. Here is the early edition of the wisdom of "Broken Windows":

> Based on its analysis of a carefully controlled experiment carried out chiefly in Newark, the Foundation concluded, to the surprise of hardly anyone, that foot patrol had not reduced crime rates. But residents of the foot-patrolled neighborhoods seemed to feel more secure than persons in other areas, [and] tended to believe that crime had been reduced. (Wilson and Kelling 1982, p. 1)

> These findings may be taken as evidence that the skeptics were right—foot patrol has no effect on crime; it merely fools the citizens into thinking they are safer. But in our view . . . the citizens of Newark were not fooled at all. . . . They knew that having officers walk beats did in fact make their neighborhoods safer. . . . But how can a neighborhood be "safer" when the crime rate has not gone down—in fact may have gone up?" (p. 2)

The authors go on to outline a theory of how enforcing rules of order and removing strangers and menacing behavior enhances citizen's feelings of security. They urge that police resources be devoted to marginal neighborhoods rather than very high-crime areas "where the situation is hopeless" (Wilson and Kelling 1982, p. 16). In its most celebrated early statement, the argument for "broken windows" police strategies neither placed priority on control of serious and violent crime nor claimed that even successful implementation of the strategy worked to reduce crime.

This modest refusal to expect even successful police strategies to reduce rates of crime was issued early in 1982, late in the era of "nothing works." By the late 1990s, however, the claims for order maintenance policing had expanded exponentially, and serious and violent crime had gone from being peripheral to the priorities of police resource deployment to being the central concern of the order maintenance regime.

In 1996, in a book he coauthored with Catherine Coles, George Kelling, coauthor of "Broken Windows," was still invested in the potential benefits of policing strategies to "reduce fear and strengthen the community"; but he also claimed more concrete benefits: "There is growing reason to believe that order maintenance activities will have a major impact on crime" (Kelling and Coles 1996, p. 248). Kelling and Coles suggest four different mechanisms that account for this major impact and tell us that "this is a finding of critical significance for neighborhoods already facing high levels of crime"; there is no mention of either the results of the careful experiment in Newark or the theory that the highest crime areas of a city should be regarded as "hopeless," both elements in "Broken Windows."

Of course, one difference between 1982 and the late 1990s was the environmental impact of declining crime, particularly in New York City. Not that the experimental results in Newark were displaced by a second careful evaluation; instead, city-wide crime declines in New York were the case study, as observers attributed the decline to what U.S. News and World Report called "smarter police strategies" (Morrow 1999). These new police strategies were present to soak up the public attention once declining crime rates produced a search for causes.

And George Kelling's optimism on the subject was by no measure as emphatic as that of some senior police practitioners. William Bratton, the administrative architect of the New York reorganization, entitled his 1998 book *Turnaround: How America's Top Cop Reversed the Crime Epidemic* (Bratton and Knobler 1998). The central conflict in his book concerns his battle with Rudolph Giuliani, then mayor of New York City, not over whether the policing strategies reduced the crime rate but over which of those two contestants should receive the lion's share of the credit. The scenario of "turnaround" carries a lesson of importance beyond the streets of New York City: crime declines produce an environment in which what were thought to be crime-neutral police strategies became policies that were believed to generate a major impact on crime; the only serious question in the 1990s was "Who gets the credit?"

Three Strikes: The Tiger Changes Its Stripes

On the West Coast, it was criminal law rather than street policing that captured public attention in the mid-1990s. But the crime declines that followed new penal legislation in California were too swift and too large to attribute to the usual purposes of the new laws. So, as I will show, the rationale was changed.

Whether the discretionary life-imprisonment terms of the traditional habitual criminal statute or the mandatory 25-year-to-life prison sentences mandated by California's 1994 Three Strikes and You're Out law, the architecture of habitual offender legislation can always fit neatly with one and only one of the announced purposes of criminal punishment—incapacitation. The obvious tension between notions of just deserts retribution and providing the same protracted imprisonment for offenses of widely different severity is obvious. Waiting for a second or third offense before the protracted term is imposed, and then threatening the same long term for serious and minor crimes, also does not easily fit any conception of rational general deterrence policy. Instead, the combination of emphasis on repetition and the use of a drastic incapacitation sentence seeks to identify dangerous offenders and lock them up to avoid the repetition of dangerous and violent crime. Indeed, the long term in prison is because the repeat offenders who fit the statute's criteria are presumed to be incorrigible. They are deterrence's failures.

The author of California's Three Strikes proposal, Mike Reynolds, put it this way the year before his proposal became law: "We're talking about nasty people who have truly given up their dues card on the human race. And yet, for some reason, the State of California is repeatedly turning them back out on the streets" (Podger 1993, p. B1). Pete Wilson, governor of California, put it more succinctly: "It's time to make career criminals career inmates" (Lucas 1993, p. A14).

California was already locking up the targets of this new approach prior to 1994, but the complaint was that it was failing to throw away the key. The specific Three Strikes statute that California adopted can only be justified as a scheme for incapacitating dangerous offenders. The statute requires a dangerous or violent criminal record before any of its provisions can come into operation, but then uses its 25-to-life sanction no matter how severe the current felony charge is.

While the objective of this type of legislation might have been incapacitation of the dangerous, the realities of California trends in crime and imprisonment made it difficult to explain the crime decline only in terms of benefits of keeping the dangerous off the streets. The rate at which California added to its prison population did not increase any faster after the new statute came into effect than before, as shown in figure 2.1.

While prison and jail populations did not increase quickly (Zimring, Hawkins, and Kamin 2001, p. 93), the rate of crime did drop in the years immediately after the law was passed. But the third-strike defendants would only start serving their extra prison sentences later on. If this new law had any major role in the crime decline, why was that?

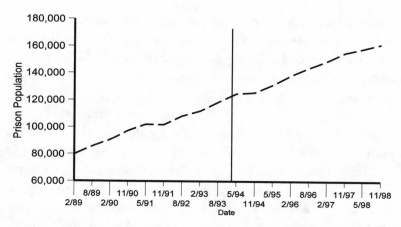

Figure 2.1. Trends in imprisonment, California, 1989–98. Source: California Department of Corrections. 1999. *Quarterly Movement Summary Report*. Sacramento: California Department of Corrections, 1999.

In a study I coauthored, we argued as follows.

> General deterrence became the reason for attributing the decline in crime to Three Strikes by a process of elimination. Since there were no large and immediate changes in the rate of incarceration to generate crime reductions, any prevention attributable to Three Strikes must be the result of the threat of punishment, which is persuading potential offenders not to commit crimes. (Zimring, Hawkins, and Kamin, 2001, p. 94)

When our study subsequently found that those offenders who were eligible for the special new punishment threatened by three strikes only showed a tiny decline in their share of total felony arrests, one economist argued (Shepherd 2002) that the large decline in crime was still deterrence, but it was the potential offenders with no strikes (and no immediate change in punishment eligibility) who were the bulk of the deterrence!

So the two case histories are a study in contrasts. The downtrend in crime rate produced a more typical response from policy supporters in the story of "broken windows" policing, a claim that the same policy simply created crime prevention benefits that hadn't been part of the original package. In the case of Three Strikes, the need to establish a causal link between a policy and an effect on crime provoked a shift also in the mechanism that supporters believed to be effective and then a shift in the audience of potential offenders who were the reason for the crime decline. Once the assumption is made that a policy shift must have caused a decline in crime, analytic flexibility as to how that happened seems to have been the order of the day.

The comparative careers of Three Strikes in California and "broken windows" policing in New York also show a strong tendency for what might be called a "favorite son" phenomenon for causal assumptions in explaining crime declines. The timing of crime declines in both California and New York City was not dissimilar. But the discourse about potential causes of a crime decline was confined to Three Strikes on the West Coast and to zero-tolerance policing on the East Coast. And both the East Coast and West Coast orthodoxies developed without reference to the events on the other coast. Not until after the millennium was any action by police discussed as causes for crime declines in California, after William Bratton became police chief in Los Angeles, and shifts in criminal law and criminal punishment were never taken seriously as a cause of victories in the war on New York City crime. In each of these "favorite son" crime decline narratives, the evidence for causation is usually before-and-after temporal comparisons, but only one intervention is the center of attention.

The only element that sets apart the stories of "broken windows" policing and "three strikes and you're out" from stories about a multitude of other possible causes of crime decline is a better record of the "before and after" changes of attitude in these two instances.

In part II, I will discuss optimistic assumptions about the 1990s performance of a wide variety of remedies that have been nominated for violent crime, from federal subsidies to hiring more urban police to youth employment, from gun controls to liberalized access to abortion. Whatever the nominated cause, there is a tendency to overreact when the crime news is good, to assume that since crime rates can go down, particular government policies can produce significant reductions in crime. We are never so ready to believe in the effectiveness of our policies as when fortune smiles upon us.

This is not a feature only of crime policy, of course. When the stock market is going up, the number of investors who consider themselves financial geniuses increases exponentially. Good news is the mother's milk of self-confidence. Such is human nature. Is there any harm in the criminal justice branch of such optimism?

The Euphoric Fallacy

Is there any error in assuming when crime rates drop that particular policies are the cause of such happy news? As a matter of logic, the answer to this question is an unqualified yes. Even the happiest events in human life often occur without obvious explanation and also without human agencies playing an important role in bringing them about. Abundant rainfall is not good evidence of the efficacy of rainmakers, even if a great deal of rainmaking activity preceded the storm. The fact that crime volumes are variable, and that this variation occurs in a desired direction, is not by itself proof that manmade policies are the causes of every observable crime decline. In addition, the stronger the urge to assume that declines are inevitably caused by human agencies, and the more powerful the vested interest of criminal justice actors to see their efforts as a cause of the benefits of lower crime rates, the more important it becomes to impose the discipline of logic on our temptation to attribute crime declines to the success of particular policies.

The temptation to assume that crime declines are caused by policy is probably reinforced by some of the weaker statistical techniques associated with regression analyses over time. To the extent that existing statistical models do not explain all the variations in crime rate noted in an era like the 1990s—and they do not—then the unexplained downward movement becomes a residual to be associated with whatever else has varied over time during an era of decline. The absence of good models for explaining crime variance over time thus makes that kind of time-series exercise a trap for false positive conclusions of causation in eras of declining crime rates. Statistical assessments over time that produce a "good fit" with the timing of a crime decline are a hazard we will encounter when examining statistical soundings on various possible causes in chapter 4. The "good fit" often happens precisely because we go hunting for policies to test after the news of the crime decline has been noticed. Studies without plausible cross-sectional controls that try to fit variations in policy to a known crime decline are almost certain to provide misleading indications of the causes of crime decline.

But isn't a 40% drop in crime and violence during the 1990s some evidence that criminal justice policies may be working? Yes and no. There is certainly more room to speculate on the impact of new policing efforts in the 1990s, when crime dropped, than in eras like the late 1980s, when extraordinary resource investments coexisted with increases in rates of violent crime. What crime declines provide is evidence of the possibility of policy effects, along with the temptation to jump to unwarranted conclusions about the agencies that caused a decline, and about the magnitude of the manmade policy effects. Part of the optimism generated in an era of crime declines is justified; much of it is not justified. The essence of what I would call the euphoric fallacy in eras of crime decline is the willingness to assume that all the good news was the natural and probable result of last year's change in police manpower or criminal punishments.

The euphoric fallacy is powerful and understandable. It will not ever leave either the political arena or the operational centers of the administration of criminal justice. Scholars and senior decision-makers will also be chronically tempted to assume human causes for good news, but a combination of disciplined expectations and the demand for more rigorous techniques of evaluation are the best hope to counter the expansive overreactions that arrive with declining crime rates.

The Search for Causes

Part II

Introduction to Part II

This part of the book summarizes and criticizes the theories that have been put forward to explain the crime decline of the 1990s. The two chapters that discuss causes have a modestly eccentric organization. Chapter 3 covers discussion during and after the 1990s of factors that had long been considered as potential crime prevention—incarceration, demography, and economic expansion. With respect to these longtime candidates for credit in crime prevention, the 1990s were a cascade of best-case outcomes—high levels of incarceration, a drop in the proportion of the population in high-risk youth categories, and unprecedented prosperity for the same nine years that crime declined. With an epidemic of good tidings, a crime decline in the 1990s should have been expected, even though only about half of the actual crime drop appears to have been caused by favorable trends in longstanding correlates of crime rates.

Chapter 4 considers a series of new explanations for declining crime that were created as theories of crime prevention because observers thought that they fit well with the timing of the 1990s decline.

But if the crime decline is why the theory was created, the temporal fit of the new theories with declining crime in the United States during the 1990s is not strong evidence of causation. One must look for other places and other times to test these novel theories with any rigor. The independent evidence for these new explanations is not convincing.

So I end my survey of existing theories and evidence with only about half the decline explained, and that half attributable to the confluence of population, economic, and incarceration trends. The available evidence stops well short of a complete or precise account of the causes of decline. This leads me into the further research reported in part III.

The Usual Suspects

Imprisonment,

Demography, and

the Economy

3

The title of this chapter was borrowed from one of the best-remembered lines of the classic movie *Casablanca*, when the police chief responds to a killing by the film's hero with an order to his officers to "round up the usual suspects." What sets the three topics to be covered in this chapter apart from the issues to be discussed in chapter 4 is their existence as hardy perennials in discussions of why crime rates rise and fall in the United States. To be sure, there has never been consensus about whether and to what extent changes in imprisonment, the age structure of the population, or unemployment and economic opportunity were related to changes in levels of crime, but the sustained discourse on these factors over several decades is important, because there is a long track record of inquiry about these factors that precedes the particular developments of the 1990s. This not only provides more data and historical context for discussing these issues but also means that the peculiar timing of crime trends in the 1990s had nothing to do with proposing these factors as explanation.

Whatever the weaknesses in the scientific case for these longstanding theories of crime causation as an influence in the 1990s, the theories were not selected only because variations in these presumed independent variables seemed to fit well with the timing of the crime drop in the 1990s.

Later chapters will explore the dangers inherent in such after-the-fact hypotheses. It is better that we begin with potential influences that have a long pedigree independent of the 1990s.

For each of the three topics, we will confront theories of crime prevention or causation and then attempt to apply existing theory and evidence to the specifics of the 1990s declines. We already know that the crime decline had multiple causes. This chapter is the beginning of an attempt to identify those elements that played an important role in the decline and to estimate the extent to which particular causes can be measured.

A good case can be made that each of the factors profiled in this chapter contributed to declining crime in the 1990s but that the cumulative impact of all three accounts for less than half of the national crime drop.

Imprisonment and Crime

No other change in the operation and output of American criminal justice in the generation after 1970 begins to approach the scale of the expansion of incarceration. Figure 3.1 shows the number of persons in state and federal prisons over the period 1960 to 2002. This total reflects persons serving sentences after conviction for crime but doesn't include those awaiting trial in local jails or serving short terms in those local facilities.

After dropping to just over 200,000 in 1972, the prison population in the United States expanded in each of the next 30 years, reaching a volume of 1,500,000 early in the twenty-first century. Two adjustments should be

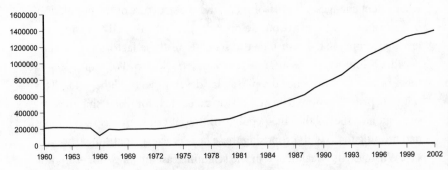

Figure 3.1. State and federal prisoners, 1960–2002. Source: U.S. Department of Justice. Bureau of Justice Statistics. Correctional Surveys (*National Prisoner Statistics and Survey of Jails*). Washington, D.C.

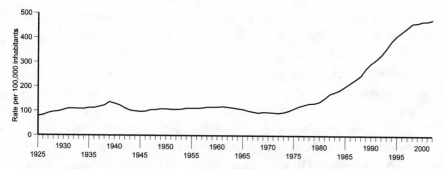

Figure 3.2. State and federal incarceration rates, 1925–2002. Source: U.S. Department of Justice. Bureau of Justice Statistics. Correctional Surveys (*National Prisoner Statistics and Survey of Jails*). Washington, D.C.

made to the incarceration statistics in figure 3.1 before discussing the impact of incarceration on crime rates. Figure 3.2 converts the prison numbers into a rate of imprisonment per 100,000 citizens, adjusting the totals in figure 3.1 to reflect the expanding population. This rate per 100,000 figure starts in 1927.

After small and trendless variations for several decades, the rate of imprisonment in the United States expands after 1973 more than threefold. Figure 3.3 reduces the time frame to the years after 1980 and includes rates of jailing for adults (incarceration pending trial and short sentences served in local facilities).

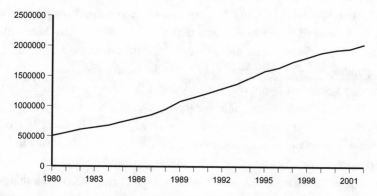

Figure 3.3. Number of persons in jail and prison, United States, 1980–2002. Source: U.S. Department of Justice. Bureau of Justice Statistics. Correctional Surveys (*National Prisoner Statistics and Survey of Jails*). Washington, D.C.

The expansion in incarceration is larger in gross numbers when jails are included, but the rate of increase is moderated because jail populations grew at a slightly lower rate.

There are two ways that increasing the number of persons incarcerated might reduce crime rates in the communities from which these persons are extracted. Physically removing persons who have been active offenders will avoid whatever offenses these persons would commit in the time they are not free to offend in their home communities, a phenomenon typically called incapacitation (Zimring and Hawkins 1995). Raising the penalties threatened for particular criminal offenses might also reduce offenses committed by potential offenders other than the punished person. To the extent that increases in actual imprisonment and therefore in levels of threatened punishment reduce the number of crimes committed, the effect is usually called general deterrence (Zimring and Hawkins 1973).

The crime prevention theories of incapacitation and general deterrence are a study in contrasts. Incapacitation effects do not depend on the rationality or will of the incapacitated person but rather on the isolation of a potential offender by physical force. If there is any consistency in the propensity to commit crimes so that today's offenders could be expected to commit crimes tomorrow if free to do so, the question to be addressed is not whether incarceration reduces crime rates but by how much (Zimring and Hawkins 1995).

There are many more contingencies in the theoretical machinery of general deterrence, more moving parts that must work for marginal changes in threats to reduce offense rates. And the methods ordinarily used to search for marginal general deterrent impacts of imprisonment overlap with those used to measure incapacitation effects (Blumstein, Cohen, and Nagin 1978). So apportioning any reduction in crime rates achieved by expanding rates of incarceration between deterrence and incapacitation is no easy task. Most criminologists regard incapacitation as a more frequent and more likely outcome than marginal general deterrence of changes in levels of imprisonment for common crimes and would be likely to credit incapacitation rather than deterrence as the mechanism that leads to imprisonment increases reducing crime (see, e.g., Conklin 2003). Economists, who tend to regard threatened penalties as the price the system charges for crime, are more likely to presume diminished demand for crime as the price goes up and thus expect marginal general deterrence as a routine output of increases in threatened penalties (Coase 1977).

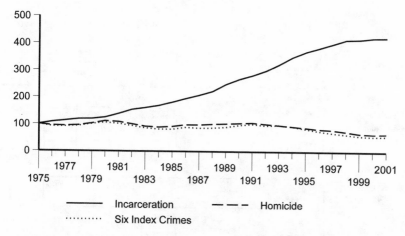

Figure 3.4. Trends in incarceration, homicide, and index crime, United States, 1975–2001. Sources: U.S. Department of Justice. Bureau of Justice Statistics. Correctional Surveys (National Prisoner Statistics and Survey of Jails). Washington, D.C. U.S. Department of Justice. Federal Bureau of Investigation. *Uniform Crime Report.* Washington, D.C. (Homicide and index crime.)

Since a huge increase in incarceration was the major policy change in American criminal justice in the last three decades of the twentieth century, one would expect many observers to give this boom in imprisonment the lion's share of the credit for declining crime in the United States. One problem with such an assumption is that massive doses of increased incarceration had been administered throughout the 1970s and 1980s with no consistent and visible impact on crime. Figure 3.4 tracks the rates of incarceration for adults and trends in homicide over the period after 1975.

While the rate of incarceration steadily increased throughout the 1970s and 1980s, the homicide rate (and that of most other index crimes) cycled down, then up, then down, then up again in the 16 years after 1975 (prior to 1991).

Some Ironies of Timing on Crime and Imprisonment

The roller-coaster pattern in U.S. crime and the uninterrupted increase in incarcerated populations do not produce any clean pattern in the aggregate. Figure 3.5 breaks the 25 years after 1975 into five-year periods, showing trends in total incarceration (prison and jail) and aggregate index crime

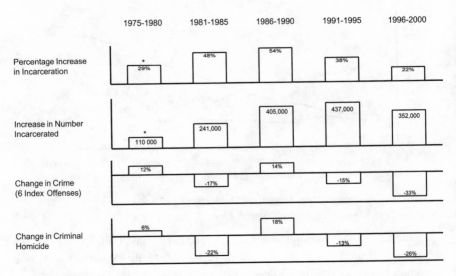

Figure 3.5. Crime and incarceration in five-year intervals, United States, 1975–2000. Note: Jail populations were available only for 1973 and 1978, so 1975 jails were estimated in linear interpolation of those values. Source: U.S. Department of Justice, Bureau of Justice Statistics, Correctional Surveys, Washington, D.C. 1975–2000 (incarceration); U.S. Department of Justice, Federal Bureau of Investigation, *Uniform Crime Report*, 1975–2000, Washington, D.C. (crime).

other than larceny and homicide. Larceny is excluded from the crime index because it is weighted with trivial cases and is a majority of all offenses.

The best measure in theory of marginal deterrent power would be the percentage change in incarceration, because that is a measure of the relative shift in incarceration risk over time. The best measure of the change in total volume of crimes averted due to incapacitation would be the aggregate increase in numbers incarcerated. Yet trends in neither of these measure is a reliable predictor of periodic trends in crime since 1975. The largest proportional increase in imprisonment in the United States is the five years after 1986, a period of increasing crime. The lowest relative increase is the 22% for the period 1996–2000, during which the majority of the declines in crime that were outside previous cycles took place. The high proportional growth in the first half of the 1980s did come with a clear (but short-lived) crime decline.

When testing the potential for incapacitation, the number of extra bodies removed rather than the relative change in threat conditions or imprisonment rate should be the best predictor of crime decline. Because the jurisdiction maintaining the cell makes no difference, jail and prison numbers must be combined to estimate incapacitation. The top period for new incarceration, 1991–95, is associated with declining crime rates, but the second largest incapacitation period was 1986–90, the five years that are the central puzzle in any account that would give major credit to punishment shifts in changing crime rates. Why did crime rates increase during a period when there was a 54% increase in incarceration—the largest proportional increase in American history—and a net increase of 405,000 persons were added to the inmate population? Obviously, there must have been offsetting factors at work in the United States of the 1980s, but none of the demographics or economic trends of that era appeared to be criminogenic.

The grossly uneven record of crime results during the era of escalating imprisonment means that no stable estimates of prison-based incapacitation, or of deterrence, or of their joint effect can be derived from study of the trends in incarceration and crime for the entire period.

The economist Steven Levitt puts it this way when analyzing the era of uninterrupted prison growth prior to 1991:

> The crime experience from 1973 to 1991 is not well explained by the factors identified in this paper. Driven almost exclusively by increased incarceration, I would have expected crime to fall substantially over that time period. Instead, violent crime either remained roughly constant if one believes victimization data, or rose sharply if the reported crime statistics are correct. The real puzzle in my opinion, therefore, is not why crime fell in the 1990s, but why it did not start falling sooner. (2004, pp. 33–34)

Any explanation of the 1990s decline that features the imprisonment trends of that era must also account for the lack of consistent effect in the 15 years prior to the 1990s. This has not been an easy task.

Incapacitation and the Paradox of Diminishing Returns

From one perspective, it turns out that the late 1990s are the least likely time in the United States expansion to expect major crime reductions from incapacitation. The problem with expecting big gains from incapacitation late in a prison expansion is diminishing marginal returns. The essential point is rather simple: where incarceration is a limited resource, police, prosecutors, and judges will want to lock up those most likely to reoffend seriously first.

If there are 50,000 cells in California, the 50,000 who fill them will be the most dangerous offenders we have. Double the space available, and those in the system will search for the next most dangerous 50,000. The number of crimes prevented with this second increment will probably be fewer than with the first 50,000. Indeed, the better the system was at isolating the most dangerous high-rate offenders when making the first 50,000 decisions, the larger the drop-off we expect in the incapacitation savings from the second group. And the phenomenon of diminished returns can be expected even if the system's decision-makers do not seek to isolate the most dangerous offenders first, because the offenders with the highest rates of offending will be caught earlier and more often than the less active. "If current policies make it much more likely that such extremely high rate offenders are already behind bars, the marginal return from further incapacitation will be much smaller" (Zimring and Hawkins, 1995, p. 51).

But the large crime declines of the 1990s came at the tail end of the largest prison expansion in American history. Between 1973 and 1995, the prison system had doubled, then doubled again. From the standpoint of selecting dangerous offenders to continue increasing the incarceration population, the system must have been dipping much deeper into the dangerousness barrel, if not scraping its bottom. Every serious commentator on incapacitation has pointed out this likelihood (see e.g. Spelman 1994, 2000; Cohen and Canela-Cacho 1994, p. 356), but how then might one account for the fact that the last decade of the prison buildup was associated with a much larger apparent dent in the crime rate than the first 15 years?

One conclusion that this peculiar timing invites is that the marginal incapacitation of 1990s incarceration played a rather modest role in the crime decline, and commentators like William Spelman and Steven Levitt place a pretty low upper limit on the prison part of the decline, no more than 27% for Spelman (2000), somewhat less for Levitt (2004). Others would reduce these estimates by up to half (Donohue and Siegelman 1998). A second technique is to search for a theoretical reason that the 1990s variety of "end of expansion" imprisonment might produce so much more impact.

Elasticity and Its Discontents

After acknowledging the diminishing marginal returns phenomenon, William Spelman tries to explain some of the large crime declines of the 1990s in terms of a concept of "elasticity":

Bed for bed, prisons become less effective as they fill up. On the other hand, the effects of prison expansion are usually measured not in terms of beds or cells, but in terms of percentages. Because a one percent increase in prison population is a lot more prisoners after 25 years of expansion than before, an apples-to-apples comparison requires that we examine the elasticity (which depends on the percentage increase) rather than the offense rate (which depends on the numerical increase). (2000, p. 112)

Readers who find this analysis confusing should not worry about their confusion. The central point Professor Spelman is making is that a 1% increase in a prison population of one million is twice as large as a 1% increase in a prison population of 500,000. This doesn't make the later increase more cost-effective, it just makes it larger.

The reason for the confusion is the use of the term "elasticity" in a discussion of incapacitation effects. The term comes from economics, where it refers to the relative effect of price changes and the quality of goods demanded (or supplied). If we were thinking about the deterrent impact of changes in the prison sentences threatened on the crime rate, then an analogy with price effects would have some appeal—elasticity would be the degree to which an increase in threatened penalty decreases the number of offenses.

But there is no mechanism remotely analogous to supply or demand in the mechanics of incapacitation. So the concept of "elasticity" adds nothing to the process of determining incapacitation effects. We are always interested in the impact of adding 100 prisoners; or 1,000; or 1,000,000; and the number of offenses this will avoid. There is no reason to think that the effectiveness of each 1,000 additional prisoners will be as great in the late 1990s as in the late 1980s, and since the volume of prisoners added was just as large in the late 1980s, there is nothing to explain why the crime rate rose in the first period and declined in the second.

Deterrence as a Fallback

Perhaps one way to read the 25-year record is as evidence that the incapacitation effects were always relatively modest but that marginal general deterrence, the increased effectiveness of threatened punishments, kicked in in the 1990s. This is possible but untestable. The difficulties in constructing plausible methods of measuring marginal general deterrence are longstanding and notorious (Zimring and Hawkins 1973, pp. 249–367; Blumstein, Cohen, and Nagin 1978). The percentage increases in imprisonment were larger in the late 1980s than in the early or late 1990s. It is always possible to theorize some "tipping point" in threatened punishment that might explain accelerating deterrence, but it is never possible to test such a theory on the crime data that generated it. The possibility of deterrence is an untestable consolation prize that should only be a last resort in analysis of the last quarter of the twentieth century, and it may not be necessary.

A Focus on Cumulative Effect

Analogies with concepts such as elasticity make obscure one aspect of the growth of imprisonment that is both obvious and fits with a larger crime impact at the end of a sustained growth rate. The way figure 3.5 expressed incarceration growth was in five-year intervals. But if growth is steady, it is the total (and therefore cumulative) growth of imprisonment that represents the total incapacitative impact of a particular stock of persons in prison. Figure 3.6 tells us this story in its cumulative dimension.

While figure 3.5 told us that the percentage of added prisoners during 1995–2000 was 22% of the number present in 1995, figure 3.6 shows that the number of additional prisoners added to the 1975 base by then was 406% of that base, by far the largest total increase over the 25 years. And most of those extra prisoners were in fact added after 1995, since most

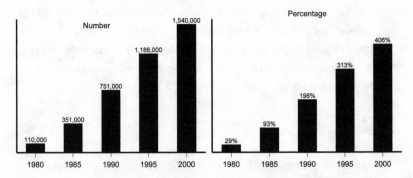

Figure 3.6. Cumulative change in incarceration over 1975–2000. Source: U.S. Department of Justice, Bureau of Justice Statistics, Correctional Surveys, *National Prisoner Statistics and Survey of Jails* (1975–2000), Washington, D.C.

prisoners leave prison after three or four years. The largest impact of crimes avoided per year from this 25-year buildup would be expected to come at the end of the time period. While the crime increase in the late 1980s remains a mystery, the late-blooming dividend from cumulative incapacitation in the 1990s should come as no surprise. It is not a tipping point but the additive nature of the impact of increments in prison populations that provides the throw weight for maximum incapacitation. We should expect the amount of crime reduction shown in the last period of figure 3.6 to be five times as great as in 1975, discounted somewhat for the lesser number of high-rate offenders in the added volume.

Incapacitation Assessments and the Role of Incarceration in the Crime Decline

I began the discussion of prison influences by noting that the role of incarceration in reducing community crime rates is undeniable, but the difficulty is in estimating the extent to which variations in incarceration rates will cause changes in crime rates. In the specific context of explaining the 1990–99 crime decline, existing data and analysis do not much narrow the margin of error in guessing the following.

1. What proportion of the experienced decline was caused by increased levels of incarceration?
2. What was the effect of the additional incarceration on rates of specific offenses, particularly on homicide, rape, and robbery?

There are no truly powerful methods available to test incapacitation effects and a fairly wide range of results found in published studies. A best guess of the impact of post-1990 changes in incarceration rates on post-1990 declines in the crime rate would range from 10% of the decline at the low end to 27% of the decline at the high end (compare Spelman 2000 with Donohue and Siegelman 1998).

The only way to break any estimate down further to an estimate of murders, rapes, and robberies avoided is with heroic assumptions. But the methods of estimation are very weak. Models to predict crime generally are not strong; models to predict specific types of crime are even more premature and fragile.

The margin of error associated with estimates of the crime reductions from recent imprisonment may or may not have policy significance. Even at the high end of existing estimates, there is doubt that additional imprisonment would be cost-effective (see Levitt 2004; Spelman 2000). At the low end, the entire decade of marginal crime prevention was a losing proposition.

The last piece of bad news on the incapacitation front concerns the prospect for better measurement. There is no great improvement on the horizon for estimating the impact of imprisonment shifts on the total volume of crime or on individual crimes. So the incapacitation issue is likely to remain for some time, a mixture of certainty that some crime prevention results when additional offenders are incarcerated and substantial uncertainty about the volume of crime prevented and its social value.

One important footnote to estimating the impact of expanding incarceration on crime in the United States comes from the data on Canada reported in chapter 5. Canada had a broad crime decline at exactly the same time as the United States but without any increase in incarceration as a potential explanation. To the extent that observers search for the same causes for these simultaneous declines, the incarceration boom south of the border must be deemphasized.

Can Demographics Help Explain the 1990s Crime Decline?

Different demographic categories in any population have quite different propensities to produce official statistics on crime. Arrests for most categories of common crimes are concentrated at the young end of the age distribution—among youth and young adults. Males are much more likely than females to commit most crimes, and many disadvantaged minority populations have much higher than usual rates within the high-risk age and gender categories. These characteristics of the distribution of arrest statistics are part of the well-established conventional wisdom of criminology.

But can paying attention to the different growth rates of different population groups help us understand the rise and fall of crime rates over time? A predictive approach that emphasizes changes in the composition of a population as an explanation for increases and decreases in crime rates over time would only be important if the risks associated with various different age, gender, and economic classes stayed close to constant and if the growth rate of different parts of the population varied substantially.

No matter how great the risk differences between men and women for serious crime, for example, taking those differences into account is not a good way to explain any crime trends of the last 50 years or to predict any changes in the future, because there has been no significant change in the ratio of males to females in the population, particularly in that age sector of the population that has any significant involvement with common crimes. If the ratio of young males to young females is stable, it cannot be an important part of explaining or predicting a change in crime over time.

The other key element in using demographic categories to explain and predict crime changes is that whatever risk relationship one finds or projects for a part of a population has to be predictable in the future.

To return for a moment to the demographics of gender, there was in fact some theorizing in the 1970s and 1980s that crime rates would increase because the relative involvement of females in crime would increase as the social distinctions between male and female gender roles diminished over time (Adler 1975). This was a prediction based on social rather than demographic change, but it turned out not to apply in the 1990s, because the predicted shift in crime propensities for the most part did not happen.

Can we assume that the relative risks of different age and social class categories will remain stable? If not, demographics might still be useful in explaining historical crime trends but couldn't be used to predict future changes in crime rates because of expected demographic changes.

A Short History of Demographic Crime Explanation

The use of demographic analysis in explaining crime trends has a recent vintage and a reputation for accuracy that is uneven at best. The major event that produced an emphasis on demographic change in discussions of crime was the post–World War II baby boom. But this demographic shift did not become important in discussion of crime trends until after the fact of the increase in crime that developed in the decade after 1964.

By the 1970s, observers trying to comprehend the reasons for the jump in crime rates had developed theories about the baby boomers. Here is James Q. Wilson, writing about "Crime amidst Plenty: The Paradox of the 1960s":

> Well before the war in Vietnam had fully engaged us or the ghetto riots had absorbed us, the social bonds—the ties of family, of neighborhood, of mutual forbearance and civility—seem to have come asunder. Why?

That question should be, and no doubt in time will be, seriously debated. No single explanation, perhaps no set of explanations, will ever gain favor. One fact, however, is an obvious
beginning to an explanation: by 1962 and 1963 there had come
of age the persons born during the baby boom of the immediate
postwar period. A child born in 1946 would have been sixteen in
1962, seventeen in 1963.

The numbers involved were very large. In 1950 there were about
24 million persons aged fourteen to twenty-four; by 1960 that had
increased only slightly to just under 27 million. But during the next
ten years it increased by over 13 million persons. Every year for ten
years, the number of young people increased by 1.3 million. That
ten-year increase was greater than the growth in the young segment
of the population for the rest of the century put together. To state it
in another way that focuses on the critical years of 1962 and 1963,
during the first two years of the decade of the 1960s, we added
more young persons (about 2.6 million) to our population than we
had added in any preceding ten years since 1930. (1974, p. 12)

The impacts Wilson theorized from this youth population explosion
started with the arithmetic of population but did not end there. A 13-
million-person expansion to the 27-million-youth population of the nation is 48%, so that the volume of crimes attributable to that age group
might be expected to increase 48% if rates stayed constant. The crime rate
would go up less than that, because the population of the nation as a whole
went up. With a constant rate per 100,000, the impact of this youth population expansion on the total index crime rate of 1960 would be about 13%.
But Wilson thought that the sheer size of the youth cohort produced more
than a larger group with the same propensities as earlier youth groups:

The result of this has been provocatively stated by Professor
Norman B. Ryder, the Princeton University demographer: "There
is a perennial invasion of barbarians who must somehow be civ-
ilized and turned into contributors to fulfillment of the various
functions requisite to societal survival." That "invasion" is the
coming of age of a new generation of young people. Every society copes with this enormous socialization process more or less
successfully, but occasionally that process is almost literally
swamped by a quantitative discontinuity in the numbers of per-

sons involved: "The increase in the magnitude of the socialization tasks in the United States during the past decade was completely outside the bounds of previous experience."

If we continue Professor Ryder's metaphor, we note that in 1950 and still in 1960 the "invading army" (those aged fourteen to twenty-four) were outnumbered three to one by the size of the "defending army" (those aged twenty-five to sixty-four). By 1970 the ranks of the former had grown so fast that they were only outnumbered two to one by the latter, a state of affairs that had not existed since 1910. (1974, pp. 12–13)

The specific theory Wilson puts forward is that the larger size of the youth cohort relative to adult populations breaks down the efficiency of the socialization process that civilizes the young and reduces crime rates. If Wilson was implying that larger youth cohorts systematically have higher crime rates, statistical analysis does not support that generalization (Steffensmeier et al. 1989). But perhaps Wilson only expected this type of cohort effect in extreme cases.

Figure 3.7 uses population and UCRs data to contrast the type of demographic impact that could have been predicted from the baby boom cohort during the 1960s with the type of demographic impact that actually happened. What I call the "prospective" model uses 1960s arrest rates to estimate the percentage of all crime attributable to persons aged 15–24 and then estimates crime volume that would be added to that rate by a 48% increase in the cohort population at 1960s crime rates. The "retrospective"

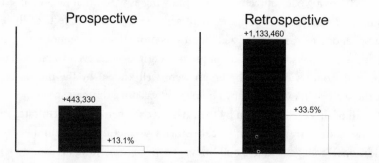

Figure 3.7. The impact of expansion of youth population on crime from 1960 to 1970, two versions. Sources: U.S. Department of Commerce. Bureau of the Census. U.S. Department of Justice. Federal Bureau of Investigation. *Crime in the United States* (1960 and 1970).

estimate shows the crime volume that the same population shift would produce at 1970 rates. This is a rough estimate that overestimates youth crime share, because group arrests are not discounted when converting the percentage of youth arrests into an estimated percentage of crime attributable to youth.

At 1960s crime rates, the largest shift in youth population of the twentieth century would have produced only a 13% increase in crime over a decade, not an epic impact. At 1970 rates, however, the same population shift produces 2½ times the increase in crime. This is still under 25% of the actual crime increase, but plays a much larger role in the total explanation of what happened.

What the "retrospective" analysis of the 1960s pattern shows is the compound effect of a larger youth cohort when rates of offenses among the young are also going up sharply. From 1960 to 1970, the expanding youth population and the increased arrest rate for the young interacted, with each trend making the other trend substantially more important. As the "prospective" estimates in figure 3.7 show, the arithmetic of population increases will rarely be a major element in movements of crime rates all by itself. But population numbers that interact with big rate changes can be quite important.

Prediction versus Retrospection

That leads to an important distinction between using demography after the fact to explain crime fluctuations and using demography to predict crime trends. Looking back at the 1960s, and knowing as we do that rates of arrest went up as the youth population increased, the compound effects of these two phenomena can be analyzed. But it was more than inattention that explains why social scientists did not predict a crime wave, even when the aging birth cohorts of the baby boom were well known by the mid-1950s. Without a rise in rates, the baby boom itself was not a dramatic headline.

All of this was forgotten by the early 1990s, when rising birth rates in the 1980s were translated into scare stories predicting fixed numbers of additional "muggers, killers and thieves than we have now" (Wilson 1995) and "by the year 2010 . . . approximately 270,000 [more] juvenile superpredators on the streets than there were in 1990" (DiIulio 1996). What supplied the impetus for these worries was remembering the 1960s, but what was forgotten was that rates of arrest were a much more important component in the crime wave of the 1960s and early 1970s than population numbers. Since movements in crime rates are notoriously hard to predict (just ask Professors Wilson, Fox, and DiIulio!), modest movements in youth populations are not a decent foundation for future crime projections.

The 1990s in Demographic Retrospect

But what about retrospection? Looking back on the 1990s, what can be said about the role of changes in the structure of population as a reason for the crime decline that was the major criminological news event of the decade? Figure 3.8 shows the percentage of the U.S. population in the high-risk age groups of 15–24 and 15–29 every five years between 1980 and 2000.

Over the 20 years after 1980, the percentage of the population in the most crime-prone years declined by a fairly substantial amount. The proportion of the population between 15 and 24 dropped by 26% during the 20 years, a change of magnitude second only to the upswing of the 1960s, and the 15–29 age group declined by 24% over 20 years. In three of the four five-year periods, crime rates declined as well, but 1985 to 1990 was a period when increasing crime rates among offenders aged 15–24 more than offset the benefits that a smaller fraction of the population in this high-risk group would have produced.

The data on the age structure of the population supports three conclusions. First, the smaller share of the population in high-risk groups pushed crime rates downward. By historical standards, the shift in the age

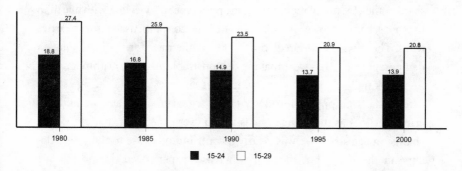

Figure 3.8. High-risk age groups as percentage of population, United States, 1980–2000. Source: U.S. Department of Commerce. Bureau of the Census. International Data Base (IDB). Available at the website of the Census Bureau: www.census.gov/ipc/.

structure was substantial in the post-1980 period. How large one estimates the movement in crime rates to have been as a result of this depends on the standard of comparison. Levitt estimates that raw age structure effects "may have reduced homicide and violent crime by a few percent, and property crime by as much as 5–6 percent" (Levitt 2004, p. 172). While that might seem a small number, it is actually a rather large fraction of the level of change we can ever expect from shifting age structure if rates of crime remain stable. An "across the board" 6% decrease in larceny over the 1990s would be about 26% of the total decline in that category and about 15% of the burglary decline in the 1990s. Moreover, the contrast between the demographic push in the 1960s and 1970s and that during the 1980s and 1990s is even more dramatic. The net swing in crime tendencies when the two periods are compared has to be an important part of the story.

But demography all by itself will never be a major explanation of crime rates dropping by half or doubling because the changes in population groups are more gradual. It is only when demographic trends interact with changes in crime rates that the combination produces dramatic swings. In the period after 1965, the increasing share of the population and its increase in rate compounded on the up side. After 1993, decreasing rates and the smaller population share created a compound effect in the downward direction.

In retrospect, the alarms James Q. Wilson sounded in 1995 were based on faulty computation as well as questionable policy analysis. The "extra million" in the adolescent population predicted by 2000 were only part of the high-risk age group he had singled out earlier when explaining the 1960s. The 15- to 24-year-olds that were his earlier focus never became a larger share of the U.S. population during the period he was viewing with alarm in the 1990s, because lower populations over age 20 compensated for the extra teens. Those who were predicting higher crime rates for the late 1990s on demographic grounds were making demonstrable errors in arithmetic.

Looking back, the demographic news after 1980 about the age structure of the U.S. population described a scenario about as conducive to crime declines as the United States would ever expect to experience. This change in age structure was clearly a contributing cause to the crime decline in the 1990s, but the sharp increases experienced during the late 1980s, despite declines in youth population, are a reminder that the modest influence of shifts in population can be overwhelmed by other social trends that influence crime rates. When rates of crime came down in the 1990s, the demography of that era made the good news better. As I shall show in chapter 5, similar demographic trends in Canada were also keeping step with that nation's crime declines.

Crime and the Economy

There is no single dominant theory of the influence of the economy on either the incidence or prevalence of crime. One reason for this was the timing of the increases of crime in the middle and late 1960s. Expanding rates of crime during periods of general economic prosperity was supposed to be "the paradox of the 1960s," and this warned criminologists off from simplistic economic explanations of fluctuations in crime rates.

A second reason for the absence of consensus theory on crime and the economy was the lack of good criminological theory that would link crime rates directly to marginal changes in general economic conditions. Still, there are statistical indications that rates of some offenses rise and fall with changes in rates of unemployment. And claims are frequently made that improvements in economic conditions reduce crime, sometimes even independent of fluctuations in unemployment. Ayse Imrohoroglu and his associates, for one example, generate a model of the United States from 1980 to 1996 that counts the improving economy as the second leading cause of a decline in property crime (only increased probability of apprehension is more important), despite the model showing that "the effect of unemployment on crime is negligible" (Imrohoroglu, Merlo, and Rupert 2004, p. 707). But because there is no empirically based orthodoxy of explanation of the role of economic factors in crime rate fluctuations, it is open season on finding models of crime and teasing out economic influences. There is widespread agreement throughout most social sciences that legitimate economic opportunities and the economic conditions that produce or extinguish opportunity should play an important role in adolescent and young adult behavioral choices. But how?

Two Theories of Impact

There are two quite straightforward hypotheses about the relationship between crime rates and levels of noncriminal economic activity that are both plausible and empirically supported. The first theory relates to crime as an income source: to the extent that persons engage in crime to obtain money, the increase in other economic opportunities for potential offenders should increase rates of noncriminal behavior to produce income and thereby reduce rates of criminal behavior for income. This approach would expect to see increases in legal income opportunity result in lower rates of offenses that produce income—theft, robbery, drug sales, and prostitution are classes of crime where monetary gain is a primary motive. This will be complicated to some extent by increases in criminal consumption patterns that may also occur with rising income from legitimate sources (Raphael and Winter-Ebmer 2001).

A second approach to crime and economic opportunity stresses the impact of work and schooling as competing with crime as a focus of use of time and social associations by potential offenders. The greater the opportunities to participate in work and study, the less time is available for the social patterns that generate the highest risks of all kinds of crime—property crime and violent crime, income producing as well as income depleting. Larger legitimate opportunities increase the number of potential offenders who are diverted into time allocations and patterns of social interaction that generate less risk of crime than the social interaction of males without occupations with other unemployed males. The study in depth of urban social pathology in the last third of the twentieth century makes crystal clear the conditions of maximum risk for extreme criminal involvement (Wilson 1995). Full-time employment or schooling is a diversion from that highest risk lifestyle.

What remains to be demonstrated is whether and to what extent sustained economic expansion makes an impact on opportunity at the bottom of the opportunity structure. But there is some evidence that this happened in the 1990s. What is beyond controversy is the extraordinary and sustained growth of the American economy during all but the first year or two of the 1990s. What is not as clear is the extent to which the longest sustained period of economic expansion can be given any significant credit for the longest sustained crime decline.

The Economic Record of the 1990s

The usual measure of aggregate economic trends is changes in gross domestic product in the United States. When the 1990s are described as the longest continued expansion in the twentieth century, this is the index that is used. The pattern after 1990 is shown in figure 3.9.

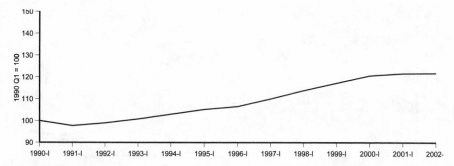

Figure 3.9. Real gross domestic product per capita, quarterly (1990 = 100 in constant dollars [chained 2000 dollars]), United States, 1990–2002. Source: U.S. Department of Commerce. Bureau of Economic Analysis. Available at the website of the Bureau of Economic Analysis: www.bea.doc.gov/bea/dn/nipaweb/TableView .asp?SelectedTable'253&FirstYear'1990&LastYear '2002&Freq'Qtr.

After a recession in 1991–92, the aggregate economic activity expanded in every quarter for eight years in the United States. Not all of the elements of aggregate economic performances are directly linked to crime reduction, of course. Greater wealth might increase the demand for illegal goods and services and thus the rate of some "victimless" crimes. What's good for General Motors in this sense may also be good for cocaine sales. Greater wealth might also increase the volume and value of property worth stealing, which could increase rates of theft. And much new wealth—stock gains, dividends, executive compensation—would seem to be irrelevant to the social and economic forces that determine street crime rates.

But sustained periods of economic growth create jobs and increase wages, two aggregate measures of economic activity that have been directly linked to rates of some forms of crime. Figure 3.10 tells the official unemployment rate story for the United States after 1990.

Over the eight years after 1991, the unemployment rate dropped by about half. There are two ways that lower rates of unemployment might reduce crime rates. First, lower unemployment rates will reduce the number of cases in which loss of a job might motivate criminal activity to replace earnings (Fagan and Freeman 1999, p. 236). Second, finding jobs (when more are available) might divert potential criminals from committing crime and provoke desistance from previous patterns of criminality. All of these would produce positive associations between unemployment rates and crime rates; and Ted Chiricos (1987) reported a positive relationship

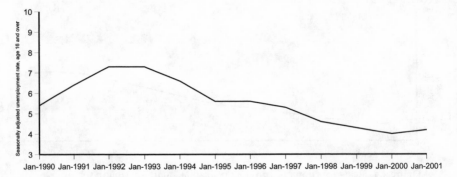

Figure 3.10. Monthly unemployment rate, United States, 1990–2001 (seasonally adjusted). Source: U.S. Department of Labor. Bureau of Labor Statistics. *Labor Force Statistics from the Current Population Survey.* Available at the website of the Bureau of Labor Statistics: www.bls.gov/cps/cpsatabs.htm.

between unemployment and property crime when reviewing 63 studies (Fagan and Freeman 1999, p. 237). The magnitude of the positive unemployment effect is hard to pin down. In their 2001 analysis, Steven Raphael and Rudolph Winter-Ebmer estimate that "slightly more than 40% of the decline (in overall property crime rate between 1992 and 1997) can be attributed to the decline in unemployment" (2001, p. 281). This claimed impact is at the high end of current estimates.

Unemployment is not the only labor statistic that is relevant to crime rates. An environment of rising wages, particularly for entry-level and unskilled work, may also reduce crime, independent of its effect on unemployment. Presumably, higher wages for entry-level work might both attract youth who would choose crime at lower legitimate entry wages, and higher incomes might discourage criminal activities for supplementary income. There is some work on this pattern in the United States (Grogger 1998) using individual-level data. A more adventurous regression study

> obtained strong results using aggregate data from 352 counties
> over a 17-year period (1979–1995). . . . The results showed the inverse relationship of wages with both property and violent crime
> rates. The effect is stronger for property crime . . . the results are
> specific to young, unskilled men, the population group most
> likely to commit these offenses. (Fagan and Freeman 1999, p. 25)

Figure 3.11 shows trends in real wages for the United States over the period 1985–2002. Figure 3.11 uses estimates in constant 2003 dollars of wages for the tenth percentile and twentieth percentile of U.S. wage earners, the two areas where new workers would be concentrated. A deflation using the consumer price index is the method of constant dollar calculation.

Inflation-adjusted wages stayed flat from the mid-1980s through 1996, with the 1996 levels actually below wage levels in 1973. After 1996, the tenth-percentile wage that best represents entry level increased 15% in the next five years. While that seems modest, it was by far the largest increase in any period since 1973. The twentieth-decile group was also flat until 1996 and then increased 13% from then through 2001.

All the data on labor market trends can be influencing both economically motivated crime and time allocation influences on crime rates.

My final data set from the economic trends of the 1990s takes the measure of the number of late-teenagers not involved full-time in either work or school. By lumping full-time work and schooling, I am trying to measure the proportion of youth fully involved in legitimate activities. Economic propensity increases rates of work by providing jobs and increases school participation by providing family and public support for higher education.

Figure 3.12 shows trends in the highest risk group from a time allocation perspective of young persons with the greatest amount of time for persistent criminality, those neither fully occupied at work or school.

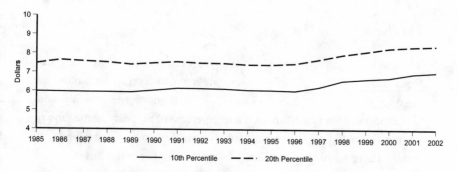

Figure 3.11. Annual estimates of first- and second-decile wages in 2003 dollars, United States, 1980–2002. Source: U.S. Department of Labor. Bureau of Labor Statistics. *The State of Working America* 2004–2005. App. B. Available at the website of the Bureau of Labor Statistics: www.bls.gov/cps/cpsatabs.htm.

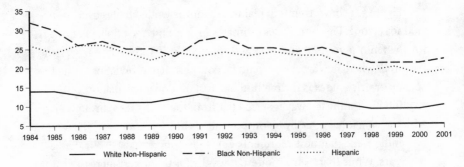

Figure 3.12. Percentage of youth ages 18–19 who are neither enrolled in school nor working, by race and Hispanic origin, United States, 1984–2001. Source: U.S. Department of Labor. Bureau of Labor Statistics. *Labor Force Statistics from the Current Population Survey.* Available at the website of the Bureau of Labor Statistics: www.bls.gov/cps/cpsatabs.htm.

The trends in figure 3.12 tell two pieces of good news. First, the rate of nonengagement in school or work is down for all significant groups by the late 1990s—down a third for older African American and Hispanic teens. Second, the noninvolvement rates, as measured by the Department of Labor, stays low even after unemployment increases after 2001. The magnitude of the decline from mid-1980s levels looks large. How much independent impact that would have on crime rates is still an open question.

The Elusive Bottom Line

The economic circumstances of the 1990s were good news on the crime front, but the magnitude of the aggregate impact on crime rates of all the positive economic trends is very much an open question. At the low end, we have Steven Levitt's estimate of 6 or 7 percent of property crime (2004). Higher estimates might account for as much as 40% of total property crime. There is, however, a danger with the higher estimates: they are based in part on fluctuations in crime and economic data from the 1990s—the problem alluded to in the introduction of this chapter. But the range of published economic effects estimates, from one-quarter to 40% of the total property crime decline, is a substantial part of the 1990s story.

A Decade of Maximum Impact

One other feature of the economic performance of the 1990s is important in the overall portrait of that decade. The contribution of economic growth to public finance, to crime prevention, to economic mobility, and to many other aspects of the American infrastructure was as positive as we are likely to see in the foreseeable future. Thus, whatever economic growth has to contribute to control of crime in the United States is probably observable in the record of this remarkable decade. Income inequality expanded in most of the 1990s, but the sustained job growth had also created an entry-level opportunity structure near the end of the decade that was quite broad.

The timing of the largest part of the economic expansion fits better with the second half of the 1990s crime decline than with the first half. Yet because much of the earliest part of the decline may have been normal cyclical fluctuation (see chapters 1 and 5), the post-1996 economic expansion is well timed to contribute to the element that distinguishes the 1990s from earlier postwar crime downturns, the length of the downtrend (see chapter 1).

Three Noncandidates

There are three long-nominated factors in American crime and violence that scholars have not nominated as major influences on the national decline in crime of the 1990s: rehabilitation programs, a general decline in drug use, and variations in gun control. In each case, what keeps the issue off the list of candidates is the lack of a plausible nationwide independent variable. In the drug control debates, the decline of crack cocaine in cities has been cited as an influence on 1990s homicides and will be discussed in the next chapter. But other illegal drugs continued to be chronic problems. The big declines in survey research estimates of national drug use happened in the late 1980s, when crime was increasing. So there was no general drug use decline to isolate as a cause in the 1990s.

Nor were there any indications that correctional or crime prevention programs had national-level impact on crime. One of the interesting contrasts throughout the 1990s was that the public belief that crime controls were working did not extend to any programs treating offenders or potential offenders.

The role of firearms in the crime patterns of the 1990s is a more complicated story. Firearms are an important influence on the death rate from criminal violence in the United States but have no clear relationship to rates of nonrobbery property crime or aggravated assault. So the place to look for gun policy effects would be in homicide trends. Figure 3.13 shows the volume of handgun homicides, other gun homicides, and nongun homicides from 1990 to 2000.

Handgun homicides increase in the first three years of the 1990s, peaking in 1993, then drop by 43% in the next seven years. Nongun homicides decline by 28% after 1993, so that two-thirds of the handgun homicide decline is not specific to handguns.

But what of the 15% drop in handgun killings that isn't reflected in nongun homicide trends? One major piece of federal firearms control legislation passed in 1993, the peak year of handgun killings in the decade. But the major change in handgun regulation provided in the Brady law—a waiting period for firearm purchase record checks—should have reduced killings more in those states previously without record checks where the change in regulation was greatest. This evidently did not happen in the early years of the new law (see Cook and Ludwig 2000).

The only other shift was a change in dealer fees and regulations that might be linked to reduced handgun sales, but how this might have major impact is not obvious. So the lower rate at which handguns were added to the market may have also reduced handgun use, but no major public policy shift seems to have caused that change at the national level. In New

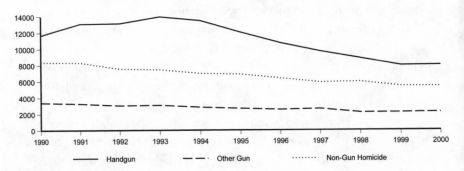

Figure 3.13. Handgun homicides, other gun homicides, and nongun homicides, United States, 1990–2000. Source: U.S. Department of Justice, FBI, *Uniform Crime Report*, 1990–2000.

York City, by contrast, changing effectiveness of gun controls may have played an important part in that city's stunning success during the 1990s, a possibility I discuss in chapter 6.

Conclusion: A Crime Prevention Trifecta?

The three forces I have examined in this chapter—imprisonment, demography, and economy—are not new considerations in the discourse about crime trends. All three have long been seen as influences on crime rates. It turns out that the 1990s was a decade when each of these three influences was operating with maximum historical impact in a crime-preventive direction. The incapacitative throw weight of more than a million and a half additional prisoners was operative by the late 1990s. Despite the fact that marginal contributions from the prisoners who were a net addition of stock were less than in earlier years, the total incapacitation effect was maximal in the late 1990s. The decline in the share of the population in the highest risk age groups was a demographic blessing often overlooked during the 1990s. For most of that decade, the rhetoric about youth population trends and the facts were headed in opposite directions. And the economic expansion was both very big and the longest on record. This trifecta of crime-preventive forces had never before happened in the seven decades of recorded crime trends in the United States.

Could incapacitation, demographics, and the blessings of prosperity explain the whole of the 1990s crime decline? In considering this question, the reader must first remember that the 40% or so crime decline that is measured from the very top of crime rates in 1991 may also contain cyclical declines without any clear causes. If a 10% decline in crime was due to a regression from a cyclical peak, that would only leave 30% of crime to be explained by substantive changes in the American environment. Since the triple experiment that happened in the 1990s had never happened before, why couldn't the concordance of demography, imprisonment, and prosperity account for a 30% reduction? This is possible, but the margin of error for estimating the influence of each of the three influences on crime is substantial. The range of crime reduction that these factors might explain is well less than half at the low end but as much as two-thirds at the high end. I will revisit the issue of the impact of prison and demography after my analysis of crime trends in Canada in chapter 5.

Whether the high-end or low-end estimates seem more plausible, what is indisputable in retrospect is that watching trends in incarceration, in the economy, and in population trends should have made a substantial crime drop very much less of a surprise as it was happening than proved to be the case. By 1996, at the latest, many of the trends discussed here were in evidence or should have been.

Progeny of the 1990s

Three New Explanations

of Decline

4

What separates the theories to be examined in this chapter from the topics covered in the previous chapter is that this chapter's explanations were inspired by the declining crime rates of the 1990s and the opportunity that declining crime presented for new explanations of good news. Not all the theories considered here were totally novel in the 1990s—police and policing are central to government activity intended to control crime. But as I showed in chapter 2, variations in levels of policing or in strategies of police deployment were not regarded as a major influence on crime prior to the 1990s.

I will consider the three theorized causes of crime declines addressed in this chapter in increasing order of novelty—first police, then the rise and fall of crack cocaine, and finally the impact of increased access to abortion that, advocates claim, caused a shift in the crime-risk profile of birth cohorts in the 1970s. After an introductory discussion of the definition and special problems of theories that were inspired by the 1990s' decline, I will give unequal attention to the three explanations covered. The section on police is shorter than it might be because national-level police effects seem implausible in the 1990s. But chapter 6 reopens the impact of policing in greater detail when considering the crime decline in New York City.

Over half of this chapter—and a substantial data appendix—addresses the thesis that crime declines in the 1990s were caused by the coming-of-age of population cohorts that were altered by the impact of elective abortion in the United States in the 1970s. There are two reasons this theory and its testing demands sustained attention. It is of substantive interest as a carefully constructed and original theory of the latent impacts of legal changes. And it is also of methodological interest as an illustration of the special problems and opportunities confronted when the known facts of a crime decline inspire a new theory of causation and then serve as the evidence for its truth.

A Counterfeit Novelty?

My classification as "novel" here the theory that police are responsible for crime reduction might seem like a contradiction of both history and common sense. Police are, after all, one of the two major government investments in criminal justice (the other is prisons), and police dominate the detection of crime and the apprehension of offenders. In what sense can we call it novel to suppose that the number of police we hire or the way we deploy them might have an important impact on crime rates?

I have already shown in chapter 2 that the conventional wisdom of the 1970s and 1980s doubted the ability of changes in police tactics or manpower allocations to make any sustained difference in crime rates. Charles Silberman most famously asked us to "abandon the quixotic faith that there is a police solution to the problem of criminal violence" (Silberman 1978), and even enthusiasts for "broken windows" did not claim the power to reduce crime until the mid-1990s.

But doubts about the capacity of policy activities or organizations to make a major dent on crime rates were not merely an artifact of the pessimistic 1970s. David Bayley, one of the top three or four academic experts on policing in the United States, starts his 1994 volume *Police for the Future* with a series of unconditional assertions in his introductory chapter, which he calls "The Myth of the Police": "The police do not prevent crime. Experts know it, the police know it, but the public does not know it" (p. 3).

He goes on to summarize the empirical evidence on police impacts in the following terms: "First, repeated analysis has consistently failed to find any connection between the numbers of police officers and crime rates.

Second, the primary strategies adopted by modern police have been shown to have little or no effect on crime" (Bayley 1994, p. 3).

This was the orthodox social science view in the mid-1990s, and claims for major crime prevention dividends from police numbers or tactics can thus be regarded as both (1) new in the 1990s and (2) dependent in large measure on the link between police activity and crime rates during the 1990s. It is this dependence on the crime decline of the 1990s that justifies the special scrutiny I give to new theories of crime prevention in this chapter.

The second novel theory of crime prevention I will consider in this chapter concerns the "rise and fall of crack cocaine" as an explanation of 1990s (post-crack) crime declines. The crack story is a mix of old and new. The links between illegal drugs and crime have been investigated and disputed for decades. During the 1980s, a major explanation for increases in homicide and other violence after 1984 was the arrival of smokable "crack cocaine" in inner-city neighborhoods. But the new wrinkle in the 1990s version of drugs and crime was attributing a sustained and relatively gradual decline in crime to the abatement of the crack epidemic in the 1990s. The standard theory of drugs and crime was only to explain increases in crime and violence. The 1990s variation of that theme was to attribute good news on the crime front to the passing of an epidemic.

The third new causal theory of crime decline to emerge from the 1990s was to view the decade's crime drop as a delayed effect of selective high-risk birth reductions caused by elective abortion opportunities in the 1970s. This theory was completely new to criminological discourse at the turn of the twenty-first century, so its credentials as innovation are beyond doubt. Beyond doubt, too, is the fact that the 1990s crime decline is a crucially important element of the empirical evidence that advocates use to support a general theory that elective abortion legislation has a preventive effect on crime.

A Methodological Concern

The new theories of crime prevention discussed in this chapter vary substantially in the mechanisms they say reduce crime, but they share one common characteristic that requires special caution: they use the 1990s crime decline as evidence to prove that these newly discovered mechanisms prevent crime.

Since it was the events of the 1990s that generated the new theories, the close fit in time between when crime declines occurred and when they would be expected is weaker evidence of the causal linkage than if the theories had been in place before the declines happened. The theories in this chapter are not independent of the 1990s. They were derived from these events in the United States and cannot therefore be tested against the timing of the crime decline as if the close fit in timing had not been known before the theory was proposed. Testing a theory only against the history that provoked it is a specially constrained empirical inquiry. The chances of coincidental timing are inescapably greater.

This handicap for new hypotheses is no excuse for ignoring promising new possibilities. But it should inspire caution in drawing inferences based only on 1990s events in the United States, and it should provoke a wide variety of different types of tests of causal theory in environments other than those that generated the theory. On the basis of the evidence surveyed in this chapter, I am not prepared to conclude that any of the three theories discussed had a proven role of any magnitude in the 1990s crime decline.

Two Theories of Police Efficacy

The crime decline of the 1990s produced not one but two discrete theories of changes in policing as a major influence on crime rates. The first explanation of policing as crime prevention emphasized a quantitative approach—increase the number of police in American cities, and the crime rate will decrease. The second theory focused on new and more effective tactics for deploying police resources.

Did Size Matter?

The expansion of police manpower was an important part of the 1990s by most measures, and some observers gave credit to larger numbers of police in explaining the crime decline.

The major political milestone in this story was President Clinton's focus in the federal crime legislation of 1994 on a legislative initiative to fund 100,000 new police at the municipal level. The six-digit round number and the scale of the promise captured public attention and neutralized crime as a partisan political issue. The call for 100,000 cops countered Republican calls for financial aid to state prison construction and federal standards for tough sentencing proposals. There was no clear emphasis on what particular types of police deployment were to occur. The major premise of the Clinton proposal was that there was a shortage of urban police in the United States, and more cops could play a major preventive role by operating in the same way that existing police forces used manpower. While some of the current buzzwords in 1990s police administration—terms like community policing, zero tolerance, broken windows, and the like—were mentioned in the discourse on funding an expanding scale of urban police, the heavy emphasis was on more police rather than different policing as the crucial ingredient in the federal recipe for safe streets.

But more police to do what? Variations in police car patrol manpower were not supposed to reduce crime (vide Kansas City, as discussed in chapter 2), and while foot patrols made citizens feel better, they didn't seem to reduce crime either (Kelling et al., 1981; see also Wilson and Kelling 1982). One critical problem with assessing the influence of levels of police services on crime rates is that it is a classic "black box" problem: one will know how many police there were but not what they did. Without any explicit theory of how police influence crime rates, the only evidence for the effectiveness of police at the margin would be found in the statistical correlation one derives. If there are substantial problems measuring both levels of police resources and crime, and additional problems of identification that must be estimated or neutralized, regression studies of police effects on crime can be a real mess. By and large, they are.

Despite the political call for 100,000 extra police, the actual per capita expansion of police was more modest. Steven Levitt puts the expansion in police at 50,000 to 60,000 and provides a ballpark per capita expansion estimate of 14% (Levitt 2004, p. 177). Professors John Eck and Edward Maguire argue that there is an uncomfortably large margin of error in any ballpark guess in national-level police manpower expansion. "The size of police agencies . . . is undoubtedly growing . . . inaccurate methods of counting police make it difficult to know by how much" (Eck and Maguire 2000, p. 216).

Can we use previous studies of the impact on police on crime rates to estimate the influence of expanding police forces on crime in the 1990s? There have been two efforts to do this, and they present a rather startling study in contrasts in both methodology and conclusions drawn.

In 2000, Eck and Maguire produced a 60-page summary of research to date on the effects of quantitative and qualitative changes in policing, with over 100 references to previously published work. They surveyed 41 regression studies on the quantity-of-police and crime issue. After excluding all cross-sectional studies for inadequate identification restrictions and a number of other studies for failure to plausibly deal with identification problems, they say, "we were left with nine studies containing twenty-seven separate dependant variables" (Eck and Maguire 2000, p. 217). Presumably these "dependent variables" are 27 different crime rates that police manpower levels might influence.

> Police strength has no effect on crime in fifteen equations (55%), a positive effect in four equations (15%) and a negative effect in eight equations (30%). Thus, even when we examined only the most rigorous studies, we could not find consistent evidence that increases in police strength produce decreases in violent crime. Overall, the research suggests that hiring more police officers did not play an independent or consistent role in reducing violent crime in the United States. (p. 217)

Steven Levitt published a shorter examination of possible causes of crime reduction 3½ years later, and his analysis reviewed the empirical research on police and crime with great circumspection. Professor Levitt cites one review of literature he does not rely on and then mentions only four studies—each by an economist who concludes that more police reduce crime rates—including two studies done by himself. The first and most famous Levitt study on this topic produced elasticity estimates for different crimes that ranged widely (Levitt 1997) and most of which turned out to be not statistically significant when a computer programming error is corrected (McCrary 2002). He then generated a later regression analysis using firemen rather than local election cycles as his identification strategy, which produced a tighter range of elasticity estimates for various crimes (Levitt 2002). He then used a single elasticity estimate from this fireman exercise to reach the conclusion that "using an elasticity of crime with respect to police of −0.48, the increase in police between 1991 and 2001 can account for a crime reduction of 5–6% across the board" (Levitt 2002, p. 177).

In reaching this global conclusion, Professor Levitt does not mention the earlier Eck and Maguire analysis, even though it appeared in the only scholarly book published on the topic of his 2004 article. This failure to consult or acknowledge scholarship outside economics on a question like police seems to me an example of what a federal judge once called "the cross-sterilization of the social sciences."

But whatever the flaws of Levitt's quick-draw estimates of police manpower effects on crime, the marginal growth of police during the decade and the lack of an independent basis for estimating manpower impacts leave a relatively small margin of error for determining the role of the quantitative expansion of policing in the 1990s decline. The moderate growth in policing certainly had no more than a 5% impact on crime rates and probably much less than that.

Still, if the impact of police numbers is ever an important question, we are not well equipped to study it. Because there are few natural experiments with sharp increases in police manpower, measuring the impact of changes in police levels on crime will probably remain the domain of regression analysis. Without good and consistent models for the other factors that influence crime rates, it would be charitable to call such exercises an inexact science.

Because of all the substantial problems associated with studies of police manpower over time, the best hope for reducing the margin of error on estimates of effects is a triangulation of proof, where a variety of differently imperfect methods lead to generally consistent conclusions. But this is exactly the wrong place to use partial samples of existing studies of comparable quality or to ignore analyses or analysts with whom one disagrees! So Professor Levitt's selectivity of citation would be a problem on any question but could be a disabling strategy on this question.

The quantitative increase in police may have played a small role in the national crime decline. But perhaps not. There is no clear theory about how numbers of police should reduce crime, so current estimates of police effectiveness rely only on widely varying regression results.

The Quality of Policing

Far more than the sheer number of police was changing in big cities of the United States over the period after 1985. Declining faith in preventive patrol and encouraging evaluations of a series of innovative efforts produced widespread emphasis in police forces on new programs of community policing, well established by 1990 and still flourishing at the turn of the century. The momentum to change strategies of urban policing has been one of the truly important developments in criminal justice in the United States in recent years. Has it also been an important cause of the national-level crime decline during the 1990s?

Probably not. The responsibility for the organization and deployment of police is decentralized into thousands of local departments, including hundreds of city police departments. So any truly national-level change in policing over a short time would seem unlikely. With the crime decline spread widely and fairly evenly across so many different types of police agency during the 1990s, changes in the style of policing at the local level are an unlikely cause of such a pattern.

There is also reason to believe that truly dramatic changes in policing were not widespread during the 1990s. The gap between rhetoric and reality in progress toward community policing was substantial, according to informed observers (Eck and Maguire 2000, pp. 218–224). The number of departments endorsing the rhetoric of "order maintenance" during the 1990s was smaller than the community police partisans, but there is no reason to suppose any smaller gap between verbal descriptions and organizational change for these departments. So there is no clear evidence of substantial substantive change at the national level in strategies of street policing that would justify linking police strategy to national-level crime declines.

A City-Level Policy Experiment

Nonetheless, the very features that make national-level impacts of changes in police organization unlikely produce very good opportunities to test the impact of police strategy changes at the city level. The modern big city is the level of government that both reports crime and provides the administrative structure for police operations. A substantial change in police organization and strategy that was city-wide in scope would be a natural policy experiment that might produce city-level shifts in a variety of dependent outcomes, including the quantity and quality of reported crime.

The city of New York conducted something close to this city-wide policy experiment in policing beginning in 1994. Just as the data make it unlikely that changes in police strategy drove national-level crime rates down, the best evidence from New York City suggests that simultaneous changes in the quantity and quality of policing reduced crime in New York much more than the national baseline trend. I reviewed some of the evidence for the special nature of the New York decline in chapter 1; I will sympathetically examine the argument for policing as an important influence on New York City crime in chapter 6.

For present purposes, however, the important lesson from New York City is that methods of policing can make a difference in crime outcomes. The reasons for doubting any important national impact of changing policing strategies in the 1990s are more closely tied to the decentralized nature of police governance and the marginal and uneven pace of change in policing, not to any inherent limits of police activity as a crime influence. Chapter 6 will show that the received wisdom that the police don't influence crime rates will probably require extensive qualification once the lessons of the 1990s are thoroughly understood.

Crack Cocaine and Its Aftermath

A major puzzle in the story of late twentieth-century American crime patterns concerns the second half of the 1980s. This was a period when both the demographics and the policy changes should have produced either flat or declining crime with smaller cohorts of youth in the population and the largest proportional expansion of prisoners in the modern era. But crime rates, particularly rates of urban violence, turned up after 1985, powered by substantial increases in homicide in the age group 15–24. Why this age group? Alfred Blumstein outlined the most plausible explanation of this in an introductory essay to his and Joel Wallman's collection on the crime decline:

> The evidence available so far is largely consistent with the earlier hypothesis (Blumstein 1995) of the sequence that created the rise phase: introduction of crack in the mid-1980s; recruitment of young minority males to sell the drugs in street markets; arming of the drug sellers with handguns for self-protection; diffusion of guns to peers; irresponsible and excessively casual use of guns by young people, leading to a "contagious" growth in homicide and possibly robbery also. Cork (1999) provides some strong evidence supporting this connection. (Blumstein and Wallman 2000, p. 39)

If the growth of crack cocaine in the late 1980s fueled the expansion of crime and violence in that era, to what extent might the 1990s declines in crime and violence also be the product of removing the criminogenic elements of crack markets? Such a theory is the social science equivalent of the observation that "the nice thing about hitting your head against a stone wall is that it feels so good when you stop." To what extent can we attribute the drop in rates of crime and violence to the removal of the pathological influences of expanding crack markets?

Professor Blumstein is uncertain how much credit is due to the abatement of crack effects in the crime decline. "A significant aspect of the improvement involved undoing some of the factors that contributed to the growth of the late 1980s"—but which factors and to what extent can we regard them as undone? The closer one stays to the increases and decreases in gun violence by young minority males in the period from 1985 to 1998, the better the fit with the rise and fall of crack cocaine markets. Even within the homicide-among-youth category, the rise of crack cocaine is a more persuasive account of the increase in youth homicide than is the withering of cocaine as an explanation of decline. The Blumstein analysis shows clearly that the increasing homicides after 1985 were specific to young offenders using guns and further concentrated in big cities. And the drop in homicide after 1993 was just as clearly concentrated in minority youth and gun cases, as shown by figure 4.1 (fig. 2.18 in Blumstein and Wallman 2000).

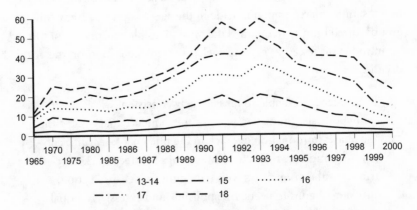

Figure 4.1. Trends in murder arrest rate by age (individual young ages), United States, 1965–2000. Source: Alfred Blumstein. "Disaggregating the Violence Trends," fig. 2.18, in Blumstein and Joel Wallman, eds. 2000. *The Crime Drop in America*. New York: Cambridge University Press.

There are, however, two reasons why a group that has experienced a greater-than-normal increase in homicide events (in this case, handgun homicides by black youth) might fall faster and further than rates that had remained relatively stable. One reason the more volatile rate might drop more is that the same substantive factors that pushed rates up among the high-growth group turned around and pushed rates down. But what is the dynamic of decline in youth violence after the peak of crack markets? Even as crack cocaine commerce slows down, the substantive features of streets and neighborhoods that had generated danger might not spontaneously recover.

Which leads to a second possibility: the very fact of a large increase in the late 1980s may make a larger than usual decrease in the 1990s more likely as a "regression toward the mean" phenomenon that might not be closely linked to the decline in crack markets. The greater the increase in homicides has been, the larger the drop we can expect, if only because the higher peak leaves room for a larger drop to take place before normal historical levels are restored. Something close to regression toward older historical averages may operate after a crack epidemic.

If the drop in gun violence among minority youth in the first few years after exceptionally high peak levels might just as easily be regression effects as the result of pacification of local drug markets, any longer term decline in violence might not be either regression or the end of crack. The longer declines in violence persist, the more likely it becomes that any continual decline is a result of neither regression nor the easing of crack market consequences but rather the result of substantive changes in the later 1990s. So drops in homicide in 1995, 1996, and perhaps 1997 can more easily be linked to either crack relaxation or regression than the decreases that persisted to the very end of the 1990s. Why would the deconstruction of crack effects be spread so evenly out over a relatively long period of time? For this reason, Richard Rosenfeld correctly argues that this hypothesis "does not account for the length and breadth of the decrease in youth violence" (2004, p. 87).

Crack in the Context of a General Crime Decline

What makes the crack story persuasive in the early and middle 1990s is the way it fits with so many of the circumstantial details of increases followed by decreases in minority youth gun homicide. But the very specificity of the crime pattern linked to crack cocaine renders the story vulnerable when explaining the broad crime drop of the 1990s. One problem is that the crack/gun violence influence should not cause all varieties of crime to go up and then decline. Thus, Rosenfeld concludes that the crack hypothesis "says nothing about the drop in property crime rates or the long-term decline in violence among adults" (2004, p. 87). Rosenfeld is making a limited but important point—that there are many elements of the 1990s decline that the proliferation and then abatement of drug markets in big cities did not cause. What, after all, should be the impact of variations in crack cocaine markets on rates of auto theft, rape, or robbery? This puts a natural limit on the breadth of decline that crack might explain, without, however, casting any doubt on the drug market explanation for falling youth homicide rates in the mid-1990s.

There is a second respect, however, in which the breadth and evenness of the 1990s crime decline may challenge the importance of the crack cocaine story as a major influence on even the decline in homicide. To the extent that the broad decline in official crime was evenly spread across crime categories, there is no apparent crack-violence downdraft bigger than the general decline to observe during the 1990s. Homicide rates went down at the same pace as rape, robbery, and burglary, not at a faster rate. But none of these other crimes should be sensitive to variations in crack markets. So why didn't the overall homicide rate decline faster than rape and burglary? The larger drop in minority youth homicide rates that can be observed might simply be regression rather than a substantive impact of changes in cocaine commerce. The drop in youth violence, on that reading, would only be the downswing of an epiphenomenon because the peak homicide rates of minority youth had much farther to drop before reaching their long-term levels (see Zimring 2004).

This use of the breadth of the crime decline as an argument against crack abatement as a major influence on homicide is a strong reservation if and only if one accepts the characterization of the declines across crime categories in the 1990s as spread evenly, and as presumably being all effects of the same causes. That reading of the period would only allow a minor role for crack cocaine developments in the larger pattern of decline in lethal violence.

But any pressure toward disaggregation in the explanation of crime declines might allow for a much larger role for crack cocaine influences. To what extent is the aggregate decline in all crime categories a composite with many different subsidiary causes and only a superficially similar bottom line? In that setting, the power of the crack story could be substantial. But the more unitary one's conception of the crime decline, the smaller the probable role of the crack story in explanation of the aggregate. On current evidence, the generality of the decline in the 1990s and the similarity of declines across categories remain very much open questions.

The Case of the Unborn Offender

The growing literature that addresses the possible link between increasing access to abortion in the early 1970s and decreasing crime in the 1990s demands sustained attention for three reasons. First, it is a genuinely fresh theory about the causes of variations in crime rates, not so much counterintuitive—like the famous "More Guns, Less Crime" argument of John Lott, Jr.—but instead an overlooked possibility that deserves serious consideration once it enters the conversation. Second, the magnitude of the abortion influence that its proponents claim is very large, between a third and a half of the total crime decline. And this huge abortion dividend is not being urged by cranks: John Donohue and Steven Levitt are among the most prominent practicing scholars of law and economics in the United States and probably the two most eminent economic researchers with a special interest in crime and its control since Gary Becker.

The third claim the dialogue on crime and abortion law makes on our attention is the extraordinary difficulty of using trends in crime to test the delayed effects of legal change that happened decades earlier. It would be hard to pick a more complicated hypothesis to test empirically, and the growing literature on the subject provides a window into the different approaches of different social sciences to a formidably difficult problem. It is easy to imagine making the issue into the subject of a book-length examination of the promise and limits of various empirical methods for the study of the impact of law on behavior.

I will not try to write that book in these pages but will instead take my time in setting out the theories advanced on the abortion question, the evidence that has so far been introduced in the literature, some "missing links" in the evidence developed to date on abortion effects, and some further data that might provide a more powerful test of the theory than now exists. A close reading of this developing debate tells us quite a bit about the current limits on our knowledge, but it also shows at least one clear path to more powerful tests of important questions.

Three Theories of Crime Reduction

John Donohue and Steven Levitt outlined a variety of ways abortion might influence in an article published in the *Quarterly Journal of Economics* in May 2001. The first possibility was lower cohort size:

> Legalized abortion may lead to reduced crime either through reductions in cohort sizes or through lower per capita offending rates for affected cohorts. The smaller cohort that results from abortion legalization means that when that cohort reaches the late teens and twenties, there will be fewer young males in their highest crime years, and thus less crime. (2001, p. 381)

The two other potential impacts of available abortion concern the qualitative impact of giving control over fertility to women:

> More interesting and important is the possibility that children born after abortion legalization may on average have lower rates of criminality for either of two reasons. First, women who have abortions are those most at risk to give birth to children who would engage in criminal activity. Teenagers, unmarried women, and the economically disadvantaged are all substantially more likely to seek abortions. Recent studies have found children born to these mothers to be at higher risk for committing crime in adolescence. . . . Second, women may use abortion to optimize the timing of childbearing. A given woman's ability to provide a nurturing environment to a child can fluctuate over time depending on the woman's age, education, and income, as well as the presence of a father in the child's life, whether the pregnancy is wanted and any drug or alcohol abuse both in utero and after the birth. Consequently, legalized abortion provides a woman the opportunity to delay childbearing if the current conditions are suboptimal. Even if lifetime fertility remains constant for all women, children are born into better environments, and future criminality is likely to be reduced. (p. 381)

The three separate parts of the theory of abortion effects each proceed with a theory of the proximate impact of abortion availability on the quantity and risk circumstances of live births that is followed by delayed impact on crime rates at some period after birth that is 15 or more years in the future. Table 4.1 provides a graphic and time representation for the three hypotheses outlined by Donohue and Levitt.

There is a clear distinction between the type of proximal impacts predicted by the increased utilization of abortion reducing the total number of births, which should measurably reduce the birth rate, and those special

Table 4.1

Proximate and ultimate impacts of abortion legalization—Three Donohue and Levitt theories.

Period: 1970–73 to present	Proximate result[a]	Ultimate result[b]	Crime impact
More abortions	Fewer births	Fewer young men and fewer crimes	Lower crime volume
More abortions of pregnancies that would produce babies at socio-economic risk	Fewer single mother births	Lower risk youth population	Lower crime rate per 100,000 youth
	Fewer mother-in-poverty births	Lower risk youth population	
	Fewer teen mother births	Lower risk youth population	
	Fewer disadvantaged minority births	Lower risk youth population	
More abortions of pregnancies that would produce socially or psychologically mistimed births	Better timing of births by mothers age, marital status, economic circumstances, or mother's psychological condition	Lower risk youth population	Lower crime rate per 100,000 youth; perhaps lower crime rate per 100,000 youth in specific previous high-risk groups

[a]Timing of each proximate result is 7–9 months.
[b]Timing of each ultimate result is 15–20 years.

characteristics of women who take advantage of legal opportunities for abortion who would otherwise produce children at much higher than average risk, thereby increasing the crime rate of the entire birth cohort. The first theory suggests that the number of births changes, while the second and third theories predict changes in the circumstances children are born into. While Donohue and Levitt present two different theories of qualitative selectivity, many of the same demographic characteristics will be influenced by a higher abortion rate among higher risk mothers. Whether the lower early rate of high-risk births is evidence of lower eventual fertility or different birth timing will not be easy to measure. But many other aspects of family structure at birth can be measured.

The Donohue/Levitt Study

What makes it difficult to link 1970 and 1973 abortion law changes to arrest patterns in the 1990s is the variety of other factors that influence crime and arrest rates over time and the extraordinary difficulty of constructing rigorous causal tests that can discriminate causes of crime with assurance. The way Donohue and Levitt outline their hypotheses in the 2001 study suggests one natural next step in testing for a causal relationship between abortion law effects and lower eventual crime rates: to test for the presence and magnitude of the proximal effects—the effects on births in the 1970s—that they believe have led to the eventual crime decline.

This is not the path of Donohue and Levitt. They mention an analysis suggesting a 5% reduction in live births as a consequence of abortion, but they do not report data on the risk environments of birth and early childhood in the 1970s and 1980s. This failure to study the earlier stops on the causal chains they have constructed is probably a matter of the intellectual style of econometrics, which is typically a regression exercise that focuses on the presumed independent variable and the presumed dependent variable, and seeks only to create statistical controls for all other possible influences on the dependent variable. I have had reason to criticize this strategy in the past (Zimring and Hawkins 1997) and will show what data on the proximate variables look like for abortion and fertility later in this chapter. For now, however, it is prudent to attribute these missing links not to any deviant scholarly tendencies of these authors but to the predominant style of American econometric method.

In keeping with the style of this approach, the strategic aim of the Donohue and Levitt analysis is to fashion comparisons of crime statistics in the 1990s that should reveal whether the later changes in crime are associated with the earlier changes in abortion policy and utilization.

The authors provide a summary of their evidence that increases in abortion use is a major cause of later crime reduction in the United States:

> First, we see a broad consistency with the timing of legalization
> of abortion and the subsequent drop in crime. For example, the
> peak ages for violent crime are roughly 18–24, and crime starts
> turning down around 1992, roughly the time at which the first
> cohort born following Roe v. Wade would hit its criminal prime.
> Second . . . the five states that legalized abortion in 1970 saw drops
> in crime before the other 45 states and the District of Columbia,
> which did not allow abortions until . . . 1973. (Donohue and
> Levitt 2001, pp. 381–382)

Two further comparisons are put forward as indicators that the increase in abortions drove crime rates down:

> First, there is no relationship between abortion rates in the mid-
> 1970s and crime changes between 1972 and 1985 (prior to the point
> when the abortion-affected cohorts have reached the age of
> significant criminal involvement). Second, virtually all of the
> abortion-related crime decrease can be attributed to reductions
> in crime among the cohorts born after abortion legalization.
> There is little change in crime among older cohorts. (Donohue
> and Levitt 2001, p. 382)

The authors emphasize the fact that abortion rates don't influence crime rates prior to 1985 and that the crime declines are evident only among younger offenders as evidence that a change in the quality of births is the only likely cause of such a pattern.

Abortion and Crime: Some Academic Reaction

While the Donohue and Levitt argument has received sustained media attention, most of the discussion of it in academic circles has remained within economics. The approach that Richard Rosenfeld, a certified criminologist, took to the Donohue and Levitt article is typical in both its tone and its level of attention of the criminological reaction. Writing in the Scientific American of this analysis, Rosenfeld gives the authors a pat on the back and a quick dismissal:

> Economists . . . Donohue . . . and . . . Levitt . . . offer an intriguing alternative to conventional demographic explanations of the crime drop. They attribute as much as half of the crime decline during the 1990s to the legalization of abortion in the 1970s. This change resulted in fewer births of unwanted children to low income women, thereby, they claim, preventing the crimes those disadvantaged children would have committed some 15 to 20 years later. Though not implausible, the analysis implies that youth homicide trends should have slackened earlier than they did. (2004, pp. 86–87)

A more extensive tug-of-war over the plausibility of an abortion legalization dividend involved Ted Joyce, an economist with a significant history of studying abortion, who published a critique of the original study (Joyce 2004a), to which Donohue and Levitt replied (Donohue and Levitt 2004), after which Joyce responded in turn (Joyce 2004b).

Two general points about this exchange deserve preliminary mention. The first is that both sides in this debate subscribe to the methodological assumptions and preferences of econometric inquiry. In that sense, their dispute about abortion impacts can be seen to be a narrow one. But the assumptions and style of economic analysis are about all the identified common ground that develops in the dialog. The two sides take opposing positions in the initial dispute, and there little common ground is identified as the discourse develops. So there are multiple differences of opinion on whether the most plausible reading of the abortion law changes in the 1970s and crime drops in the 1990s is that the former caused the latter.

Ted Joyce doubts that counting the rate of abortions per 1,000 live births gives a reliable reading of unwanted births avoided at any time, but particularly after the mid-1970s. He shows (as Donohue and Levitt also acknowledge) that abortion rates far exceed any lowering of the birth rate by a factor of three or more to one. Whether this means that many of the legal abortions after 1970 were illegal ones before the changes in law is disputed, and neither side has very good data on the subject.

Joyce argues that there is no clear negative relationship between rates of abortion and rates of fertility (except in the early repeal states during the early 1970s). He then puts great stress on his reading of the crime rate trends in these early repeal states between 1986 and 1990. The lack of differential impact in this period is evidence of no substantial liberalization evident to Joyce (2004a, pp. 6–8), while Donohue and Levitt attribute this lack of early impact to greater exposure to crack problems during the 1980s (Donohue and Levitt 2004, p. 29). But Donohue and Levitt do not discuss another possibility if these early states had more crack impact— might they also have had larger regression declines, particularly among the 15- to 24-year-olds who experienced the largest jump in the late 1980s and very early 1990s?

Each side in the econometric abortion access impact debate presents statistical analyses that are plausible but far from proof that crime reductions have direct links to abortion frequencies. With all the complicated statistical apparatus that is used in the exchange, these are still uncontrolled comparisons of crime levels in a decade where many of the determinants of crime fluctuations cannot be well specified.

A second econometric critique of the evidence on abortion, released by Christopher Foote and Christopher Goetz in late 2005, revealed that the calculation supporting the theory that those who were not born because of elective abortion would have had higher crime propensities does not sustain that interpretation when corrected (Foote and Goetz 2005). This is another "inside job," in that the basic methodological strategy is not challenged, only the results.

Another econometric study, by John Lott, Jr., and John Whitley, argued "that legalizing abortion increased murder rates by around about 0.5 to 7 percent." One mechanism the authors mention in support of this scenario is that "legalizing abortion increases out-of-wedlock births and single parent families" (Lott and Whitley 2001). Lott is famously involved in a dispute with John Donohue over Lott's study of the impact of liberalized permit-to-carry legislation on crime rates. (Compare Lott 1998 with Donohue and Ayers 2003.) So the motive of Lott's regressions contradicting Donohue's findings is easier to determine than the validity of his exercise. The study was not published.

One notable exception to the all-economist lineup in the discourse on abortion is a collaboration between public health researchers and a statistician that has produced two studies of the impact of changes in abortion law on homicide rates. Susan Sorenson, Douglas Wiebe, and Richard Berk first studied the impact of Roe v. Wade (decided early in 1973) on the annual volume of reported homicides of infants (under age 1) and younger children (aged 1–4) in the United States. This was an attempt to study what the authors call "a more proximal potential association between legalized abortion and homicide" (Sorenson, Wiebe, and Berk 2002, p. 239). The theory is that the reduction in both total and unwanted births might also reduce fatal instances of parental loss of control. But there was no statistically significant decline in infant killings noted in this analysis. For deaths from homicide among children aged 1–4, there was no decrease in rate in the early and mid-1970s, but the authors report some encouraging trends a few years after Roe v. Wade (p. 244).

The study of child abuse is careful to check for changes in death statistic reporting categories, so the data portrayed are a credible reflection of behavioral trends. However, there is very little evidence of behavioral change in the data set. The short-term trends in infant killing are flat (see Sorenson, Wiebe, and Berk, p. 248), and the long-term trends are up—and neither of these indicates any downshift in high-risk parenting. The killing volume among children under age 5 is also up, so that the decreasing rate at which this class of homicide was increasing certainly cannot be viewed as an absolute improvement in the quality of parenting among the highest risk parents. There are no controls in this study for the size of the population at risk.

In one respect, the study of child endangerment in the 1970s is not the same subject as the Donohue and Levitt analysis because Sorenson and her colleagues are testing for the criminality of parents rather than postabortion children. But trends in child abuse killing are also one direct test of whether the rate of highly dangerous environments for young children changed in the 1970s. There is no indication of change in the homicide data.

When the same team of researchers study homicide trends in the 1990s, however, their news is much more cheerful. Using interrupted time series methods, they find a decrease in homicides when the post-Roe babies are grown and also note that the decrease is concentrated among the youngest age brackets (Sorenson, Wiebe, and Berk, 2002). This is a more straightforward temporal test of homicide trends than multivariate regression, but the study does not mention the possibility that homicide rates that went up drastically only among those under age 25 might also drop more substantially among the young as a regression toward more historic proportions of homicide (see Zimring 2004). That this study only concerns homicide—where the regression danger might be more pronounced than other crime—makes it less indicative of a broad decline than would otherwise be the case.

The Search for Missing Links

This section will revisit the debate about the impact of abortion legalization by examining trends in live births and particular categories of live births that are thought to be markers for risks of crime. I begin with figure 4.2, which shows the number of births recorded in the United States by year from 1965 to 1990, with the vertical lines for the 1973 Roe v. Wade decision and early legalization (in five states) in 1970.

The number of births starts at 3,760,000 in 1965, a volume that is not equaled again until 1980 and that dropped unevenly through the mid-1970s. The year with the lowest total births in the series is 1973—the very first year when Roe v. Wade would have any effect on birth rates—but the biggest drop recorded in births was in 1972, and the period immediately after Roe v. Wade was decided is characterized by very flat birth numbers between 1973 and 1976, followed by increases in the later 1970s. To the extent that what Donohue and Levitt call cohort effects depend on a reduction of the size of the population born after legalization, any cohort dividend from Roe v. Wade would be minimal. Using the 3,258,000 births in 1972 as a baseline, the average birth volume in the four years after that was about 3% lower, but then the volume turned up, so that the average number of new births was 6% higher in 1979 than in 1972. By the end of the decade, there were approximately 500,000 more births than a stable 1972 rate would produce.

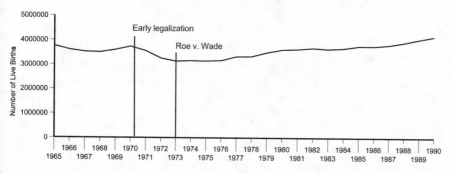

Figure 4.2. Live births by year, United States, 1965–90. Source: National Center for Health Statistics. 1990. Hyattsville, Md.: U.S. National Center for Health Statistics.

This does not mean, of course, that available abortion failed to reduce the level of births in the United States from what they would have been with no Roe v. Wade. I have no reason to doubt that birth numbers might have been higher in an atmosphere of restricted abortion. But most of the drop in births that happened in the United States happened earlier than 1973. And all of the post-1980 cohorts of births are very large by historic standards. So any crime decline that was a function of a smaller number of births would have been quite modest in size and very short in duration.

Qualitative Change

The heart of the Donohue and Levitt theory is that "women who have abortions are those most at risk to give birth to children who would engage in criminal activity. Teenagers, unmarried women, and the economically disadvantaged are all substantially more likely to seek abortions" (Donohue and Levitt 2001, p. 381).

One leading indicator of whether there were fewer children of this high-risk type after Roe v. Wade is trends in live births with demographic characteristics that are thought to be high risk. Figure 4.3 charts the proportion of all births where the mother was listed as single, where the child was recorded as African American, and where the mother was both single

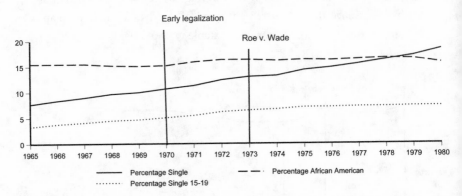

Figure 4.3. Percentage of total births to single mothers, African American mothers, and single mothers aged 15–19, by year, United States, 1965–80. Source: National Center for Health Statistics. 1990. Vital Statistics, 1990. Hyattsville, Md.: U.S. National Center for Health Statistics.

and aged 15–19. The percent single and percent African American are proxies for socioeconomic risk factors, and the single teenager category is a proxy for socioeconomic risk and undesired timing. The first two categories are not good indicators that a particular child is at risk (which is part of the moral of this exercise), but both factors play important roles in the Donohue and Levitt theory of infants at risk. The vertical lines in the figure showthe early legalization threshold (1970) and the year of Roe v. Wade (1973).

I take three morals from figure 4.3. The first is that the period when abortion was legalized in the United States saw no important shifts in the percentage of births with markers of socioeconomic risk. The proportion of births that were African American was stable throughout the period, while single motherhood and teenage single motherhood grew very quickly after 1965. There was also no change in trends associated with the key liberalization years. The proportion of all births to single women grew three points (from 7.7 to 10.7) between 1965 and 1970 and another 3½ points (from 10.7% to 14.3%) between 1970 and 1975. The percentage of births to teen single mothers grew from 3.3% to 5.1% between 1965 and 1970 and then grew from 5.1% to 7.1% between 1970 and 1975.

The second lesson from figure 4.3 is that the number of children born into risk marker settings didn't decrease in the immediate aftermath of abortion liberalization; it increased substantially. The highest risk category Donohue and Levitt identify in their theory is teen single mothers. Just over 123,000 children were born to single teen mothers in 1965; by 1970, there were over 190,000 births in the category, a 55% increase; by 1975, 222,500 children were born to teen single mothers, another 17% increase from a higher base.

While it might be argued that the decrease in the rate of increase in the teen single mother cohort might have been an abortion dividend, this kind of increase would be expected to increase crime rates as the cohort matured rather than push them down. Indeed, conservative pundits were using birth data and juvenile crime numbers in the mid-1990s to talk about "moral poverty" and to predict a "coming storm of juvenile violence" as recently as 1996 (Council on Crime in America 1996). That lends a counterintuitive charm to arguments published five years later that selective abortions had actually produced a generation of children in the 1970s who were environmentally less at risk than the cohorts that had preceded them. The same cohort was supposed to be the bad seed, according to one set of predictions, and a low-risk group of wanted children, according to another.

Economic Risks in Childhood

Figure 4.3 does not attempt to classify the births of the 1970s in terms of the economic circumstances of their families. In large part, this is because the economic circumstances of families may change over time, so that economic trends through childhood years rather than at birth should be examined.

What we were hearing about trends in child poverty for those born in the 1970s was not good news for most of the 1980s, but there was some improvement during the economic expansion of the 1990s. It is not clear when during the course of child development economic limits are most debilitating. For educational development, the critical deficits may come pretty early, while for entry into the labor market and for job mobility, the economic conditions that are current when youth are in their teens may be more important.

When we look to the economic trends for children during the 1980s, the data are not encouraging. The measurement of child poverty over time in the United States is both complicated and controversial. But despite these complexities, the standard accounts of the economic status of children during the 1970s and 1980s were not encouraging. Daniel Lichter, using one standard measure, reports: "The trend in child poverty has been one of substantial reductions during the 1960s which leveled off during the 1970s and then increased in the 1980s and early 1990s" (1997, p. 123).

The most optimistic sociological analysts are willing to project stability in child poverty (Duncan and Rogers 1991), but they caution: "a rare opportunity to reduce childhood poverty offered by the dramatic decrease in family size and the rapid increase in educational attachments has been squandered" (p. 549).

These overall trends do not mean that access to abortion has had no beneficial effects on the economic status of some women and children. What is missing, however, is any measurable improvement in the aggregate of child poverty as a risk condition for future crime involvement. There is no evidence that the population at risk because of child poverty decreased in the 15 years after abortion access was secured in the United States.

Abortion and the Demography of Crime Risk

A review of the proximal circumstantial evidence on births and child welfare indicators provides little evidence that supports the three Donohue and Levitt theories of abortion dividends. Were fewer babies born? Only slightly fewer, and only for a short while. By the end of the 1970s, the volume of births had turned up. Were fewer babies born to African American mothers? No. Were fewer babies born to single mothers? Quite the opposite. Were fewer babies born to single women who were ages 15–19 at the birth, the group most likely to have a high proportion of badly timed pregnancies? No. Were fewer babies born who would grow up as children of poverty? Evidently, no, at least not through the early 1990s. There is no basis, then, in such aggregate statistics to either predict or explain declines in crime rates.

Again, it is important to distinguish between two different propositions when considering the impact of this proximal circumstantial evidence. On the one hand, none of this data shows that access to abortion failed to reduce births or various kinds of births thought to generate higher risks of crime. This cannot be established, because there is no clear indication of what levels of various kinds of births would have occurred if the law hadn't changed. That is the "counter-factual condition" that can only be debated with several layers of circumstantial evidence. So we cannot make definite statements, vide Donohue and Levitt, about whether crime rates during the 1990s might have been higher than they were if abortion policies had not changed.

But Donohue and Levitt are trying to explain a crime decline, and it is here that the proximal evidence runs out of logical fuel. How can more babies born to single mothers aged under 19 generate fewer crimes when they grow up? How can a stable or larger group of poor children explain half of a crime drop? It is here that the positive signs on the demographic arithmetic of risk categories are particularly troublesome.

But the final lesson I draw from the discouraging appearance of figure 4.3 in light of the very good news of the 1990s crime decline concerns the limits of demographic determinism as a method of predicting crime trends in the United States. Both the crime trend predictions of Donohue and Levitt and the "coming storm of juvenile crime" prognostications of the mid-1990s are nested in assumptions of demographic determinism, the notion that circumstances at birth or early in childhood will determine later outcomes such as criminal careers. It is certainly the case that risk factors in infancy and childhood might determine the relative risk of an individual toward crime compared to others in his cohort. There is that much to the notion of risk and protective factors. But the aggregate level of crime in one era versus another is not merely the sum of individual risk and protective tendencies.

I have in previous work suggested that the elements one might examine to predict which youth in a population might have higher than average rates of violence might not also be efficient predictors of levels of violence either cross-sectionally or over time. Thus, even if the rates of crime among poor youth are higher than among nonpoor youth, it is by no means certain that changes in the proportion of a youth population that is poor will increase or decrease the crime rate (Zimring and Hawkins 1997, pp. 217–218). Whether for this or other reasons, using demographic trends as the basis for predicting variations in youth crime rates has been a very high-risk venture in recent times (Zimring 1998, pp. 49–65). This suggests that caution should be exercised in assuming that shifts in the composition of a youth population have caused variations in the total crime rate.

Power over Fertility and Crime

Donohue and Levitt focus on abortion as one method that women use to limit unwanted births. But many methods exist to limit births, and the history of birth control first available to women after midcentury is rich and complicated. Among the major landmarks in the demographic history of the 1960s were oral contraceptives and intrauterine devices. Two things happened together during the 1960s: increasing availability of contraception and declining female fertility. (I am grateful to Bryan Sykes for a tutorial on these matters. See Sykes, Hangartner, and Hathaway 2005.)

Figure 4.4 shows fertility rates by year in the United States for white and African American women as well as an aggregate total. The racial disaggregation is provided because of the emphasis on African American patterns in Donohue and Levitt's work.

With the exception of a two-year period at the beginning of the 1970s, the 20 years after 1960 were an uninterrupted period of declining fertility for women in the United States, as might be expected during a period when advanced chemical and mechanical methods of female contraception became widely available. There was a continuous downturn in fertility, presumably

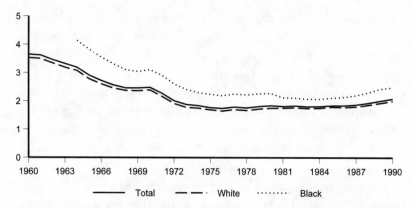

Figure 4.4. U.S. total fertility rate (TFR) by race, 1960–90. Note: To compensate for missing data, values for the African American TFR have been linearly interpolated for 1961–63. Source: National Center for Health Statistics. 1990. Hyattsville, Md.: U.S. National Center for Health Statistics.

linked to the increasing power of women to control fertility while remaining sexually active. If this reproductive autonomy was a major influence on crime, then why didn't the obvious benefits appear in the late 1970s, and why did the middle and late 1980s produce a sharp increase in crime? Donohue and Levitt do not consider this broader trend in fertility control, so the question of why abortion might have an unique impact isn't addressed. It took a demographer, Bryan Sykes, to raise this issue by providing the broad demographic context that is necessary to a balanced perspective on fertility and its consequences.

An Invisible Advantage?

None of the preceding statistical analyses disproves the connection between a reduction in unwanted children because of abortions in the early 1970s and lower crime rates in the 1990s. But the new problem introduced by the data in this section is that there were no visible signs of changes in the demography of births to match the theories of lower risk advanced. Any increase in the wantedness of American babies was not reflected in the marital status of their mothers or the proportion of births involving teen single mothers. To an extraordinary extent, Donohue and Levitt must now be positing unmeasurable and intangible qualitative changes in birth rates that generate major impacts on crime rates two decades later. There is a dissonant "man bites dog" charm to economists betting on the high magnitude of wholly intangible aspects of birth cohorts generating crime declines, but the problem of evidence is awkward. The absence of post–Roe v. Wade indicators of shifts in birth risk circumstances puts enormous weight on the later crime trends in the early legalization states, perhaps more than that comparison can bear. Might there be other methods available to test whether increasing access to abortion generates lower crime rates?

Indeed, there are. It turns out that the rules about abortion were changing in a number of developed nations in the last half of the twentieth century. The last part of this discussion of abortion and crime will suggest transnational comparisons as a method of expanding the range of empirical tests of the Donohue/Levitt hypothesis.

Comparative Data on Abortion Access and Crime Trends

A brief survey of changing patterns of legal regulation of abortions provides a tutorial about both the potentials and the limits of international comparisons in sorting out the impact of access to abortion on crime rates. The good news is that sharp changes in the legal availability of abortion were the rule rather than the exception during the early part of the last third of the twentieth century. Abortion reform swept through the developed nations in one of two patterns during the 1970s. For those nations that had already made abortions available to women who would apply for permission from doctors or other authorities, the 1970s usually brought a shift to abortion on demand for the early stages of pregnancy. This is what I shall call "two-step" abortion liberalization. Two-step nations included Great Britain, most of Scandinavia, and France. Canada also had a two-step process, but its first reform came in 1969 and fully elective abortion only in 1989. For those nations that had not previously made lawful abortions available (e.g. the United States and Italy), the 1970s liberalization tended to be a "one-step" reform directly to electoral abortion on the woman's request. Both shifts were part of a redefinition of abortion as the woman's prerogative rather than that of the state or organized medicine.

The many nations that removed restrictions on abortion provide three advantages over the Donohue/Levitt U.S.-only research design. First, many different developed nations are better than just one nation to test a theory of selective birth limitations on crime that should have general applicability. Second, testing the impact on other nations will not bump into the problem generated by the fact that the 1990s crime decline in the United States inspired the abortion theory. There have been no self-conscious searches for explaining crime declines in England, western Europe, or Canada. If a decline is discovered, there will not have been the same bias in selection.

The third advantage of a multinational test is that only the United States is known to have experienced the "youth only" homicide epidemic of the 1980s that made analysis of younger versus older age cohort arrest trends a particular hazard for the 1990s. If the same age breaks are found in trends over time in arrest, it will be easier to believe that larger drops in the younger age groups are the product of influences other than regression. So the drop among younger offenders that is regarded in the U.S. case as evidence of abortion impacts should carry over to other nations.

Some Preliminary Data

Appendix 1 reports on a series of empirical soundings on crime trends in the wake of abortion liberalization in western Europe, Canada, and Australia. The western European nations were my choice for this analysis, while Canada and Australia were added to test claims that have been made by others that abortion effects have been identified in those nations.

The first notable finding about crime trends during the 1990s in western Europe was the absence of crime drops as broad and as deep as those observed in the United States. While rates of abortion were comparable to those in the United States in nations like France and England, crime trends were much less pronounced. Only in Italy, which liberalized abortion in 1978, did significant drops in homicide occur during the 1990s. So there was substantially less of a crime decline to explain in those jurisdictions that were not selected because of crime declines.

The second notable pattern in the limited data I was able to obtain was the lack of clear evidence that arrests or convictions dropped more substantially among younger age groups than among older age groups over the 1990s. The distinctive fingerprint of probable abortion liberalization in the United States was that the drop in crime noted during the 1990s was concentrated in younger offenders, those young enough to have been born after the liberal abortion law changes. I was able to find data on conviction and prosecution for homicide in Italy and England and for a broad variety of offenses in France. Jane Sprott and Carla Cesaroni had earlier

American River College Library

published data on arrests in Canada for homicide (Sprott and Cesaroni 2002). Some data is available for Australia and for its largest state, New South Wales. In none of these analyses is there a distinctive pattern of crime participation by the young dropping more substantially than among the older age groups during the 1990s (see appendix 1).

The age-specific patterns of crime involvement over the 1990s is the clearest indication that can be developed of the role of changes in abortion regulation on crime declines. The existing data reported in appendix 1 are far from complete and are not transparently reliable in some cases. But the absence of a clear trend concentrating crime reduction among the young is not encouraging news for theories of major abortion liberalization impact.

The materials reported in appendix 1 are only a small down payment on the statistical explorations of crime and abortion policy in developed nations since the 1960s that I hope to see. But the current collection of data is consistent with three substantive conclusions. First, it is by no means impossible that the avoidance of unwanted births through induced abortion contributed to the reduction of crime in developed nations in recent years. The second conclusion, however, is that currently available evidence on abortion and homicide trends is not strongly supportive of abortion dividends, either because the trends in homicide are not themselves supportive of an effect or because the age trends in convictions don't point to policies that have only influenced births in recent decades. The use of age-specific trends as a confirming indication of abortion policy effects is both a tribute to the ingenuity of Donohue and Levitt and a disconfirmation of age-specific abortion effects in two nations with very significant homicide declines, Canada and Italy.

The third conclusion I reach from even the preliminary soundings reported in this book is that any abortion policy dividend that might later be determined to exist in the wide variety of nations that should share in the benefits of greater birth selectively will be much smaller than the estimates generated by the 1990s-based regressions of Donohue and Levitt in the United States. How a policy that did not decrease the birth rate of any identifiable risk group of babies could nonetheless reduce a homicide rate by almost 2 per 100,000 in the United States (half the total decline) would be on a par with the miracle of the loaves and the fishes. The data from other nations will either be consistent with far more modest youth crime reductions or with no discernable impact. This more restrictive field of choice is not atypical of the results generated by broad comparative studies.

Why were the Donohue and Levitt estimates of magnitude so high? The organizing principle of this chapter is that there is special danger in testing the magnitude of an impact in a time period where the decline in crime is one reason for establishing the theory of decline. The big drop in crime in the 1990s was one original basis for the abortion dividend theory. Any theory that fit well with the actual crime declines of the 1990s might get credit for crime drops that were in fact unexplained.

The problems associated with "U.S.-only" theories of crime declines are yet another reason why transnational comparisons are useful in criminological research. And the next chapter of this book, an examination of crime trends in Canada, is my major effort to provide a context for understanding trends in the United States by paying attention to data far outside our borders.

Two New Perspectives

Part III

Introduction to Part III

The statistical adventures reported in chapters 5 and 6 break new ground in the study of the U.S. crime decline. Chapter 5 discovers the amazing parallel between Canadian crime trends in the 1990s and those in the United States. The close fit between Canada and United States trends in timing, breadth, and magnitude suggests that similar mechanisms were at work to reduce crime on both sides of the border. But several of the economic and justice policy shifts that happened in the United States were not operating in Canada. So chapter 5 opens an entirely new approach to study of causation in the United States.

Chapter 6 covers more familiar real estate—the study of crime in New York City—but uses New York as a laboratory for new theories about the linkage between crime and social structure in urban American life. New York City received a double dose of crime decline in the 1990s, with serious crimes such as murder, robbery, and auto theft dropping by more than 70%. A substantial part of New York's larger than average decline was the result of more and different policing.

But the most important lesson from 15 years of dramatic crime decline in New York City is that spectacular changes in crime can be achieved without fundamental structural or social change. New York City in 2006 has the same populations, schools, transportation, and economy as in 1990 but 75% less homicide, robbery, and auto theft. Even more important than parsing out the credit for the city's crime drop is understanding that relatively superficial changes in the public ecology of a major city can create major shifts in public safety.

Which Twin Has the Toni?

Some Statistical Lessons

from Canada

5

The fact that a chapter in this book is devoted to crime and crime control in Canada proves the hazards empirical evidence presents to well-laid research plans. What might have happened in Canada during the 1990s played no role in any south-of-the-border discussions of crime declines in the United States before the research for this book was launched, and the comparative study of the G-7 nations reported in chapter 1 was intended to demonstrate the distinctiveness of the U.S. pattern during the 1990s. Except it didn't. Trends in Canada looked quite similar to those in the United States over the 1990s, when aggregate changes in rates of common crimes were comparted.

So this chapter will report on my attempts to fill out a United States–Canada comparison. First, I will present more detailed records of Canadian crime trends over the period after 1980 and compare the Canada with the U.S. experience. Second, I will revisit some earlier theories of causes by discussing trends in Canadian economic, demographic, and criminal justice indicators that parallel some of the U.S. data sets that were examined in chapters 3 and 4. A concluding section will discuss the lessons to be learned from a United States–Canada comparison. The similarity of crime trends in the 1960s and 1970s, as well as the detailed comparison of U.S. and Canadian crime trends during the 1990s, makes a powerful circumstantial case that a cyclical dynamic that began early in the 1990s has played an important role—independent of government policy—in the crime decline during the decade on both sides of the border.

Crime Trends in Canada—A Closer Look

The starting point for my special interest in Canada was a series of one-decade crime rate comparisons of Canada and the United States, with aggregate percentage changes reported only over the decade. The results of this analysis are repeated in figure 5.1.

Using official crime statistics for seven offenses, the declines in Canada and the United States are of similar magnitude (in percentage terms) for two crimes—sexual assault and homicide; are greater in the United States than in Canada for three crimes—auto theft, robbery, and burglary; and are greater in Canada than in the United States for two crimes, theft and serious assault. The Canadian decline is almost as broad as the United States one—six out of seven rather than seven out seven offenses—and almost as deep: the six crimes that decline in Canada average a 33% drop, while the six biggest drops in the United States average 35%. The aggregate crime trends in these two contiguous nations are by no means identical, but they are very close indeed.

Several methods are available to provide a thicker account of crime trends in Canada than the one figure 5.1 provides. Data could be collected

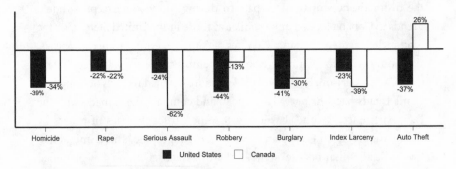

Figure 5.1. National-level crime rate declines, Canada and United States, 1990–2000. Sources: U.S. Department of Justice. Federal Bureau of Investigation. *Uniform Crime Report.* Washington, D.C.: Government Printing Office. Statistics Canada. Ottawa.

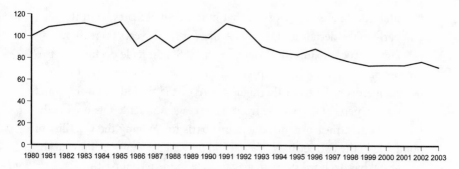

Figure 5.2. Rates per 100,000 of criminal homicide by year, Canada, 1980–2000. Source: Canada. Integrated Meta Data Base (IMDB). No. 3302.

for a longer period of time than the 10-year comparison, for each year of the period under study, for a wider variety of crimes than the seven reported in figure 5.1, and for big cities and various regions across Canada; and official crime statistics could also be compared to other data trends to test whether the changing statistical categories were really the result of shifts in rates of offense commission. With the help of the Centre for Criminology at the University of Toronto, I did all of these things. The story that develops is more complicated than figure 5.1 in many respects, but the decline in serious crime in Canada remains broad and substantial, and quite similar to the United States when its details are examined.

My presentation of the crime data will divide the Canadian crime categories into violence and property crime; I will launch the discussion of violent crime with homicide.

Violent Crime in Canada

Figure 5.2 starts Canadian crime reporting at the top of the seriousness scale with annual rates of reported criminal homicide arrests by year for the period 1980–2000. The Canadian offense category corresponds almost exactly with the murder and nonnegligent manslaughter category used by the FBI in the United States, and the Canadian police data is comprehensive.

The rate per 100,000 of Canadian homicide starts much lower than that of the United States and stays much lower throughout the reports. There is fluctuation in the 1980s, a high rate for the period reached in 1991, and steady decline thereafter throughout the 1990s. The timing of the

Canadian decline is very close to that in the United States, with the high year early in the decade and steady decline for many years thereafter.

Figure 5.3 compares the Canadian and U.S. homicide declines on two dimensions of variability—expressing the 2000 homicide rates first as a percentage decrease from the highest rate of the period 1980–2000 and second as a percentage decline from the average homicide rate during the 1980s. The first measure introduces one basis for judging the volatility of homicide in the two settings. The second percentage shows us how far the 2000 total has declined from an average rate in the recent past.

When measured as a decline from recent average, the decline in Canada is about three-quarters that found in the United States.

The pattern for rape and other types of sexual assault in Canada is harder to compare with the United States, because there is no single rape category in Canada after 1983. The 1983 reforms did away with offenses that required sexual penetration and instead divided sexual assault into two aggravated grades and a broad residual category: (1) assault with injury or wounding and assault with a weapon, and (2) a more general sexual assault offense that would include all other forcible rapes but also many other sexual impositions. The two most serious forms of sexual assault declined substantially over the 1990s, while the more general category declined less. For the most serious forms of sex assault, the Canadian rate started low and went lower, with a percentage decline at 65% for the most serious forms of sexual assault, a decline much greater than the fall in the United States rape rate. For less serious forms of sexual assault, the rate of

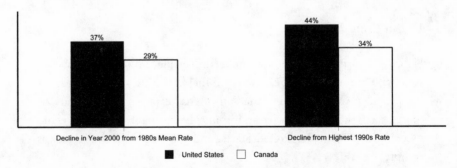

Figure 5.3. Two measures of homicide decline in Canada and the United States. Source: U.S. Department of Justice. Federal Bureau of Investigation. *Uniform Crime Report*. Washington, D.C.: Government Printing Office. Statistics Canada. Integrated Meta Data Base (IMDB). Ottawa.

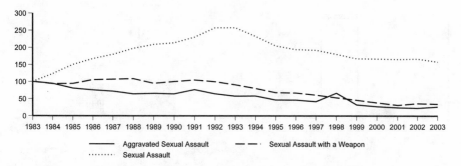

Figure 5.4. Sexual assault rates for Canada, 1983–2003. Source: Statistics Canada. Integrated Meta Data Base (IMDB). Ottawa.

reported offenses was much higher (about twice U.S. rape), and the 1990s decline was equal to that in the United States.

Figure 5.4 shows the trends over time for the two aggravated forms of sexual assault and for the general sexual assault offense by year after the 1982 legal reforms.

The general assault offense climbed steadily throughout the 1980s and topped out in 1992 and 1993 about 150% higher than its initial reported rate. After 1993, the rate dropped steadily until reaching a plateau from 1999 onward. The decline from peak rate in the 1990s is substantial, but there is no real 1980s base rate that will serve as a reliable baseline. The wounding aggravated sexual assault rate declined throughout the 1980s and 1990s, and had dropped almost two-thirds by 2000. The sexual assault with a weapon offense was stable for its first 10 years and then dropped sharply after 1992.

The puzzle in these data is not the fact of a 1990s decline in sex crime but uncertainty about its magnitude. If the two most aggravated forms of offense are the best indicator, the rates dropped by two-thirds, while the drop during the 1990s of the general sex assault category was half that size. I report a sharp drop in sex crime killings in Canada in appendix 2, and this suggests that the higher drops in serious sex crimes are plausible.

Figure 5.5 completes the analysis of sex assault by comparing the two national patterns.

Sex crime rates in both nations drop from their 1990s highs, but return to rates that are not significantly below 1980s levels. When the general sexual assault category (which is broader than U.S. rape) is the standard, the decline is still one-third greater than that of rape in the United States.

Which Twin Has the Toni?

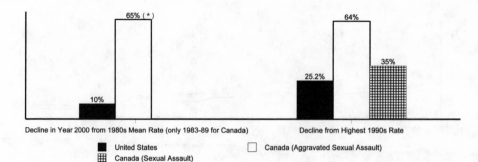

Decline in Year 2000 from 1980s Mean Rate (only 1983-89 for Canada)   Decline from Highest 1990s Rate

■ United States   □ Canada (Aggravated Sexual Assault)
田 Canada (Sexual Assault)

Figure 5.5. Two measures of decline for rape (U.S.) and two forms of sexual assault in Canada. Note: 1982=100. Canada (sexual assault) was 3.3% higher than 1983. Sources: U.S. Department of Justice. Federal Bureau of Investigation. *Uniform Crime Report.* Washington, D.C.: Government Printing Office. Statistics Canada. Integrated Meta Data Base (IMDB). Ottawa.

When the most serious Canadian sex category is used, the Canadian drop is more than twice that of the United States.

Serious Assault

The trends for Canadian assault, nonfatal attacks involving injury or weapons, provides a mixture of large decline at the serious end of the spectrum with flatter rates for lesser offenses. This is shown in figure 5.6.

The most serious offense class of assault, level 3, was down 40% over the 1990s and had a rate in 2000 that was down from the average for the 1980s after a change in classification in 1982 and that is greater than the U.S. decline. But less serious level 2 rates were reported at a rate slightly higher than the

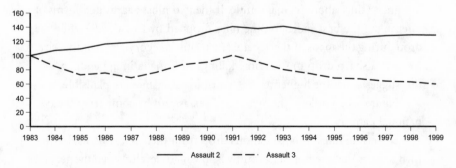

Figure 5.6. Percentage change in assault levels 2 and 3, Canada, 1983–99. Source: Statistics Canada. Integrated Meta Data Base (IMDB). Ottawa.

early rate in 2000, and this was a 10% increase over the 1980s average for class 2 assault. Some of this contrast may simply be a result of more emphasis on reporting marginal assault cases. But there is no reason to suppose that the rates of life-threatening and less serious attacks need to follow the same trends (see Zimring and Hawkins 1997, ch. 3). The same pattern of decline in serious assault and increase in "other assault" occurs in the United States in the 1990s, if we can use the trends in arrest rates for the *Uniform Crime Reports*' part 2 "other assaults" as an index of reported offenses. The incidence of the "other assault" offenses is not available in the United States.

Serious assault peaked in 1993 and declines by more than 30% by 2000, while the lower grade of assault stayed much closer to its 1993 high rate for the rest of the decade. The decline in level 3 aggravated assault in Canada was much greater than the decline in aggravated assault in the United States.

The fourth category of violent crime in Canada—robbery—declined only 13% during the 1990s, but when longer range trends are consulted, a mixed picture emerges, as shown in figures 5.7 and 5.8.

The robbery rate is volatile in Canada, and it peaked later in the 1990s than other offenses (1993) but then dropped by 26% from that high. This 26% drop was much closer to the other violent crime declines in Canada and seems, by that measure, another example rather than an exception to the general Canadian decline. But even if the Canadian drop was 26%, the U.S. robbery decline was almost twice as great. And the U.S. decline was more than a third lower than mean 1980s robbery rates in that nation, while Canada in 2000 was only 7% below its 1980s robbery rate.

Because reports of different grades of robbery seriousness are not maintained in Canada to match the assault and sex crime reports, I tried

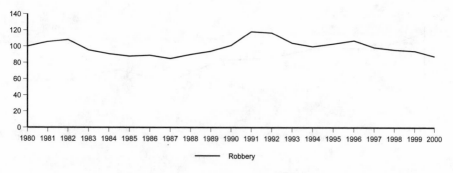

Figure 5.7. Trends in reported robberies, Canada, 1980–2000. Source: Statistics Canada. Integrated Meta Data Base (IMDB). Ottawa.

Which Twin Has the Toni?

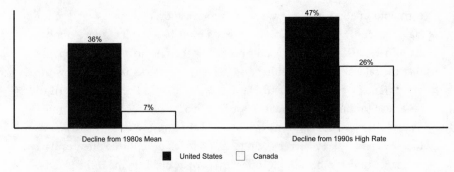

Figure 5.8. Two measures of decline in robbery, United States and Canada. Sources: U.S. Department of Justice, Federal Bureau of Investigation, *Uniform Crime Report*. Washington, D.C.: Government Printing Office. Statistics Canada. Integrated Meta Data Base (IMDB). Ottawa.

to test whether serious robbery might have declined more than the overall category in Canada. Since the Canadian statistics do not segregate firearm robbery or robbery with a weapon, the homicide statistics were searched for robbery killings. A similar exercise for rape killings is reported in appendix 2—as an index of life-threatening sexual assault.

Figure 5.9 shows the trend in robbery killings over the period between 1992, the first year they were specifically reported, and 2000.

Using the 1992 total of 58 cases as a 100% baseline, there was a steady decline over the 1990s, and the total drop exceeded 50%. While the drop from year 1 to year 2 is the second largest in the series, there is every evidence that the downtrend is sustained. So a palpable decline in life-threatening robberies over the decade seems likely.

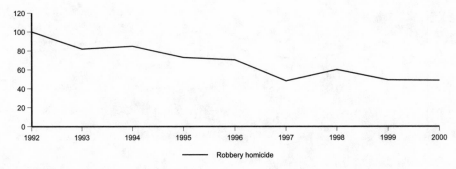

Figure 5.9. Percentage change in rates of homicide involving robbery, Canada, 1992–2000. Source: Statistics Canada. Integrated Meta Data Base (IMDB). Ottawa.

Property Crime

The national summary for Canada reported steep declines for both theft and burglary but an increase during the decade for auto theft. Two of these three aggregate statistical patterns must be restated substantially, given the findings of my further inquiry.

Theft is the most common offense reported in every major nation, and Canada is no exception to that pattern. The larceny theft category used in the Canadian statistics reported in chapter 1 was restricted to property over a minimum value level, and that level was changed twice in recent reporting. In each case, the minimum value for inclusion was raised substantially, and each increase produced a precipitous drop in the number of theft cases reported in the category, as shown in figure 5.10.

The sharp drops that twice accompanied the change in minimum dollar level for includable theft ruin the major theft category in Canada as an indicator of trends in theft over time. But the solution to this problem is not difficult, and our revised theft category turns out to be directly comparable to the statistical reporting of theft in the United States.

Figure 5.11 combines all thefts reported at all levels of property value by year in Canada.

The total theft rate started high in 1980, at just over three cases per 100 population, and stayed high until 1992, when a steady decline dropped the rate from 3.5 per 100 citizens in 1992 to 2.2 per 100 in 2000. The drop from the highest recent rate to year 2000 was 37%, and the drop from the 1980s average rate was 31%.

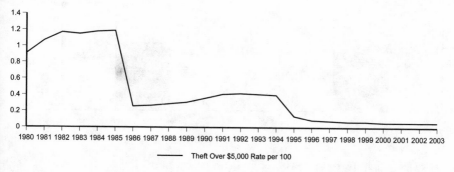

Figure 5.10. Canadian index theft, rates per 100, 1980–2003. Note: Minimum value changes after 1985 and 1994. Source: Statistics Canada. Integrated Meta Data Base (IMDB). Ottawa.

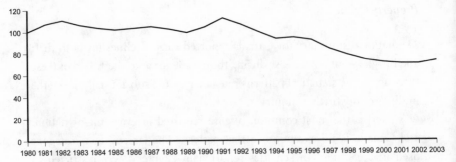

Figure 5.11. Trends in theft reported by year, Canada, 1980–2003, all values. Note: 1980 = 100. Source: Statistics Canada. Integrated Meta Data Base (IMDB). Ottawa.

It turns out that the total theft measure that I resort to for Canada is also the way U.S. larceny has been reported in the UCRs since 1973. Prior theft reporting had only included larceny over $50 in value, but this had created incentive to keep reported index crime rates low by understatement of the value of goods taken. The inclusion of all theft in the index means that the bulk of all the criminal acts counted in the UCRs' part 1 index offenses are larceny theft offenses.

Figure 5.12 compares U.S. and Canadian larceny drops when measured against prior trends.

The decline in most measures was half again as great in Canada as in the United States. Because larceny thefts are so numerous, the somewhat larger drop in this category in Canada (31% versus 18% from the 1980s)

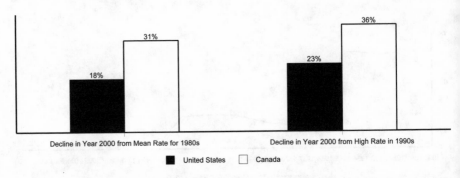

Figure 5.12. Two measures of decline in theft, Canada and United States. Sources: U.S. Department of Justice. Federal Bureau of Investigation. *Uniform Crime Report.* Washington, D.C.: Government Printing Office. Statistics Canada. Integrated Meta Data Base (IMDB). Ottawa.

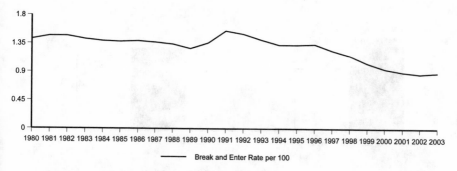

Figure 5.13. Breaking-and-entering rates per 100, Canada, 1980–2003. Source: Statistics Canada. Integrated Meta Data Base (IMDB). Ottawa.

means that the drop in Canadian crime numbers in the aggregate crime rate index total might be larger than the percentage drop in the United States. But this would involve the unweighted aggregation of petty theft and homicides, a dubious measure.

Burglary, which the Canadian system calls breaking and entering, was the only property offense that remained close to its original statistical portrait after supplemental inquiry. The category was down 30% in Canada during the 1990s, compared to a 41% decline in the United States during the 1990s. Figure 5.13 shows trends in rates of breaking and entering in Canada from 1980 to 2000.

The official rate of breaking and entering started at just over 1,400 per 100,000 in 1980 and was flat with a slight downward drift all through the decade. The rate then jumped in 1990 and 1991, reaching its high for the period in 1991, and then dropped steadily for the rest of the decade. By 2000, the rate has dropped below 1,000 per 100,000 for the first time in the series, more than 40% below the 1991 high. The temporal pattern is quite close to that of several other Canadian offenses, with increases at the very beginning of the 1990s and a sustained and steady decline thereafter. The break-and-enter offense peak was 1991, the same year as homicide, level 3 (serious) assault, and one year before the peak level of theft. For all these offenses, the steady decline after a high early in the decade consumed the rest of the decade.

Figure 5.14 compares the burglary declines in the United States and Canada on the two standard measures I have been reporting, the shift from recent high points and the drop from 1980s average rates for the burglary offense.

Which Twin Has the Toni?

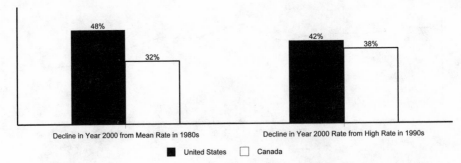

Decline in Year 2000 from Mean Rate in 1980s   Decline in Year 2000 Rate from High Rate in 1990s

■ United States   □ Canada

Figure 5.14. Two measures of change in burglary (U.S.) and breaking and entering (Canada). Sources: U.S. Department of Justice. Federal Bureau of Investigation. *Uniform Crime Report.* Washington, D.C.: Government Printing Office. Statistics Canada. Integrated Meta Data Base (IMDB). Ottawa.

The level of breaking and entering in Canada in 2000 was 38% below the 1991 high point and 32% below the mean level recorded for the 1980s. The U.S. burglary decline was about the same during the 1990s (42% versus 38%), but the decline from the mean rate in the 1980s was half again larger in the United States than in Canada (48% versus 32%). Therefore, both declines are real and not connected to regression from earlier historically atypical periods. Both declines were concentrated in the same time period, the middle and late 1990s, and both declines were very long in duration. The Canadian rate dropped in eight of the nine years after 1991 and was flat during the sole nondecline year (1996). The bigger gap when the baseline is mean rates in the 1980s shows that burglary rates started trending down earlier in the United States.

The Puzzle of Auto Theft

Only one crime category other than the less serious types of assault shows any increase during the 1990s in Canada, and that offense is auto theft. The rate of auto theft reported by Statistics Canada increased 26% during the 1990s, a contrast with every other offense and a sharp contrast to the trends of the other two nonperson property crimes, which both declined over 30% in the 1990s. Figure 5.15 shows annual reported rates of auto theft in Canada during the 1990s.

The annual totals for auto theft add somewhat to the puzzling divergence of car theft from larceny and breaking and entering. Three-quarters of the increase in auto theft happened in one year—1991—and the pattern after that was a mild upward trend.

In the United States, auto theft is regarded as among the most reliably reported offenses in the UCRs' part 1 crimes (see President's Commission on Crime 1965) and is also a behavior where reliable nongovernmental measures can be used to test official statistical trends. Both the reputation for reliability and the capacity for independent auditing are products of the widespread institution of automobile theft insurance. Because insurance companies require that citizens pursuing theft claims report losses to the police, the official rate suffers less from nonreporting than burglary and larceny. The institution of insurance also creates a separate statistical system that can be consulted for trends in auto theft that produce insurance claims. I found data for six Canadian provinces with private insurance and one with a government program, and I report on this in appendix 2. The rate of auto theft claims goes down during the 1990s in the six private insurance jurisdictions (see appendix 2), but only two of the most populous provinces were in the sample. An additional report on Quebec also shows declines and is discussed in appendix 2. No data were available on the proportion of drivers insured against theft or on the proportion of losses that lead to claims over time.

The data I found is not sufficient to definitively resolve the conflict between official and insurance-based estimates of theft. If there were national totals for insurance claims, I would prefer them to the crime report estimates where the two methods disagree. For present purposes, however, it is sufficient to conclude that a decline in auto theft as well as the other six categories of crime in Canada is a distinct possibility during the 1990s.

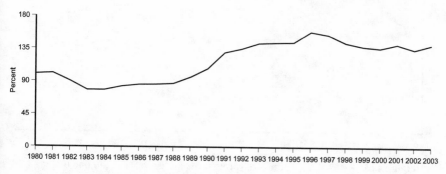

Figure 5.15. Percentage change in auto theft rates, Canada, 1980–2003. Source: Statistics Canada. Integrated Meta Data Base (IMDB). Ottawa.

Which Twin Has the Toni?

Crime Policy, Demography, and the Economy in Canada

This section addresses a few of the policy and social change dimensions that have been viewed as potential causes of the decline in crime south of the Canadian border. In view of the Canadian crime trends in the 1990s, one natural question is whether there were important parallels as well between the two neighbors in crime policy trends. Without exception, the answer to this question is no; nor did the Canadian economy have a breakout decade in the 1990s to parallel the U.S. trend. The only obvious crime-related change the two countries share is in the age structure of Canada's population.

Figure 5.16 starts a short tour of criminal justice policy with Canadian data on prisoners in federal and provincial custody since 1980. The figure uses rate per 100,000 of the two levels of imprisonment combined. We start with imprisonment because increases in this measure were the major change in the United States.

The variation in rate of imprisonment was minimal throughout the two decades, with a high rate of 116 per 100,000 in 1994 and a low rate of 98 per 100,000 in 1980. During the first four years of the 1990s, the rate increased by 6%, but then it fell by 12% between 1994 and 2000.

Figure 5.17 compares trends in total prison populations per 100,000 in the United States and Canada, by showing the 1980 rate as equal to 100 in each nation and every succeeding year's rate as the rate derived when the year's total is divided by the 1980 rate base.

The contrast in imprisonment between these contiguous nations is stark, for the 1990s specifically and for the entire period as well. During the

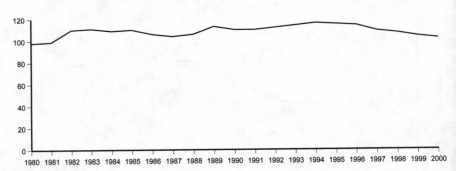

Figure 5.16. Rates of imprisonment (provincial and federal) per 100,000 by year, Canada, 1980–2000. Source: Statistics Canada. Integrated Meta Data Base (IMDB). Ottawa.

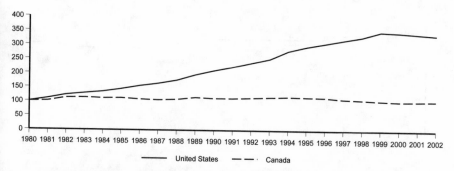

Figure 5.17. Trends in imprisonment rates, United States and Canada, 1980–2002. Note: 1980 = 100. Sources: U.S. Department of Justice. Bureau of Justice Statistics. 1990, 2000. *National Crime Victimization Survey.* Washington, D.C.: Government Printing Office. Statistics Canada. Integrated Meta Data Base (IMDB). Ottawa.

1990s, the rate of imprisonment in the United States increased 57%, while it decreased 6% in Canada. For the period 1980–2000, the imprisonment rate tripled in the United States and increased by 4% in Canada. In 1980, the American imprisonment rate was 45% higher than the Canadian rate. By 2000, the gap had expanded to more than 4 to 1. The Canadian trends thus are a perfect foil for the U.S. expansion, a place where punishment policy didn't change as a contrast to a nation where it changed by historically unprecedented dimensions. For imprisonment, Canada is the ideal control group for its southern neighbor during the 1990s.

The contrast is less dramatic when trends in police employment are compared, if only because the U.S. expansion in police employment was an order of magnitude smaller than the imprisonment boom. Figure 5.18 shows police employed per 100,000 population (solid line) from 1980 to 2000.

The number of police officers grew only 3,000 in 20 years after 1980, failing by far to keep pace with population growth. During the 1990s, the employment of police per 100,000 population fell from 204 to 183, almost exactly 10%. No precise numbers are available on the expansion in police in the United States, but there is universal agreement that there was an expansion. The estimate used in chapter 4 was Stephen Levitt's 14% for the 1990s.

What about the economy? Figure 5.19 shows the annual average unemployment rate for Canada and the United States from 1980. A complete parallel to the U.S. "youth neither at work nor in school" was not available.

Which Twin Has the Toni?

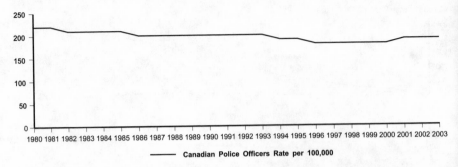

Figure 5.18. Police officers in Canada and police officers per 100,000 population in Canada, by year, 1980–2000. Source: Statistics Canada. Integrated Meta Data Base (IMDB). Ottawa.

There are some similar cyclical patterns in each nation, but the contrast in total joblessness during the 1990s is great. Canadian unemployment remained higher throughout the 1990s than it was in 1980, while U.S. unemployment dropped in every year after 1992. In 1998, when Canadian unemployment finally touched its 1980 level, the U.S. rate was 40% below its 1980 standard. For Canada, the unemployment rate trends after mid-1997 are much more favorable than earlier, but this is a full five years after crime rates start to fall steadily.

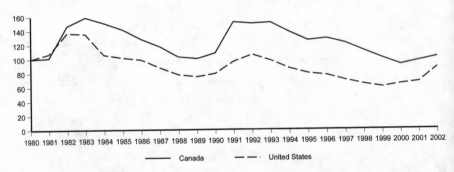

Canada   — — · United States

Figure 5.19. Annual average unemployment rates (seasonally adjusted), Canada and United States, 1980–2002. Note: the rates are adjusted so that 1980 levels equal 100. Actual Canadian unemployment in 1980 was 7.5%; U.S. unemployment in 1980 was 7.1%. Sources: Statistics Canada. Integrated Meta Data Base (IMDB). Ottawa. U.S. Department of Labor. Bureau of Labor Statistics. *Labor Force Statistics from the Current Population Survey*. Available at the website of the Bureau of Labor Statistics: www.bls.gov/cps/cpsatabs.htm.

The clear implication from Canadian criminal justice and economic data in the 1990s is negative. There is literally nothing in Canadian police, punishment, or economic statistics that would predict or explain a broad decline in crime.

Demographics

The one area where the Canadian trends do parallel those in the United States in a way that would predict declining crime is in the changing age structure of the population. Figure 5.20 shows the percentage of the population in three high-arrest-rate age categories for 1980, 1990, and 2000.

The total population aged 15–29 dropped from 29% of the Canadian total in 1980 to 24% in 1990 to 20% in 2000, a net decrease of almost one-third. Even this good news is not without its puzzles in Canada. The decline was just as great during the 1980s—when crime rates didn't go down—as during the 1990s, when crime rates did. We saw exactly this pattern in the United States in chapter 3, but crack cocaine was part of the explanation in that context. What happened in Canada?

The decline in high-arrest-risk age groups in Canada is equal to that experienced in the United States and not small-scale. If, however, it is a major reason for the Canadian crime decline, then the similar decline in risk populations on both sides of the border had a much higher impact on crime rates than current thinking would estimate (Levitt 1999).

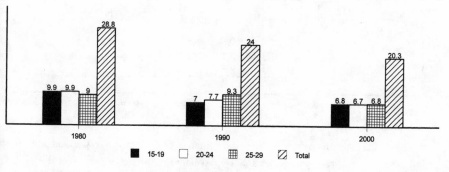

Figure 5.20. Variations in the population percentage of high-risk age groups, Canada, 1980, 1990, and 2000. Source: Statistics Canada. Integrated Meta Data Base (IMDB). Ottawa.

Which Twin Has the Toni?

Abortion in Canada

There is one other aspect of demography that may have played a role in Canada's crime decline, the impact of increased access to abortion in previous decades. As shown in chapter 4, Canada was a "two-step" jurisdiction: a first generation of reforms allowed abortion on restricted grounds after a formal permission process. This procedure was established in 1969. Twenty years later, Canadian courts struck down the restrictions and permission requirements and established abortion at the election of the pregnant woman. Only the first stage of reform could have altered the birth of persons old enough to be at high risk for arrest during the 1990s. Figure 5.21 shows rates of abortion reported in Canada by year. The figure includes some abortions that Canadian women received in the United States, where wider availability than in Canada compromised Canadian standards after 1970, but many U.S. abortions were probably not reported and counted. Figure 5.21 provides annual data for the United States as well.

The Canadian abortion level after 1969 was modest by U.S. standards for two reasons. The first is that the legal change in Canada was not as permissive as the first-trimester elective structure that followed Roe v. Wade in the United States. The second reason is that even with fully elective abortion (produced by judicial decision after 1989), the abortion rate in Canada is lower than the U.S. level. But during the period 1970–85, when the last of the criminally active cohorts of the 1990s were born, the U.S. abortion rate averaged six times the Canadian rate.

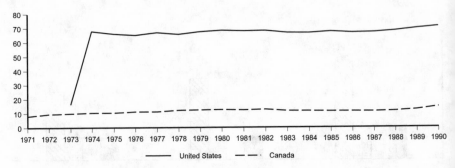

Figure 5.21. Abortion rates per 100,000 women of reproductive age, Canada and United States, 1971–1990. Source: U.S. Department of Commerce. Bureau of the Census. International Data Base (IDB). Available at the website of the Census Bureau: www.census.gov/ipc/www/idbnew.html.; www.johnsonsarchive.net/policy/abortion/#st.

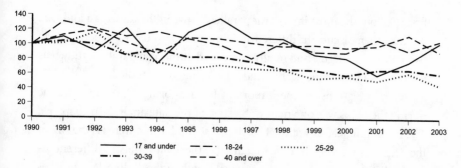

Figure 5.22. Persons accused of homicide by age, Canada, percentage change between 1990 and 2003. Source: Canada. Statistics Canada. Integrated Meta Data Base (IMDB). No. 3315. *Homicide Survey.* Ottawa.

One test of whether lower risk birth cohorts generated declines in crime that was discussed in the previous chapter was the shifts in the age distribution of arrest for index crime (Donahue and Levitt 2001) and for homicide (Berk et al., 2003). Figure 5.22 reports the distribution of homicide arrests over time for standard statistical age groups over the 1980s and 1990s.

The differences in arrest by age over time are not consistent with major postabortion cohort effects in Canada. The two age groups that would include 100% postabortion reform cohorts during the 1990s, juveniles and those aged 18–24, do not have larger than average declines in homicide arrest risk over the 1990s. The age group with the largest decline over the 1990s, 30–39, contained no persons born after 1970 during the crime decline. The age group with the second largest decline, 25–29, had no post-1970 birth cohort members until 1995 and did not have a majority of its members in that category until 1998.

Similarity and Contrast in Canadian Crime

Why an entire chapter on Canada in a study of the crime decline in the United States during the 1990s? I will argue that there are very important similarities between the crime patterns in Canada and the United States during the 1990s, and that these extraordinary similarities should modify prevailing hypotheses about both the causes of crime decline in the United States and the way these theories are tested. In this concluding section, I will

Which Twin Has the Toni?

first spell out the most important parallels between the Canadian and U.S. declines, then discuss the differences in magnitude and pattern between the two national patterns, and finally address what this comparative study tells us about the U.S. crime decline and how it should be studied.

Compiling a list of the important features of the U.S. crime decline during the 1990s was one major objective of the data analysis in chapter 1. The important features of the U.S. decline I emphasized were (1) the size of the decline, (2) its geographic breadth, (3) the wide variety of different offenses that declined, and (4) the atypical length of the decline. What makes the Canadian experience significant is that crime in Canada displays all four of these characteristics during the 1990s and does so at exactly the same time as the U.S. decline. Each of these dimensions requires separate comment before their cumulative importance can be considered.

What brought attention to the crime decline in the United States was its size. From the turn of the 1990s to 2000, five of seven index crime rates went down by around 40%, while the other two decreased more than 20%. Canadian offense levels also went down by substantial percentages, although often from a lower base rate. Five of the seven Canadian offenses for which there are U.S. index crime equivalents declined by a percentage that was 70% or more of the U.S. total. The U.S. decline was geographically broad, which was demonstrated in chapter 1 with regional and big-city comparisons. The same pattern of geographic spread appears in the six-city Canadian comparison I report in appendix 2, because Canada's big cities are so widely distributed through its territory.

A third special feature of the U.S. crime decline was the wide variety of serious offenses that produced substantial crime drops. All seven "index" offenses recorded substantial 10-year declines, and five of the seven offenses were closely clustered around 40%. The United States has been more prone than other nations to experience the same trends in violent and property crimes (Zimring and Hawkins 1997, ch. 2). For the same 10-year period, Canada had declines in six of the seven U.S. index offenses, with very significant declines in five of the seven. Less serious forms of assault and sex assault did not decline in Canada, but if U.S. UCRs part 2 assault arrest trends are a good index of trends in nonserious offense rates, the same pattern also holds in the United States.

These first three shared characteristics of U.S. and Canadian crime make a strong but not conclusive case for the proposition that the two nations were participating in a shared temporal trend that had a powerful impact on crime rates. The two features of the comparison that push the parallel well beyond coincidence are the similarities in length and timing of the two declines.

When the U.S. trend in the 1990s is compared with crime dips in the previous four decades, what sets the 1990s apart is not the steepness of the crime decline but its length. What made the 1990s decline twice as large as the drop in the first half of the 1980s was that it lasted twice as long. This was the only sustained multicategory decline in the post–World War II period in the United States, and one of two long-range trends. Inspection of Canada's rates of breaking and entering, homicide and theft, reveal the same sustained period of decline—eight out of nine years is the mode. So the Canadian crime decline exhibits the same unusual length of trend as that of the United States.

For each nation, the long downtrend is unusual, and these unusual downtrends happen at almost exactly the same time! After relatively high rates at the very beginning of the 1990s, the down years begin in 1992 and 1993 and persist through the decade. This common timing of uncommonly long trends pushes the phenomena well beyond plausible coincidence. Whatever is generating the long decline in the United States is probably an important influence in Canada as well, and vice versa. But what is this dynamic? I will explore this issue after addressing some differences between Canadian and U.S. patterns.

Differences

There are three potential differences between U.S. and Canadian crime during the 1990s: (1) the scale of crime in the two environments at the beginning of the 1990s; (2) the extent of the crime drop; and (3) the slightly narrower band of offenses that declined in Canada. The first clear difference between the two nations relates to the much higher rates of some violent crimes in the United States than in Canada. At peak levels in 1991, the homicide rate in the United States was about four times as high as that in Canada. This difference in scale has impact on the absolute dimensions of a decline. The 34% decline in Canadian homicide over the 1990s was a decline in rate per 100,000 that is much smaller than the 39% decline in the United States—less than one homicide per 100,000 in Canada versus more than three per 100,000 in the United States. To a lesser extent, this difference of scale also applies to robbery and rape rates, but not to theft and break-and-enter rates. Where the U.S. and Canadian base rates differ substantially, similar percentage declines involve significantly different volumes of crime. But it is worth noting that Canadian crime decline in the 1990s is just as great in those offenses where Canadian rates are high as where the scale is smaller. Canadian theft decreases more than U.S. theft, and so does assault, yet both are very high-volume events in Canada.

The second dimension of difference is that the percentage decline observed in the United States trends is somewhat higher for three crimes—burglary, robbery, and of course auto theft—than in Canada. The modal change in the United States is about 40% for most crime categories and closer to 30% for Canada. For three offenses, however—serious sexual assault, life-threatening violence and theft—the official statistical declines in Canada are significantly larger.

The third difference in the seven categories of FBI "index" crime and Canadian equivalents is that fewer of the Canadian offense categories showed substantial declines. Auto theft increased in the 1990s in the official statistics, and robbery only declined by 13%, less than half the average in Canada for the other five index crime equivalents. Even if the 25–30% decline in auto thefts estimated by insurance trends was the true story in Canada, the U.S. decline was substantially larger. Robbery did drop in Canada by 26% from its high point.

There are other, less serious offenses in Canada in the assault and sexual assault category without any pattern of significant decline—but these offenses probably did not decline in the United States either. So auto theft and robbery are the only clear distinctions. And my best guess is that about 75% of the percentage drop noted in U.S. crime can be found in Canada as well during the 1990s.

What is the substantive impact of these differences in pattern between Canada and the United States? Is Canada's crime decline sufficiently attenuated by these factors to be a variety of "U.S. crime drop lite"? The appropriate way to answer this question is to ask whether the commonalities in the two nations' experience outweigh the differences, and I believe that they do. The close fit in timing and length, the broad geography, and the high decline in most crime categories create strong presumptive links between the Canadian and U.S. patterns. The gap in the average percentage decline provides some room for crediting some decline to agents working only in the United States (such as increments of incarceration and police) as potential causes of the larger U.S. declines. But most of the declines over the decade are parallel to the point where joint causes are likely to be the reason for the cooccurrence of this long and large decrease.

Joint Causes?

But what joint causes might have operated in Canada and the United States throughout the 1990s? This uncomfortably open question is of obvious importance to rethinking the causes of the U.S. declines. Looking for the common causes of the U.S. and Canadian decline is principally a process of elimination, and the first candidates for exclusion come from the contrasts in criminal justice policy and economic environment considered earlier in this chapter. The sharp differences in imprisonment trends mean that increased incapacitation is not a plausible reason for the crime declines jointly experienced by the United States and Canada. To the extent that this approach is persuasive, investigators should look to the differences in crime decline that favor the United States rather than to the declines that the two nations have in common when searching for crime reductions that increased imprisonment might have caused. That would substantially reduce the amount of crime that the prison trends might have plausibly prevented.

The Canadian decline in police per capita also removes increased police manpower as a candidate for explaining the common decline, and the stable rates of unemployment would push the U.S. economic boom into a competition with prisons and police to explain an aggregate additional decline in the United States of 10% or so.

What would explain the 30% or so of slow and steady decline over the nine years following 1991 in the United States and Canada? The only traditional theory of decline supported by parallel U.S. and Canadian data trends is the decline of high-risk age groups as a percentage of the population. But even if all of the decline in youth share of population that occurred in both the 1980s and 1990s is counted toward the crime decline that was confined to the 1990s, it would be difficult to find many criminologists who would expect that feature alone to produce a crime decline greater than 10%, and even that 10% should have been spread more evenly across two decades in both countries.

But the demographic similarity between Canada and the United States over the period 1980 onward invites, if it does not demand, a reconsideration of the magnitude of age structure effects on crime. The two-decade decline in the share of the population aged 15–29 might well explain as much as a 15% decline in crime on a cumulative basis. Why the visible impact of this decline is concentrated in the 1990s is a separate mystery, but need not be compelling evidence against the eventual statistical power of the population shifts that are the only visible mechanisms of crime prevention at work in both nations during the 1990s.

Then there is the possibility of lower risk birth cohorts after liberalization of abortion as a joint cause of decline. But Canada only felt the effect of its first-stage 1969 reforms during the 1990s (plus the impact of abortion availability in the United States). The Canadian abortion rate was one-sixth of the U.S. rate, and the Canadian homicide arrest data do not show arrests are down more among postreform age cohorts in the 1990s. So it does not seem likely that abortion effects were a visible part of the Canadian decline. Unfortunately, that means that a large part of the joint decline cannot be tied to any concrete causes. The process of elimination has, in this sense, been too successful.

There are in the joint crime declines of these two contiguous nations during the 1990s strong indications of powerful cyclical forces that are not obviously tied to variations in governmental actions or to social phenomena that depress crime rates. The key evidence comes from Canada. Nothing is happening in Canada in the 1990s that didn't also happen in the 1980s that is known to influence crime. Yet crime went down in a persistent and pronounced pattern only in the later decade. It is prudent to suppose that the same dynamic is at work in the United States. But what dynamic might that be?

There are in economic fluctuations and other collective behavior many apparently cyclical phenomena that cannot currently be derived from variations in other phenomena with causal influence on rates. Whether these cycles are truly independent or merely unexplained to date we cannot know. But strong cyclical effects not connected to other causes are a possible influence on crime that cannot be dismissed. If such effects were operating in Canada in the 1990s, they were very probably operating in the United States as well. And ignoring this potential influence can be a very risky protocol for research on the causes of crime declines.

If there are strong cyclical influences on crime in Canada and the United States during the 1990s, multivariate regression exercises that do not incorporate them in models run a double hazard—such studies may identify factors that are in the models as causal simply because the residual effects not explained by other elements are so great. And regression models may also greatly overestimate the impact of influences in the model by failing to account for cycles.

The Mysterious Prospect of Crime Cycles

There is something more to the notion of cyclical variation in the two nations than simply variation over time not linked to known third causes, but how much substance to confer to the notion of "crime cycles" is not obvious. And this ambiguity is intellectually unsatisfactory. To what extent do we risk a term like "cycle" becoming a slogan that is imprecise and mysterious, a branch of criminological astrology? But even skeptics must acknowledge the downward momentum in Canada with no explanation in view. The prudent view of the Canadian events after 1991 is to assume that cyclical variations without any further current explanation play a major role in the Canadian decline, and for that reason can also be expected to be an important part of the U.S. story as well. As I will soon show, the 1990s is not the first time that Canadian and U.S. trends have converged.

Why the Canada–United States Concurrence?

When considering the concurrence of crime trends in the United States and Canada, it is suitable to begin with visual evidence of trends over several decades. Homicide rates are different in the United States and Canada, but when one creates a time series of trends that use a common starting point of 100 representing the 1961 rates for each nation the figure will show trends over time that are not obscured by the difference in base rate. I start at 1961 because that is the first year of Canadian national-level homicide reporting. Figure 5.23, constructed by Professor Anthony Doob of the University of Toronto, tells a four-decade story.

Trends over time in these two neighbors were by no means identical. Homicide increased in Canada after 1974 for two years when the U.S. rate had topped out in 1974, and U.S. homicide dropped more in the early 1980s than in Canada, but the similarity in trend is striking over the long run. The major increases in each nation were concentrated in the same decade, and so was the era of major decline.

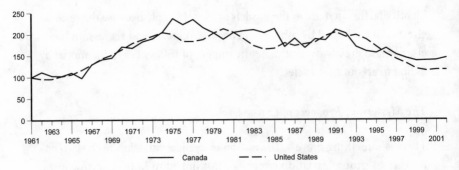

Figure 5.23. Homicide trends, United States and Canada, after 1961. Note: Canada, 1961: 1.28 = 100. United States, 1961: 4.8 per 100,000 = 100. Sources: U.S. Department of Justice. Federal Bureau of Investigation. 1970–2003. *Uniform Crime Report.* Washington, D.C.: Government Printing Office. Statistics Canada. Integrated Meta Data Base (IMDB). Ottawa. Data compiled by Professor Anthony Doob.

What is there in the two contiguous nations that produces the tendency for concurrent crime cycles? Canada and the United States share a long and open border, and there were also common demographic trends during the 1980s and 1990s. But the two economies, while interconnected, did not have strongly parallel trends in the 1990s. And the substantive reasons for an underlying similarity in crime trends are by no means obvious. Why do theft and homicide trend down together in 1990s Canada? Why do the United States and Canada trend down together for both sets of offenses in the 1990s? This is a compound mystery as of 2006, an issue that invites a great deal more statistical and theoretical inquiry. It is also a question that has suddenly become an important part of sorting out the causes of the crime decline in the United States.

Conclusion: Some Lessons for South of the Border

There are extraordinary parallels in timing, breadth, and magnitude between the crime declines of the 1990s in the United States and in Canada. If these common trends had common causes, this should produce three important changes in current thinking about the United States branch of the crime decline. The first change mandated by the Canadian story is a downgrading of emphasis on economic forces and criminal justice policy shifts as primary causes of U.S. crime drops. Crime dropped in Canada in the mid-1990s, while unemployment increased. Canadian imprisonment decreased during the 1990s, and so did the population-based rate of police employment.

If a Canadian decline that is 70% as large as that in the United States can take place without any economic or policy causation, that leaves prisons, police, and the economy competing for statistical scraps in the United States—for the 10% or so decline in robbery and burglary that separates the United States and Canada, and perhaps for major credit on auto theft.

By contrast with the diminished credibility of prison and jobs, the demographic shifts that occurred on both sides of the border have a much more plausible claim to major influence on declining crime because they are present in equal measure in both nations. For both the United States and Canada, the drop in the youth and young adult share of total population was almost a third in the two decades after 1980. In both nations, however, the apparent impact of the two-decade shift only became evident in the 1990s. If the total impact of this two-decade shift was manifest in the 1990s, demography might explain a crime decline of 10% or slightly more.

The third change in perspective suggested by the parallel trends in the two countries is the possibility that large portions of the two-nation crime drop do not have discrete policy or economic causes. The central puzzle of the Canadian 1990s was a crime decline much greater than could be explained by any visible causes. Canada did share with the United States a shrinkage of the proportion of national population in the high-arrest-rate groups aged 15–29. But if this alone were to cause a crime decline of 30% in 10 years, it would require a demographic effect more than three times as great as current estimated magnitudes. It is much more prudent to conclude that at least half of Canada's crime decline cannot be explained by old or new theories of crime causation. But if this holds for 60% of the Canadian decline, then it suggests that about 40% of the U.S. crime drop may also defy standard explanation.

The Canadian crime decline greatly exceeds any observable changes in the nation that might plausibly be expected to reduce crime, so cyclical forces beyond the current ability of social science to explain must get credit for a large share of Canada's decline. If this is so, those elements of the U.S. decline that resemble Canada in timing and magnitude must also become attractive candidates for a cyclical explanation. Without the Canadian parallel, a cyclical explanation of the U.S. crime decline would seem to most observers to be sentimental mysticism. With the Canadian example as guidance, strong consideration of cyclical influence in the United States becomes a practical necessity. The same lack of known causes that holds for the majority of Canadian crime declines may hold for 40% of the U.S. crime drop. Just as the two nations shared an unexplained crime increase from the mid-1960s to the mid-1970s, much of the shared good news of recent history seems to elude easy explanations.

New York City's
Natural Experiment

6

One large U.S. city stood head and shoulders above the rest of the nation when the statistical profile of the crime decline in big cities was reviewed in chapter 1. New York is by far the largest city in the United States, and its record of crime reduction in the 1990s was, by far, the largest of any big city in the United States. I suggested a rule of thumb in chapter 1—to estimate the drop in New York City crime, determine the average drop in any index crime category in the nation and double it. This chapter will attempt to convert that "rule of thumb" into a research methodology for assessing the impact of changes in the quality and quantity of policing on crime rates in New York City. Even more important, I will show that New York City is a natural laboratory for study of the effects of less crime on urban life, particularly for those whose lives are most at risk from crime and criminal justice controls.

When studying causes, there is no way that the history of New York City or anywhere else in the United States can be sorted through with certainty to explain the totality of the crime decline experienced in the 1990s. Instead, I want to focus on the difference between the New York City crime decline and that in the country as a whole and to search for the causes of this differential performance. At the end of the trail, we produce only circumstantial evidence of specific causes. But reducing the stakes of explanations from the totality of a crime drop in the city to the difference between the city's pattern and the general decline presents a much more plausible approach to testing the impact of particular policies. And when the whole of the city's crime decline is examined for evidence of its effects, a clear set of tools is available to assess the effects of lower crime rates on communities and groups. But little of this work has yet been attempted. The important questions can only be answered if they are asked.

This chapter's story will be told in four installments. First, I will explore the size and character of the city's crime decline, comparing what happened in New York City with the national pattern. Second, I will estimate the incremental portion of the city's total crime decline that might be the subject of a separate evaluation. This is where I argue for a "half a loaf" strategy of research.

Third, I will probe the particular history of the city during the 1990s, searching for atypical social or policy shifts that might qualify as the explanation of the city's incremental crime decline. Most aspects of social and economic change in the city parallel national trends, as does the increase in incarceration in state and city facilities. But the quantity of police and the methods of their deployment were distinctive in New York City, and there is a good fit between the timing of these changes in policing and the sharp decline of many, but not all, of New York City's crime indicators.

Fourth, I will address the lessons to be learned from the city's adventures in the 1990s. The city stands as an example of dramatic changes in the rate and risk of violent crime without major social, economic, or ecological changes. What can we learn when we shift the focus from searching for the causes of declining crime in New York City to studying the effects of declining crime on the city and its citizens? What have we learned in the variability of New York crime about the links between urban structure and rates of crime?

The Extent and Character of Declining Crime in the City

The best snapshot of the decline of crime over the 1990s in New York City comes from the comparison of crime trends in official statistics of the city during the 1990s and the rate of decline in the rest of the United States. Figure 6.1 reproduces this data, using a format suggested by John Conklin

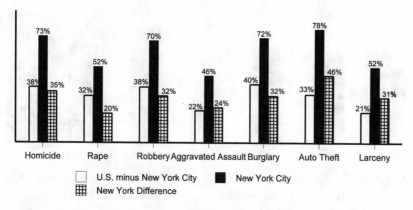

Figure 6.1. Percentage declines in seven "index" offenses in New York City and the rest of reporting areas in the United States, 1990–2000. Source: U.S. Department of Justice. Federal Bureau of Investigation. 1990, 2000. *Uniform Crime Report*. Washington, D.C.: Government Printing Office.

(2003). The white bar shows the national decline, the dark bar the New York City decline, and the mixed bar at the right-hand side shows the difference between the national and city total.

The magnitude of the city's 10-year decline is the first visually striking dimension of figure 6.1. Four of seven crime categories dropped by 70% or more during the 1990s, including two of the top three "fear crimes" in the United States, homicide and robbery. Burglary fell by 70% in the decade, and auto theft—down 33% in the rest of the United States—dropped by 78% in the city. Even the two smaller decline categories in the rest of the United States—larceny and assault—dropped by about half in New York City. The third bar in each crime category—the difference between the city decline and that in the rest of the country—is roughly equal to the magnitude of the national drop.

Using two standard measures of average, the crime drop in New York City is almost exactly twice that elsewhere in the United States. The median U.S. decline among the seven index crimes is auto thefts, 33%, while the median additional drop noted in New York City is the 32% additional decline noted for both robbery and burglary. The mean rate of crime decline in the United States without New York City is 32%, while the mean rate of additional decline in New York City shown in figure 6.1 is 31.4%.

Figure 6.2 uses one measure of decline discussed in the previous chapter—the drop in 2000 from the average rate reported in the 1980s—to

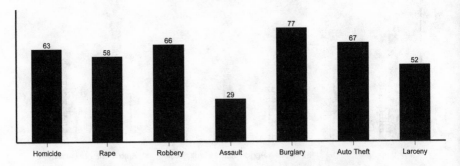

Figure 6.2. New York index crime rates, percentage decline in 2000 from mean rate of 1980–89. Source: U.S. Department of Justice. Federal Bureau of Investigation. *Uniform Crime Report*. Washington, D.C.: Government Printing Office. New York City data for 2000 and 1980–1989.

profile the seven index crimes in the city. The special value of this comparison is to measure the 2000 rate against a long-term average, to eliminate the distortion of short-term peaks and valleys in crime data. This is of particular significance for New York City, because 1990 was a high-water mark for most types of crime.

When 2000 rates are measured against longer term averages in New York City, the gap between rates at the end of the 1990s and 1980s averages is almost as great as the short-term drop for six of the seven crimes. Only assault had a crime rate in 2000 that was more than half its long-term averages. Homicide, robbery, and auto theft were down about two-thirds from their 1980s averages. For these offenses, the rate in 2000 was about one-third of its one-decade average during the 1980s, much closer to zero by 2000 than to the average crime volume of the 1980s. That is radical change. Burglary was down to less than a quarter of its 1980s rate, but readers should recall that burglary was down by almost one-half nationwide when compared with 1980s rates. (See Tonry and Farrington 2005 for international data on the decline in burglary.)

The decline in homicide by almost two-thirds from the 1980s averages is particularly noteworthy—first, because homicide is not a crime classification easily subject to manipulation or suppression in modern crime reporting, and second, because homicide was not an offense thought to be sensitive to official controls. At the other end of the seriousness spectrum in index crimes, the drop of larceny by just over half is remarkable and has no obvious precedent in large American cities. Theft is a high-incidence, diffuse, and low-visibility behavior usually regarded as difficult to influence without changing environmental controls. While changes in street policing were designed to reduce behaviors like robbery and auto theft that involve public space, there were no programatic countermeasures designed to address the city's most common index crime—theft—yet it fell by more than half from its 1980s norms.

A third method of taking the measure of the New York City decline is to examine the change in the volume of serious crimes in the city from 1990 to 2000 and the absolute crime rate in year 2000. Figure 6.3 provides New York's rate for seven offences in 1990 and 2000 and compares this rate with the mean rate for the other of the 10 largest cities in the United States in 1990 and again in 2000.

The focus in figure 6.3 is the rate of crime in New York and other large cities rather than just the convenient arithmetic of percentage changes. For 1990 and again in 2000, the graph compares the rate of seven offenses in New York City with the average rate for these offenses in the other 9 of the 10 largest cities in the United States. The average I use is the mean rate for the rest of the 10 largest cities in the 1990 census. The figure allows us to compare New York's crime rate in 1990 with that of other large cities and to show the impact of the changes in the 1990s on big-city crime in general and on New York crime. The price we pay for this actual report of crime levels is a busy and complicated graphic.

The rates of most offenses in New York in 1990 were not greatly different from the average levels for other major cities. Homicide and assault were very close to the nine-city average, while robbery rates were much higher than average and rape rates significantly lower. Of the nonperson property offenses, both burglary and larceny were lower than the big-city norm, while auto theft was equal to the big-city average.

By 2000, the rates of most offenses in New York City had dropped so precipitously that New York no longer looks like a typical big city. Homicide dropped substantially in other major cities, but after being even with the big-city average in 1990, the rate in New York in 2000 was half the big-city average, as was the officially reported rate of rape. Robbery rates in New York City were half again as much as the nine-city average in 1990 but 10% lower than the average in 2000. Assault rates were 10% higher than average in 1990 but 25% lower than that benchmark in 2000.

Prior to the 1990s, New York property offenses were in a range from equal to (auto theft) to 30% below (larceny) the big-city average. By 2000,

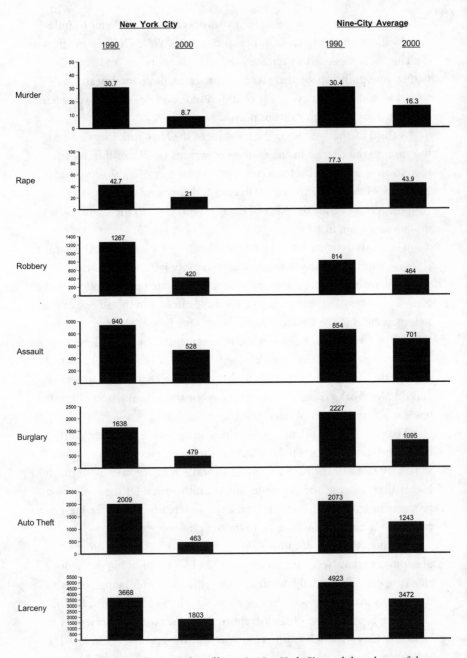

Figure 6.3. The rate of seven index offenses in New York City and the other 9 of the 10 largest U.S. cities, 1990 and 2000. Source: U.S. Department of Justice. Federal Bureau of Investigation. 1990, 2000. *Uniform Crime Report*. Washington, D.C.: Government Printing Office.

New York's burglary rate was less than half the average for big cities, its auto theft rate only slightly exceeded one-third the big-city norm, and the general larceny rate was just over half the nine-city average.

These rate declines have dramatic impact on New York's relative ranking on crime. Ranked against the other large cities in 1990, New York had the highest or second highest rate in four of seven crime categories and was lower than average only for one (rape). By 2000, New York was lower than average for all seven offenses and had the lowest of the 10 city rates for five of the seven index offenses.

Visibility and Decline

One qualitative dimension of declining crime in the city concerns whether the place where the crime occurred was publicly visible. This is a judgment that reporting police officers make that is then recorded at the city level. There is no formal auditing of the accuracy of the classifications, but there is also little incentive to biased reporting in one direction or another when individual events are classified. Figure 6.4 uses aggregate statistics retained by the police department to separately trace the decline in visible and not visible offenses for each of the four violent offenses over the 1990s.

There are two different ways to analyze the data in figure 6.4. The first is to compare visible to not visible crimes within each offense category, and for all four crimes, the drop in the visible variety of offense is significantly

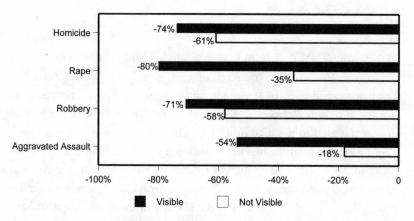

Figure 6.4. Ten-year declines in visible and not-visible violent crimes, New York City, 1990–2000. Source: Data provided by New York City Police Department.

New York City's Natural Experiment

larger than that in the not visible. This consistent pattern might reflect either that it is easier to influence crime risks in public spaces or that for some offenses, the types of offense that happen in public are very different from those that happen in nonpublic spaces.

The second possible analytic approach is to make generalizations across crime categories. An argument can be made that there is greater uniformity in the pattern over time of visible violent crime than there is in comparing the aggregate of visible and nonvisible offenses in each category. Not only is the decline in visible rape and assault much greater than in the nonvisible varieties of those offenses but also the decline in all four visible violent offenses is more similar (a range from 80% to 54%, with three of the four offenses within 9% of each other) than the distribution of violent offenses (a range from 73% to 46%, with two categories showing declines 40% greater than the other two)(see figure 6.1).

The very wide gap between declines in visible versus nonvisible rape (45%) and assault (36%) provides clear warning that a large part of that big a "visibility gap" might be the result of such crimes taking place in the nonvisible locations involving parties who know each other and might be in ongoing relationships. The very modest declines in these types of "nonvisible" offenses between acquaintances may be in part the result of greater police willingness to report and "verify" as a crime in 2000 acts that did not use to receive any official recording. This is particularly plausible because the gap between the visible and nonvisible was 3 to 1 for assault and greater than 2 to 1 for rape, while much closer for homicide and robbery.

The Scale of the Crime Decline

The size of New York City and the magnitude of the decline in rates interact to generate impressive numbers of savings in the volume of crime. The homicide rate decline of 22 per 100,000 per year in a population that exceeds 7.5 million generates a savings of more than 1,500 lives per year in 2000 compared to the 1990 death toll. The two-year saving at that rate is slightly greater than the loss of life suffered in the September 11, 2001, attacks in New York. The reduction in recorded robberies in the city was greater than 50,000 per year in one city in a decade, and there were similar reductions in burglary and auto theft. The size of the crime drop that happened in 10 years exceeded the targets and goals of even the most optimistic criminal justice and public health reform agendas of the 1970s and

1980s. Reform platforms like the National Commission on Standards and Goals for Criminal Justice risked ridicule in the 1970s by arguing that 50% declines in street crime might be achievable after a decade of concerted effort—but no reform body ever pushed the bar up to 70% reductions in a 10-year frame. In that important sense, what New York City achieved between 1990 and 2000 was a reversal in crime and violence beyond the imagination of responsible policy analysts.

The enormous changes in crime and violence in New York City over the 1990s might tempt us to conclude that this city somehow changed its character in the course of the 1990s. But any temptation to see New York as a different city at the end of the 1990s both misstates and underestimates the city's achievements. What makes the 1990s remarkable is the stunning shift in crime rates that were achieved without any fundamental change in the population composition, economy, or ecology of New York City.

Half a Loaf as a Research Strategy

A standard method of explaining variation in crime rates or other quantitatively expressed phenomena is to construct a model to explain variations over time and use multivariate regression to assess the causal role of identified factors in the observed variation. This is a popular and low-cost research methodology, but it encounters many problems in measuring the causes of crime declines in the 1990s. The governmental and social factors that influence crime rates over time are not agreed on, and the magnitude of influence of potential causes is also very much in dispute. Chapters 3 and 4 provide an uncomfortably ample number of failed models and unverifiable estimates of causal influence on crime rates. Further, the influence of cyclical trends rather than instrumental causes is of special significance during the 1990s in the United States, as discussed in chapter 5.

There are three reasons why an alternative approach is superior to attempting a comprehensive model to explain declining crime in New York City. First, all of the difficulties encountered when trying to model the totality of influences on crime in the United States as a whole are present in New York as well. A multivariate explanation of the city's crime decline is just as untrustworthy as an aggregate national version.

The second argument for trying to explain just the distinctive part of the New York City decline is the logic of triangulation of proof, mentioned in my discussion of police and crime reduction in chapter 4. An attempt to explain only the difference between New York City and the rest of the United States will undoubtedly have major flaws, but—if the method is problematic in different ways from those of the usual approach of building a comprehensive model—these two differently imperfect strategies can increase our confidence in any inferences they both support, or can underscore the fragility of results that are produced by only one of the two methods. Triangulation of proof is as close to "two wrongs make a right" as quantitative explanations come. Explaining only that part of New York's crime decline that differs from the national norm provides a novel test that may have different imperfections from rounding up the usual equations.

The third consideration that favors trying to isolate those elements in New York City that explain the city's difference rather than the entire decline is the hope that there will be a smaller number of causal candidates to explain what sets New York City apart than would be needed for constructing a comprehensive explanation for New York City crime in the 1990s.

The list of elements that changed in New York City over the 1990s (including the effects of time itself) is longer, one hopes, than the number of significant differences between the city during the 1990s and the rest of the country. Reducing the number of plausible causes that distinguish New York City is one way of "controlling for" changes in the city that are also found in the broad cross-section of the United States.

As against these advantages, there are two novel problems with what I will call a "difference" or "half a loaf" strategy. The first is that there is a less of a crime decline to explain—the method despairs of determining all of the causes of the city's crime decline. The second is that this method requires one to estimate what proportion of the total New York decline is not found in the national pattern. At the outset, then, we must make an estimate with a substantial margin of error.

There is no real sacrifice in not trying to explain all of the New York City decline, because there is no real prospect of success in explaining everything. The entire portfolio of temporal, policy, and social changes at work all over the United States during the 1990s was operating in New York City as well. There is no advantage in trying to sort out these multiple influences at the city level. Instead, there is a strategic advantage to isolating the extra crime decline that separates New York from other parts of the nation and searching for distinct influences that might explain this special performance. This is the "natural experiment" that can only happen in New York City.

But how to estimate the proportion of the New York City decline that is a candidate for separate explanation? Figure 6.5 compares two theoretically distinct methods of estimating the difference between the New York City decline and the national average. The dark bar for each of seven crimes reports the actual difference between reported New York City declines in percentages and the national average for each offense. To use one example in the figure, since homicide declined 38% in the United States outside New York City and 73% in New York, the dark bar estimate for homicide is 73% minus 38%, or 35%. The unshaded bar simply reports half of the New York City decline in each category, assuming that the appropriate measure in each crime category is half the city's decline in that category. For homicide, the light bar divides the 73% city decline by 2 to produce a 37% estimate. The first method is empirically determined, while the second is based on an assumption that since about half the total decline in index offenses is in excess of the national norm, it is plausible to assume that 50% of each crime decline falls into this category.

The primary visual lesson of figure 6.5 is that there is little difference between the observed variation from national averages in each category of crime decline over the decade and half the New York City decline. Property offenses fell slightly more than twice as far in New York City, and violent offenses slightly less. But "half a loaf," in the sense of half the total decline, is close to a precise estimate of the extra crime decline peculiar to New York City in the 1990s.

But can we safely assume that all of New York City's extra crime drop was linked to special causes within city limits? Any distribution of big-city

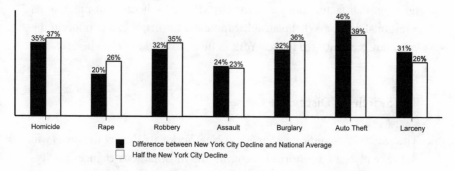

Figure 6.5. Two estimates of additional crime declines in New York City, 1990–2000. Source: U.S. Department of Justice. Federal Bureau of Investigation. 1990, 2000. *Uniform Crime Report.* Washington, D.C.: Government Printing Office.

crime declines will have a few extreme values, even if there are no special causes at work. Why not assume that most of New York's extra drop was not attributable to any particular cause? Why assume that all of the extra drop had instrumental causes?

There are a number of good reasons to doubt that New York's extreme position on the distribution of crime drops is only chance variation. New York is the biggest city by far in the nation, which makes it an unlikely candidate for an extreme position on a distribution without any substantive reason. Even if Manhattan had a big drop by chance, won't Brooklyn and Queens even out the city totals? Further, a search for other cities in the United States with very large drops finds no city with the magnitude of drop or consistency across crime categories found in New York City (see appendix 4). Chance factors alone are not likely to place New York at the very top of the crime-decline pyramid.

But the search for high-decline cities does show some large cities with much larger than average crime drops, including one of the top five cities in population. So attributing all of the differential drop in New York City to particular causes might not be justified. A more cautious statement of the approach would estimate that between a quarter and a half of the total New York City decline represents the likely effects of changes that other major cities did not experience.

So in the next section I try to find special factors at work in New York City that cannot be observed in the rest of the country that might plausibly explain substantial declines in all seven index crime rates that are roughly double the national average. The assumption is that a mix of factors beyond the reach of current analysis produced about half New York's crime reduction, but that factors unique to the city are the likely cause of much of its additional decline. What plausible candidates for major causes of declining crime are concentrated in New York in the 1990s and not elsewhere?

The Search for Distinctive Causes

The search for significant changes in New York City during the 1990s will not take place in a historical vacuum. The most famous changes in city-level criminal justice were a series of changes in the quantity and quality of police in New York City. In this section I will first discuss whether there were other nontypical changes in the city that were of sufficient magnitude to compete with the police as an explanation for the New York City difference, and I will then try to describe the multiple dimensions of the changes in policing and to determine whether separate elements of the police shifts can be identified as being responsible for measurable subsegments of the distinctive decline in the city. There was no single shift in policing in New York in the 1990s, but rather three distinct changes in policing to complicate the picture.

Alternatives to a Police-Based Explanation

The first question to be addressed is whether there were shifts in the city during the 1990s in factors plausibly thought to influence crime that were sufficiently distinct from national trends so that they might explain New York's larger than typical decline. The list of candidates for causation is taken from the theories presented in part II. Appendix 3 surveys data in New York City on the dimensions of change discussed in chapter 3, such as incarceration, demographics, and employment. The standard theories can be excluded from the competition for extra credit, but only because of the half-a-loaf strategy. As appendix 3 shows, incarceration rates did grow during the 1990s in the city, but not at a rate in excess of the national norm. In fact, the growth in incarceration in the city was lower than the 57% increase in imprisonment nationwide. The downward movement in the proportion of the population in high-risk younger age groups also followed the national trend but was smaller in New York City than nationally. For total unemployment as well, declines at the city level in joblessness were much smaller than the national average. All of these trends probably contributed to New York City's decline in crime during the 1990s, but there are no indications of unusual doses of any of these factors that might explain the additional crime decline in the city. For trends in hard drug use, appendix 3 collects a variety of data that do not suggest radical changes during the 1990s.

The two nonpolice theories analyzed in chapter 4 present a more complicated problem for analysis, in part because they cannot be quantitatively specified as can unemployment or incarceration and in part because New York City had a distinctive historical relationship with both crack and abortion reform in the 1970s and 1980s. The city of New York had a longstanding status as the nation's hard drug capital, and—at least during the middle and late 1980s—it was a focal point of concern about

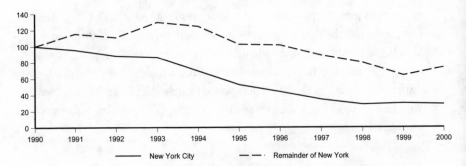

Figure 6.6. 1990 rates = 100 Trends in homicide, New York City and New York state outside New York City, 1990–2000. Source: U.S. Department of Justice, Federal Bureau of Investigation, *Uniform Crime Report*, 1990–2000, Washington, D.C.

crack cocaine. So why not believe that a more intense than typical involvement in the criminal upside of a crack epidemic would produce a larger than normal decline as the aftermath of crack epidemic? There is no a priori method of rejecting this possibility, but the breadth of the crime decline across so many categories makes it difficult to imagine that a profound aftermath of crack cocaine is a major force. The abatement of a crack epidemic might explain a much larger than normal homicide decline (73%), but why would we expect a 78% decline in auto theft and a 70% drop in burglary? Further, the official rate of hospital discharges for cocaine overdoses was just as high in 2000 as in 1990 and had climbed well beyond the 1990 rates for most of the 1990s (see appendix 3).

New York was also one of the "early liberalization" states where Donahue and Levitt expected larger and earlier than usual crime declines in the 1990s. The shift in New York to elective abortion came in 1970 instead of 1973. Might this head start explain some of the city's extra crime drop?

The critical test for the plausibility of this theory is examining whether the special character of the crime decline we find in the city happened statewide (which would be consistent with state-level abortion reform as a cause) or was concentrated in New York City (which would argue against a statewide cause). Figure 6.6 traces trends in homicide in New York City and in the rest of New York state over the period 1990–2000.

With 1990 rates at 100, the homicide total for New York State except for New York City rose until the middle of the decade and then turned down to end 25% lower in 2000 than in 1990. The out-state homicide rate decline was significantly smaller than the national average, while New York City's

73% decline was almost twice as great. The pattern in figure 6.6 suggests that city-level rather than state-level changes were the likely cause of the extra decline in homicide, and this would argue against the abortion liberalization at the state level as a prime candidate for the city-specific drop.

There is one other feature of the New York City crime decline that is inconsistent with a three-year head start in elective abortion as cause. The additional crime decline in New York City was not clustered at the beginning of the 1990s but was concentrated in the middle and late parts of the decade. Indeed, chapter 7 shows New York City has continued its decline through 2005. This is not the pattern a three-year head start should generate.

Changes in Policing—A Profile

What changed at the city level in New York City during the early 1990s was both the quantity of police in the city and the way police were deployed, evaluated, and managed. No fewer than three major elements of city policing changed. The first was the number of police officers in New York. Beginning during the term of Mayor David Dinkins in New York City, the number of full-time police employees grew from 39,400 to 53,000 in the 1990s, or 35%. Figure 6.7 compares New York City full-time police trends during the 1990s with the other 9 of the 10 largest cities in the United States

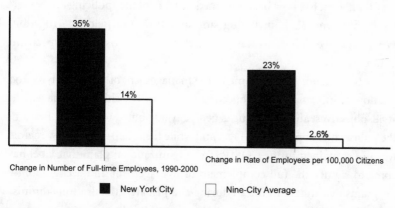

Figure 6.7. Change in full-time police employees and in rate per 100,000 population of full-time employees, 1990–2000, 10 largest cities in 1990. Source: Brian A. Reeves and Mathew J. Hickman. App. A of *Police Departments in Large Cities, 1990–2000*. Washington, D.C.: U.S. Department of Justice, Bureau of Justice Statistics.

in 1990. New York City rates are compared with the mean rates for the other nine cities.

The New York department added 35% to its police employment, which increased the rate of employees per 100,000 by 23%. The other nine large-city averages were 14% employee expansion and 2.6% increase in employment adjusted for population. No other city in the top 10 expanded by as much as 13% per capita during the decade.

Just as in crime, the size of the city and its rate of expansion interact to produce some impressive comparative statistics. The 13,631 employees added in New York during the 1990s were a larger number than the total employees in eight of the other nine biggest city police departments in 1990 and almost equal to Chicago's total of 14,909. So what New York City added in one decade was the equivalent of the third largest police force in the United States. The number of sworn officers in New York expanded by more than 9,000 during the 1990s, from 31,236 to 40,435.

And numbers were only part of the New York police story. A second major change took place in the tactical emphasis of street policing. While the labels attached to the 1990s changes in police strategy have usually been "order maintenance" or "zero tolerance," the major strategic weapons employed at street level were aggressive stops that were independent of arrests for offenses and a program of misdemeanor arrests for drug offenses, as well as a variety of public-order offenses. Both tactics have a longer history than what has now been renamed "quality of life" policing and a variety of different labels including stop and frisk and field interrogation. What the city emphasized was proactive policing across a wide spectrum of target behaviors.

A third major change came in the management of police activity and the flow of information to police management. The shift in management style, objectives, and technique is generally attributed to William Bratton, the police chief appointed in 1994, and while the totality of the new regime was not contained in the COMPSTAT organizational plan, that label has come to signify the full complement of management and accountability programs that were introduced during and just after the Bratton administration (see Bratton 1998).

The three major changes in New York City policing were interdependent and interrelated. The new manpower added did not take up policing with traditional tactics and administration but were soon part of the new priorities and tactics. The COMPSTAT management program both created many of the changed tactics at street level and used the information tion produced by aggressive street policing to create and document high-impact intervention plans. This amalgamation of manpower, management, and tactics was not only the major city-level change in New York at the time but also the only systemic change of large scope in criminal justice in the middle and later 1990s. So policing becomes the plausible cause of special New York City declines by a process of elimination.

But what aspects of the multilevel changes deserve the credit? Is there a way of separately measuring any one of the major components of police changes—say, for example, the expanding number of police—while controlling for the potential impact of the other changes? There is certainly no way to do this using aggregate data on crime and law enforcement at the city level. One can't separate the new force levels from the new tactics, because there was no control group of police added on who were deployed in traditional and more passive patrol styles. Nor is there a way of testing aggressive and expanded street-level control without the management and accountability systems. They happened together.

My view is that the only inference that can be drawn about the impact of this kitchen sink full of policing changes on New York crime levels is that there is powerful circumstantial evidence that compound major changes in the quantity of police and the tactics of policing had a major impact on crime. The only plausible independent variable in New York City's natural experiment is the whole complex of changes put in place from 1992 on. The best estimate of the level of crime reduction achieved is between and quarter and a half the recorded decline during the 1990s, and the margin of error associated with that wide range is not small.

But even if all the individual elements of the changing police environment have to share the credit with other policing changes, there turns out to be a great deal of credit to share. A decline of between 16% and 32% in serious crime is a very large prize for a police department by almost any standard. It would far exceed any previously documented decline in crime generated by variations in policing levels or strategies at the city level. Natural experiments with this magnitude of preventive effects are absent from the literature of policing or of urban history. As reported in chapter 4, the only claims for documented city-level police force effects have come from regression arguments that are weak and inconsistent in estimated magnitudes.

If the police changes in New York really produced up to half of that city's crime decline, it would mean that changed conditions of policing produced an impact in the country's largest city that was all by itself half or more of the magnitude of the nationwide decline in crime over the 1990s. And while the national-level decline was a product of multiple causes interacting with unspecifiable cyclical effects, only policing in New York would have produced an additional reduction of that approximate size. This would require major change in the social science dogma that the impact of police on crime is a myth—the received wisdom I reviewed in chapters 2 and 4 (Silberman 1978; Bailey 1994).

The Case for Single-Factor Explanations

Those few scholars who have discussed the causes of the crime decline in New York City are by no means unanimous in the belief that both qualitative and quantitative changes in policing were causes of declining crime. In two cases, the argument is made that the expansion in the number of city police alone explains New York's exceptional decline. These arguments deserve close attention.

The first published version of this "only size matters" argument was that of Steven Levitt in 2004. Discussing his doubts that changes in police strategy were an important factor in the city's crime decline, Levitt argues:

> By my estimate, the unusually large expansion of the police force in New York City would be expected to reduce crime there by 18 percent more than the national average, even without any change in policing strategy. If one adds 18 percent to New York City's crime homicide experience . . . (changing the decline from 73.6 percent to 55.6 percent), New York City is about average among large cities. (2004, p. 173)

What Levitt is doing here is not an independent analysis of New York data on criminal justice and crime so much as making an argument that the known effects of added police personnel derived from other statistical analyses are large enough that the additional manpower by itself could be expected to reduce crime by the range that New York experienced in excess of national norms during the 1990s. This becomes a rejection of the notion that COMPSTAT management or the aggressive style of street policing caused a decline, but only because there is no residual unexplained decline left for such factors to explain.

But even assuming that an 18% reduction in New York homicide is to be expected on the basis of added manpower alone, the 73% decline in New York homicide was substantially greater than the 46% drop in the mean homicide rate that figure 6.3 reports for the nine largest cities other than New York. Add 18% to a 38% national decline in homicide, and one expects a 56% decline instead of the actual 70%. So even when one plays by Levitt's rules, his result isn't obvious.

But can we assume that 18% is a good estimate of the independent effect of police numbers? I mentioned many of the problems associated with this argument in my discussion in chapter 4 of what I called quantitative police theories of crime reduction. As I pointed out there, it turns out that there is considerable controversy over whether there is any causal relation between additional police and reduced crime. There is further controversy over the extent to which police numbers reduce crime, with even Professor Levitt's two published studies producing different estimates for many offenses. All the estimates for quantitative prevention come from multiple regression exercises, with no explicit theory of how additional police reduce crime rates. The statistical correlations produce a "black box" of inferred causation without any account of what elements in police activity cause reductions.

One additional problem with Levitt's claim that his earlier estimates of the effects of police numbers fully explain the New York phenomenon is that he doesn't purport to measure any aspect of New York City's experience during the 1990s other than the number of new police and the crime decline. So Levitt's account, in effect, substitutes a black box expectation that simply hiring large numbers of police must have caused huge declines in homicide, robbery, and burglary for much more detailed theories and narratives of activities of what actually happened in New York. In my view, it would take much more reliable evidence and more precisely plausible a priori estimates of police effectiveness to support the wisdom of displacing the particular history of New York's police deployment with one-size-fits-all theories of the fixed effects of manpower increments on crime rates.

Richard Rosenfeld and his associates make a less sweeping assessment than Levitt and use New York City data more inductively, but their logic is similar. The strategy in their analysis is to build a regression model to explain variations in New York City's homicides. Among the variables assumed to be causes of reduced homicides are increases in police manpower.

The authors then argue that the additional independent or interactive effects of the COMPSTAT strategic plan cannot be established, because the additional reductions left unexplained are not statistically significant. The statistical argument here is more fine-grained than Levitt's, and the results are more qualified: "The New York rate fell more sharply than the sample average during the [COMPSTAT] intervention period, although the difference is only marginally significant at p.10. However, when the covariates are introduced in the conditional model, the difference between the New York and average homicide trends becomes non-significant" (Rosenfeld, Fornango, and Baumer 2005).

This falls far short of disproof of COMPSTAT impacts (and of street intervention effects) for a variety of reasons. The regression model for this study lacks both a longstanding pedigree in other studies of police and violence and clear external evidence for its assumed effects. The failure to find that the unexplained additional homicide variation is statistically significant would be much better evidence against COMPSTAT effects if this lack of significance was found with much higher incidence crimes such as robbery and auto theft. Of the seven traditional index offenses, homicide is the category least likely to generate a significant decline because of its low volume. The drop in homicides per year in New York City was about 22 per 100,000, while the decline in robbery rates was over 700 per 100,000. Which set of declines would be more likely to show significant residual declines when the potential influence of other factors was sliced away? There is the further problem, of course, of the stability and precision of estimates of quantitative police manpower effects. If they are half as much as these authors estimate, how much more variance is left to be explained by other police variables?

Other Strategies for Unraveling the Sources of Police Crime Prevention

I have to this point argued that the city-wide pattern in New York crime cannot apportion credit between the three changes in policing as a primary cause of crime reduction during the 1990s. But would it be possible to find variations in subunits of the city that might measure one aspect of the policing changes but not others, and then test whether variations in that dimension of policing are associated with larger drops in crime within the city? This was the aim of George Kelling and William Sousa, Jr., in a 2001 article that used rates of misdemeanor arrest as a proxy for "broken windows" policing and found that increases in an area's misdemeanor arrests over the 1990s are associated with larger declines in index crime than areas within New York City with smaller increases in arrest rates (Kelling and Sousa 2001). There are, however, several reasons why this is not strong evidence that "quality of life" policing played a major independent role in creating crime declines. First, it is not clear that misdemeanor arrest rates are a good measure of variations in "quality of life" emphasis independent of also being a function of larger police manpower or more aggressiveness in police enforcement of all laws. To the extent that there is any causal relationship between high misdemeanor arrest rates and lower crime rates, it is not possible to tie the arrest rate to a philosophy of police priority as opposed to aggressiveness in making street contacts or larger manpower concentrations.

A second problem concerns whether the variations in arrest rates are a cause of declining crime or whether precinct-level crime rates and misdemeanor arrests are both caused by other changes in policing—changes like aggressiveness at street level or intensity of patrol activities. Bernard Harcourt and Jens Ludwig (2005) couldn't get the identical data used in the 2001 study but create close approximations that are as consistent with a noncausal role for the misdemeanor arrest rate.

Can these problems be cleaned up with better measures of each individual element of police changes? Probably not. Only experimental manipulation of manpower in different work assignments holds the promise of serving as a disaggregating indication of style of policing effects inside New York City. Or perhaps some other city might wish to redirect police priorities without increasing manpower or changing styles of administration. But the record of the 1990s cannot be distilled into a test of separate elements when the variations that occurred were in fact concurrent. In that sense, our knowledge of the specific influence of particular features of the City's multiple changes in policing is a hostage to history.

It is only if reliable estimates of the effects of particular features of the police shift could be imported from other studies with confidence that credible estimates of separate police effects for New York could be constructed. We have already observed the variability of estimated effects of police manpower. Add to that the fact that the way police were deployed in New York City had some novelty, and separate estimates of quantitative and qualitative policing impacts cannot be based on a credible scientific foundation.

This is a serious limit on the capacity to estimate the costs of generating police-based crime savings. If management and tactics play a large role in crime reduction, then there might be cheaper packages of reforms that might reduce crime without the major manpower expansions of the 1990s in New York City. If not, then only major shifts in the scale of policing could claim credit for the New York result. Only new experimentation can provide answers to a high-stakes puzzle.

The lack of a plausible justification for taking any one of the city's policing innovations and awarding it principal credit for the majority of police effects is one major complication in drawing easy-to-implement policy prescriptions from the New York City experience. All that we can know from studying the New York data is that a combination of three major shifts in the content of policing had apparently major impact on crime. The only reliable prescription for a major police effect that emerges from this story is for a combination of ingredients as complicated as (and considerably more expensive than) Anacin tablets.

Worse still, even with all these New York City ingredients in place in another city, it may not be prudent to assume that the police changes that produced high volumes of crime reduction in New York will operate with equal effectiveness in other cities. That is the question I consider in the next section.

Tomorrow the World?

If the changes in the quality and quantity of policing in New York City did produce broad crime declines on the order of 17% to 35%, to what extent can we expect similar policing changes in other cities to produce the same type of results? One set of problems has already been discussed—identifying the key ingredients in the kitchen sink full of police changes that happened during New York's 1990s. But even if all the active ingredients in New York's policing changes were faithfully reproduced in Detroit or Chicago or Los Angeles, would the same dosage of independent policing variables be likely to produce the same magnitude of crime reductions?

There are three aspects of New York City in the early 1990s as a setting for police reforms that might have produced larger effects than one could reasonably expect in other cities now. The first special feature of New York in 1990 was the city's very high absolute rate of crime: the highest rates in history of murder, robbery, and auto theft in the city. This high density of crime may be associated with the opportunity for larger declines. In an environment of high crime density, police tactics that might be effective in almost all settings might suppress much more crime simply because there are greater concentrations of criminal behavior that the police efforts encounter. This would not be regression or any sort of statistical artifact. A high-crime-density environment might be an opportunity for more cost-effective reforms, and lower crime density environments (and that would include all big U.S. cities now) might have less dramatic downward potential.

The second feature that might intensify the marginal impact of effective police strategies in New York City is its extraordinary population density. The population per square mile in New York City was just over 24,000 in 1990. That same year, the population density in the nation's second biggest city, Los Angeles, was 7,400, or less than one-third that of New York. Higher population density might have a number of beneficial implications for the effectiveness of police patrol and surveillance of public areas. The sheer geographic volume of streets, sidewalks, and parks that must be brought under control is smaller in areas of high population density. The ability to use techniques of foot patrol in a cost-effective way can also be a function of density. If foot patrol is really inherently more amenable to the goals of community policing than car patrol, high-density environments present a much greater opportunity to use this more promising technique. If high population density generates the opportunity for larger crime declines, then New York City has a natural advantage over other large American cities.

One further possible advantage New York City in 1990 may have had over other large cities was its combination of low civilian handgun ownership and tight handgun control laws. In 1990, New York City had a relatively large number of handguns on its streets (75% of homicides were committed with guns, higher than the national average), but very few citizens owned guns (the proportion of suicides caused by guns was the second lowest in the nation for populous counties). This meant that when aggressive police interventions removed guns from New York streets, those guns were not as easy to replace as would have been the case in cities where 20–30% of all households owned handguns. With fewer easy replacement guns available through burglaries or purchases from gun-owning citizens, the successful removal of guns from the street might have a longer period

of likely effectiveness than in urban areas with larger civilian gun invento-
ries. One statistic mentioned earlier in this chapter might be evidence of
a further effect of gun removals having longer impact. Figure 6.4 showed
that the 1990s witnessed not only large declines in New York in "visible"
homicides and robberies but also declines almost as large in homicides
and robberies that are not visible to police in public. One reason for this
might well be that aggressive street gun removal reduced gun use even in
nonpublic places, a benefit that might not be as easy to produce in cities
with higher levels of civilian handgun ownership.

These three special characteristics of New York City that may have
magnified the impact of its police reforms do not mean that measures effective in that city would totally fail to reduce crime in other cities. In that
sense, these environmental features do not limit the generalizability of the
police changes, but they would suggest than similar levels of change in
policing might be expected to produce smaller magnitudes of crime reduction elsewhere. William Bratton, the New York City police chief cred-
ited with many of that city's reforms in the mid-1990s, may be performing
his own version of a natural experiment by having become police chief in
Los Angeles in 2002, a city with much lower population density, higher
civilian household handgun ownership, and a crime rate in the early years
of the twenty-first century that is significantly lower than New York's was
in 1990. If the same techniques of policing and expansion in force produce
smaller crime-decline dividends, there are a number of plausible explanations available to explain this more modest marginal effectiveness.

Testing the Effects of a Low-Crime Environment

While some attention has been paid to debating the causes of lower crime
rates in New York City, no scholarly attempts to use the city's experience as
a laboratory to study the effects of a lower crime rate have yet been reported. Yet New York City is the best natural setting for that type of inquiry, for the same reason it demands attention in the study of causes—
the magnitude of the city's crime decline. With twice the normal U.S.
crime decline, the city has been provided with a double dose of whatever
social medicine declining crime rates might turn out to be. If the best way
to study the impact of crime rates is to measure the impact of changes over
time—and I think it is—then the change in one decade in New York City

is the best big-city-level opportunity to examine the effects of lower crime rates without other major social changes to occur in a century. The median "index offense" rate of the seven traditional index offenses decreased by 70% in 10 years and was more than 50% below the average rate in the 1980s. Are we likely to see a change of this size again soon?

In this section, I will attempt to organize some of the important issues to examine when studying the effects of major crime declines, and I outline some of the data that can help answer basic questions. This is much more a shopping list than a report of even preliminary findings, but any progress in provoking the systemic assessment of the effects of decline is important.

Three Kinds of Questions

At the outset, it is worthwhile to distinguish three different types of questions to pursue about the effects of a lower crime environment and the sorts of data one might gather in New York City to test hypotheses.

Aggregate Impacts

The first sort of effect to examine is how the reduction in crime in the city has affected the distribution of both crime and arrests. The data one collects for this purpose consist of detailed information on victims, offenders, and arrests, as well as on the city's population. Where do the benefits of declining crime fall most heavily? Since violent crime is concentrated among disadvantaged minorities, if reductions are distributed in the same way as general patterns of both victimization and offending, the major share of crime reduction benefits will go to poor and minority populations. The good news that is implied by finding that violent crime is a regressive tax whereby the poor pay much more is that general patterns of declining crime produces some benefits that are a mirror image of the costs of crime.

And because both victims and offenders are concentrated among the same disadvantaged populations, a major crime decline might produce a double benefit—fewer victims as well as fewer offenders arrested and punished for serious crimes. The concentration of victimization is not a constant across different types of crime, of course. But for each crime, a first approximation of the benefits of a crime decline is the mirror image of the general risk of victimization. Figure 6.8 compares the race and sex breakdown of New York City homicide victims with those of the city's population for 1990.

The obvious point to be made is that the disproportionate beneficiaries of a decline in crime are those groups at greatest risk to become victims. Men are half the city's population but 86% of its homicide victims in 1990. So 86% of the drop in homicide between 1990 and 2000 is also a drop in male victims (1,413 out of 1,646). Even though African Americans and Hispanics were less than half the city's population in 1990, those groups account for 79% of all homicide victims in that census year. When the big drop in deaths happens, these two groups make up 78.5% of the decline of homicide victims of all ethnicities.

Data on crime victimization by income group is not available for the city, but national studies show clear patterns of poorer groups having

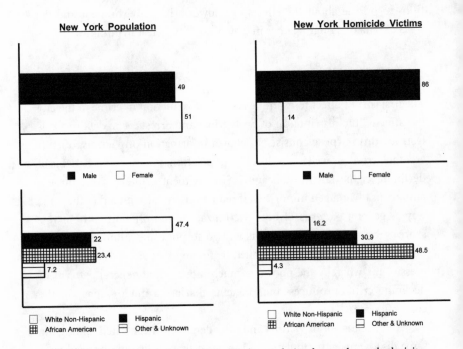

Figure 6.8. Homicide victims and New York population by gender and ethnicity. Sources: Population: U.S. Department of Commerce. Bureau of the Census. 1990 Census. International Data Base (IDB). Available at the website of the Census Bureau: www.census.gov/ipc/www/idbnew.html. Death demographics: City of New York. Department of Health. 1990.

much higher victimization. Rates of violent crimes such robbery, sexual assault, and aggravated assault are three or more times higher at the lowest end of the income categories (under $7,500) than at the highest end ($75,000) in 1996, and there is at least a 2-to-1 difference in the reported rates for all personal crimes in 1996. So any general decline in crime rates has larger positive impact among the least advantaged segments of the population (U.S. Department of Justice, Bureau of Justice Statistics, National Crime Victimization Survey 1996).

The benefits that are generated by the effect of crime declines on arrests are somewhat less straightforward. A 70% decline in homicides will produce a decline in homicide arrests almost that great (the 10-year drop in New York homicide arrests was 60.4%, from 2,101 to 833), and the concentration of arrests in minority males is even greater than for victimization. So the arrest rates for serious crimes (and the burden they represent) will decline substantially. But total arrests will not decline as substantially as serious crime arrests, and the aggregate burden of arrests may not decline at the same rate as the aggregate burden of crime victimization.

From Macro Effects to Individual Life Patterns

When the emphasis shifts from the distribution of effects to the impact of a lower crime environment on the experiences of different types of people over time, it is necessary to study defined groups of people over time. But this more expensive method of study is also of critical importance. I will illustrate the process here by outlining assessments of changing conditions on two populations—offenders being released from incarceration and high-risk youth in the city's middle schools.

ENVIRONMENTAL IMPACTS ON CRIMINAL CAREERS

If there are 70% fewer robberies and burglaries in New York City in 2000, does that mean that incarcerated offenders released from prison and jail in 2000 will commit 70% fewer robberies and burglaries than offenders released in 1990? If so, the general crime environment would have a huge effect on later criminal careers of offenders. If not, then already active offenders will be responsible for a larger share of those robberies and burglaries that do take place in 2000. If the rearrest rate of released offenders in 2000 were the same for burglary and robbery as it was in 1990, they will be responsible for three times the proportion of those crimes in the city. In either event, a major shift will have happened either in the postrelease experience of offenders or in the distribution of offenses (where the age of offenders and the proportion of offenses committed by recidivists will have gone up), or in both. Shouldn't we find out?

The data collection required for this type of analysis is not complicated. The detailed arrest profile of large groups of offenders released from custody in 1990 and 2000 over the next 36 months can provide a comparison of major crime arrest risks. This is not the equivalent of comparing either rearrest rates or recidivism rates of release cohorts, because these two general categories will be flooded by drug offense and misdemeanors arrests as well as technical parole violations. The proportion of major crime arrests is much smaller. Whether any decline in major crime arrest rates is associated with any significant decline in total rearrest or return to custody rates is not known. So the volume of serious crimes committed and arrested for might decline substantially in a population of released offenders without any significant reduction in arrests or official identification of recidivism. The rate of serious crime attributable to a group could decline, but the proportion of the group considered criminally active might not drop much at all. The threat to public health and safety might drop substantially without much change in the social or even the legal status of ex-offenders.

There turns out to be no clear way to infer the impact of environmental changes such as lower crime rates on the content and intensity of the criminal careers of individuals. The only route to getting a reading on these issues is to compare cohorts of released offenders over time. If the issue is the recidivism rate of serious crime arrests in a lower crime environment, New York City is the best major city in the world to launch such a study. But it hasn't happened yet.

An even more important question than the environmental impact of lower crime environments on formerly active offenders is the impact of lower crime rates on the life experience of youth at high risk of involvement in serious crime. Assume that the reoffending rate of released convicts for crimes like burglary and robbery has not been reduced by the 70% or more by which the rate of these offenses went down during the 1990s. If what serious crime remains in New York City is even more concentrated than it was previously in older, formerly active offenders, that would mean that the rate of robberies and burglaries committed by younger persons in the early stages of involvement with crime must have dropped more than 70% when cohorts from 1990 are compared to cohorts of the same age and social position in the lower crime environments of 2000.

Since 70% drops in the burglary and robbery involvement of ex-offenders with substantial career histories would seem unlikely, then the rates of serious crime by new recruits in high-crime areas must have declined even more than the drop in community-level rate. But if auto theft by everybody is down by 78%, could the drop in auto theft by high-risk teens in New York neighborhoods be 85%? What impact does the reduction of involvement in serious crime have on other aspects of development, including risk of arrest, law-enforcement-related handicaps to employment, school leaving rates, rates of involvement with illegal drugs, death rates, employment, and earnings? These are very important questions. They are empirical issues that cannot be approached by any means other than direct inquiry.

Many of the same warnings issued when discussing follow-up studies of released offenders apply equally to studies of the development of youth at risk in a lower crime environment. A reduction of 70% or even 80% in major crime involvement will certainly not lead to a decline in arrest rates anywhere near that large; indeed, even sharp drops in major crime commission rates may not reduce total arrest exposure for the young at all—because minor offense arrests are far more numerous than major offense arrests and because aggressive policing might more than compensate for the lower arrest experience that reduced commission of offenses like robbery and burglary might otherwise produce.

So the prevalence and incidence of official juvenile delinquency might not go down much, but the social cost of youth crime may have dropped even more substantially than the general rate of major crimes. If so, the lower stakes of youth crime in current conditions might inspire restructuring of legal system responses, and certainly a decline in serious crime by youth should substantially reduce the level of high-severity penalties in juvenile and young offender criminal court systems.

The detailed examination of criminal activity rates in lower crime environments is an important agenda item, for criminological reasons as well as for the design of rational public policy. Criminologists need to study how New York City–sized declines in crime have affected the onset, content, intensity, and length of criminal careers. Has the number of criminals in New York declined as much as the major crime rate? Half as much? At all? Have the types of crime committed changed for previously active offenders? For new recruits? Has the burden on the criminal justice system changed significantly? Has the burden of the criminal justice system on youth development in high-risk environments shifted?

A YOUTH CRIME ANALYSIS—SOCIAL STRUCTURE AND CRIME

In this connection, one puzzling feature of professional and community concern with declining crime in New York and elsewhere is the lack of concern about the risks and consequences associated with different age groups. When youth homicide rates increased starting in the mid-1980s, there was substantial focus on young persons as a risk group (Zimring 1998). The decline in crime over the period since 1993 has produced no equivalent focus. Yet there are indicators that the drop in homicide among young offenders was greater than the general decline. But the demography of good news is a much less compelling element of crime as a concern than the demography of bad news.

But a three-quarters drop in lethal youth violence would be a very important and relatively novel finding, and the difference between the New York youth homicide drop and the still-dramatic national trend during the 1990s should push us to reevaluate assumptions about how structural or fundamental the relationship is between the social and ecological conditions of urban minority poverty and chronically high rates of homicide and life-threatening robbery. There were no fundamental changes in the ecology of urban poverty in New York City during the 1990s and only modest increases in job availability and earnings at the entry level (less change than in other cities). Yet homicide arrests under age 18 fell 80% from a high of 151 under-18 homicide arrests reported in 1990 to the 30 under-18 arrests that were recorded in 2001. That 80% drop is not just a function of 1990 being a peak year. The median number of under-18 arrests for willful homicide in New York City between 1977 and 1989 was 100, 3½ times the 2001 volume and 2½ times as many under-18 homicide arrests as happened in New York in any year after 1996. Not only does the rate of homicide go down when 80% homicide arrest drops happen but also the number of kids who encounter homicide criminal charges, which have the potential to end all normal development opportunities. Youth homicides fell in New York City from being more than twice-a-week events to being twice-a-month events between 1990 and 2001. So the number of kids at maximum punishment risk in the city declined by more than three-quarters as well.

What this may indicate is that there is a looser linkage between social conditions and social values and violent outcomes than social scientists and policy analysts have been ready to assume.

The 1990s were an almost comical demonstration of bad academic bets on future rates of youth violence, as I mentioned in chapter 1. Just as the rate of youth homicide had peaked and was turning down in 1995 and 1996, several observers issued a series of very gloomy predictions . From the right came warnings of hundreds of thousands of additional "juvenile super-predators" who would be roaming American city streets by 2010 (DiIulio 1996) and "60,000 more juvenile murderers, robbers and thieves" (Wilson 1995). From the left came James Fox (1996) predicting that a continuation of arrest trends for homicide would produce "a bloodbath" by 2005.

The dire predictions of the mid-1990s were based on explicit or implicit theories of violence causation that are very widely held theories about the linkage between social environments and violent crime rates. In the DiIulio worldview, the social disadvantages of fatherless homes and pathological community settings produced what was called "moral poverty" (to be distinguished from mere financial poverty) (Council on Crime in America 1996). Fox spent less time on the underlying dynamics of the coming bloodbath but seemed more concerned with the lack of ameliorative programs and economic opportunity. But both sets of predictions were the sort of demographic determinism that projects trends in homicide rates 15 years in the future on the basis of numbers of minority five-year-olds living in tough neighborhoods.

History now shows that the crime wave predictions of the 1990s were 180 degrees wrong, the criminological equivalent of predicting an economic depression in 1993 on the brink of the longest economic expansion in the twentieth century. But why? The social and cultural conditions that evolved in the 1990s were not discontinuously different from the decade before, and the 14- to-20-year-old city dwellers of 1996 and 1997 had been brought up and educated in exactly the conditions that were imagined to be inevitable precursors to violence and predation. Nowhere was this more true than in New York City. So the changes that might explain the disappearing juvenile crime wave were not any shift in social or family structure; nor was the hip-hop culture and media emphasis of the middle and late 1990s any different from the cultural software of the early part of that decade. What, if any, are the limits to mechanical changes in crime rates and risks in the absence of changes in structure and values?

I suspect that detailed study of the youth crime decline of the 1990s, particularly in its double dosage in New York City, will force us to question how clear and uncontingent the linkage is between social and cultural conditions and rates of life-threatening urban violence. There are very few questions of equal importance to that issue in the United States, and no city anywhere that presents a better setting for such a study than New York in the 1990s.

Community Effects

The streets of New York City now have less than half the violent crime they experienced 15 to 25 years ago. What difference does this make to people living in the city, and on what dimensions? There are a wide variety of potential effects to study, but the methods to study them are not powerful. Examining changes over time in New York City will capture a very large decline in crime—but how to control for the other changes that come over time when searching for crime decline effects? Comparing New York with other cities cross-sectionally cuts the variation one can study in half. Whatever the methodological difficulties, I think it is again clear, as is the case for youth development, that New York City before and after its 1990s decline is the best place to locate a study of the effects of crime decline on big-city life.

The range of factors that declines in crime might influence is every bit as wide as the manifold aspects of urban life that crime and fear of crime can influence. This is a list that includes the incidence and prevalence in the population of crime victimization and criminal punishment, the direct negative consequences of crime, fear of crime as a discomfort and deterrent to activities and choice of living situation. An even wider range of less direct effects includes neighborhood preferences, political beliefs, attitudes toward government, and attitudes toward minority groups. The list of plausible crime-related feelings and experiences multiples like the ripples in a pond generated when a stone hits the water. Obviously, comparisons over time and between places are not capable of measuring all of this potential impact with any precision, but some preliminary indications of the breadth and magnitude of changes generated by New York City–sized declines are well worth the modest efforts needed to produce them. There is one special problem in New York City's history with testing personal and social feelings of efficacy over time—the cataclysmic impact of September 11, 2001—but there may also be clear differences between the nature and distribution of crime concerns and Twin Towers reactions that can permit separate assessment.

The distributional logic of reduced crime impacts should again favor formerly high-crime areas. The impacts of crime reduction will likely be much more substantial in such areas—typically places where disadvantaged groups reside—than in places with lower crime rates, even during periods when the aggregate crime rate was formerly high. There are two reasons to predict this. First, as already mentioned, the benefits of declines in crime rates will be concentrated among persons for whom the risk of crime was traditionally high. This must also mean that the benefits of lower crime rates will be concentrated in areas where the crime rate was traditionally high. Just as disadvantaged persons benefit disproportionately, so do disadvantaged neighborhoods.

There is a second reason that the traditionally less desirable areas of the city will have an outsized positive stake in general crime decline. These are the areas of a city and the places in its economic pecking order where the lack of private investment in special security makes the benefits of private security less available to the general population, so that people remain more vulnerable to the threat of crime than those who live in places where individual or collective nonpublic crime prevention is affordable. The simple prediction here is that a general decline in the burglary rate will have more impact on neighborhoods where buildings don't have doormen or the extensive presence of private security.

If this relative advantage prediction is correct, then the difference between wealthy and poor areas of the city should shrink over time, and formerly undesirable parts of a city with reduced crime may tend to become more desirable. That may have some unwelcome effects on longstanding tenants, as higher desirability leads to higher rents, but most of the news for all concerned will be good. In an era where most of the economic dynamics of change in the United States have generated further inequality, particularly at economic extremes, the fact that a large and general crime decline is a rare instance of "trickle up" benefits may also be worth welcoming.

Conclusion

The 1990s crime decline in New York City was twice as large as the national drop and stands as one of the most remarkable stories in the history of urban crime in the United States. While many factors contributed to the 70% drop in New York, changes in policing probably accounted for between a quarter and a half of it. Far from being one more urban legend about crime, the police changes were an important part of the city's singular achievement.

With rates of serious crime down by three-quarters in 15 years, New York City is the natural laboratory for testing the impact of reduced crime on community life and patterns of individual development. What are the benefits and risks of growing up in a lower crime environment? How is the crime that remains distributed by age and experience?

A vast amount remains to be learned about the effects of sharp crime reductions on urban life. But one central fact is already in evidence. A major city need not change in essential character to make major changes in its crime rate. So much of New York City hasn't changed since 1990 that its crime decline clearly shows the loose linkage between particular forms of urban social ecology and rates of crime.

Twenty-First Century Lessons

Part IV

Introduction to Part IV

The last two chapters of this book shift the focus from explaining the 1990s to understanding crime in the future. Chapter 7 addresses a single question—how low can crime rates drop without major changes in the character of American life. A variety of different statistical and historical patterns are consulted and the preliminary indications are good news. While the general decline ended through most of the United States at the turn of the century, there is no clear evidence of structural constraints on the decline of safety crime in American urban areas. Crime rates are quite low in low-crime U.S. cities now, and the capacity for downward movement over time in New York City suggests that neither the demographics nor economics of dense and wildly multi-ethnic populations need restrain the sharp decline of crime levels.

Chapter 8 provides my own short list of the lessons about crime and its study that have emerged from careful study of the 1990s. Explicitly comparative work provides a much thicker account of the lessons of the 1990s than inward-looking and mechanical studies of American policies and crimes. While some of the magnitude of the U.S. crime decline is more mysterious and less obviously tied to identified causes after considering comparative data, there is a deeper point that emerges from this study as the largest lesson of the 1990s. Serious crime is more variable in the United States than we had thought. We need not change the essential character of urban societies to benefit from much lower levels of violent and serious crime. Even before the specifics of engineering a safer society are worked out, the simple fact that dangerous levels of crime are not a part of our urban destiny is a reassuring prospect.

What Happens Next?

7

The lasting importance of the 1990s decline in crime will depend on crime trends and policy impacts in the coming years. Has the crime decline ended? If so, are current levels of violent and property crime a cyclical bottom from which significant upward movement can be expected? Or do the declines of the 1990s signal a new era of less crime? If so, how low can crime go without major structural, educational, or social changes?

These are obviously important questions in their own right, but trying to comprehend the present and future of American crime is also an important test of all the apparent lessons of the 1990s. How do the multitude of theories said to explain our last decade speak to what we can expect from here on? What has experience to date told us about the value of yesterday's theories in understanding current conditions?

I begin this chapter with an analysis of crime since the turn of the century. It is not a long period, and ironclad generalizations are premature, but some statistical contrasts are clear. Second, I address the potential for future change. Have we hit bottom, and if not, how low can crime fall? Can we expect cyclical patterns, and if so, how much of an increase might be on the immediate horizon? Third, I address the relationship between historical patterns of crime and the likely future. I argue that the next five years, 2006–10, will provide important data on crime trends and on the manifold effects of less crime on American society and government.

Has the Crime Decline Ended? Crime since 2000

The best way to understand the nature and significance of our most recent national crime statistics is by comparing the record of very recent history with crime trends in the late 1990s. Figure 7.1 shows aggregate trends for the seven traditional "index" offenses for 1997–2000 and for 2000–2003.

The clear change in national reported crime is from a sharp decline that lasted till the very end of the decade to essentially trendless and minor fluctuation in the opening years of the twenty-first century. In the last three years of the twentieth century, all seven of the traditional index crime rates went down, and all seven declines were in double digits. The median three-year rate decline was over 18% between 1997 and 2000, with all seven offenses showing double-digit drops. The median three-year crime trend after 2000 was a 0.3% increase in rape, and five of the seven

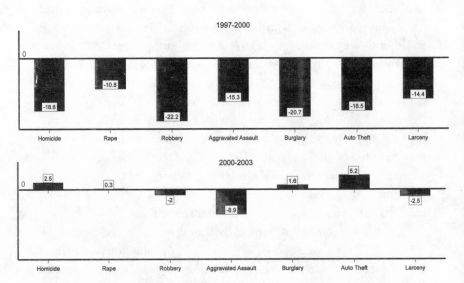

Figure 7.1. Three-year trends in seven index crime rates, United States, 1997–2000 and 2000–2003. Source: U.S. Department of Justice, Federal Bureau of Investigation, *Uniform Crime Report*, 1997–2003, Washington, D.C.: U.S. Government Printing Office.

Twenty-First Century Lessons

Table 7.1

Distribution of declining crimes, 15 cities, 1997–2000 and 2000–2003, seven offenses.

2000–2003	0	1	4	2	1	3	1	1
	0 declines	1 decline	2 declines	3 declines	4 declines	5 declines	6 declines	7 declines
1997–2000	0	0	0	0	2	2	2	9

Source: U.S. Department of Justice, Federal Bureau of Investigation, *Uniform Crime Report*, 1997, 2000, and 2003. Washington, D.C.: U.S. Government Printing Office.

aggregate three-year changes were under 3%. Only aggravated assault (down 8.9%) and auto theft (up 5.2%) showed a three-year change in excess of 1% per year. The assault decline involved the offense against the person with by far the smallest decline during the 1990s, while the mild uptick was for auto theft. The 2004 levels show a slight decline from 2003 but continue to be trendless. The overall trend in the first years of the new century was remarkably flat.

While the end of the long-term decline might generate some regret, the level pattern for crime volume overall is very good news for most citizens, because offense rates have flattened out at or near the low point in crime levels for three decades. If ever a steady crime rate were regarded as a reason for rejoicing, it would be in a nation that had just experienced a nearly 40% decrease. Our recent crime plateau has been hugging the bottom of the distribution of crime over the past generation.

But is the flat profile merely a jumble of contrasting city-level trends that even out in the aggregate, or a real sign of steadiness in crime volume? One test of this is to examine short-term crime trends in the 15 largest U.S. cities in the first years of the new century. Table 7.1 compares the distribution of crime declines for these 15 cities in the last three years of the 1990s and the first three years after 2000.

The most recent era is evenly split between cities with crime increases and decreases, with only New York City showing uniform declines and Chicago reporting declines in six offenses. Seven of the fifteen largest cities have three or more increases in the period after 2000. The contrast with the previous period is pronounced. All 15 cities reported declines in a majority of crimes, and 9 of the 15 largest cities had declines in all seven offenses.

Table 7.2 shifts the focus for the pattern in individual cities to the pattern for each crime category in the 15 cities.

Table 7.2

City-level increases and decreases in crime rate for seven index offenses, 1997–2000 and 2000–2003.

	2000–2003		1997–2000	
	Increase	Decrease	Increase	Decrease
Murder	7	8	1	14
Rape[a]	6	8	1	13
Robbery	8	7	1	14
Assault	3	12	2	13
Burglary	8	7	1	14
Larceny	8	7	1	14
Auto Theft	11	4	0	15

Source: U.S. Department of Justice. Federal Bureau of Investigation. *Uniform Crime Report.* Washington, D.C.: U.S. Government Printing Office.

[a]No report from Chicago to the FBI for rape.

In the years after 2000, five of the seven offenses show an even split between increases and decreases. Only assault shows a pronounced tendency to decline (12 of 15 cities), with auto theft showing a less clear-cut uptrend (11 of 15 cities). The contrast with the late 1990s is sharp; all of the crime categories show decreases in at least 13 of the 15 cities in the earlier period.

The pattern in the last years of the 1990s was uniform decline. The pattern in the first years of the new century is flat, with cities evenly divided between increases and decreases, generally of small magnitude. The flat overall trend is not a misleading indication of what happens at the city level; indeed, the modal performance at the city level is small changes and no definite trend.

While there is substantial variation from city to city in short-term crime fluctuations, no clear pattern emerges by geographical region or a city's prior history to predict patterns during 2000–2003. Among the cities with more increases than decreases in crime, only one—Las Vegas—shows really substantial growth, and this is not obviously connected to its region or even its very large population expansion in recent years. The other cities with only one or two out of seven crimes in short-term decline tend to be in the West or Southwest (Houston, San Antonio), and two of them also had larger than average crime declines in the 1990s (Houston and San Diego).

Two of the three cities with declines in six out of seven crime categories had smaller than average declines in the 1990s. These were Philadelphia and Chicago, and their post-2000 trends were pretty sharp declines for the new era. But the one city with declines after 2000 in all seven crime categories— New York City—also had the largest drop in the 1990s, so the cities clustered at either end do not fall into any single simple pattern. And the general pattern of level short-term trends seems more important than any patterns notable in particular clusters of cities. New York, as I will show in the next section, is an exception to that level trend tendency.

How expectable is a flat crime trend over three or four years? When the post–World War II history of reported crime is consulted, level trends are infrequent but not unheard-of. The 50 years beginning in 1950 produce 47 different consecutive three-year periods. The UCRs data on burglary and homicide show that the average three-year movement in rate was 7% for homicide and 13.2% for burglary, but a three-year variation under 3% was observed in 4 of the 47 burglary three-year observations and six of the 47 homicide reports, or about 10% of all observations. A three-year period when five out of seven index offenses had variations of less than 3% would be much rarer than flat rates of individual offenses over three years. But there are not clear indications yet that the level trends since 2000 are breaking new ground.

The fact that different crimes have different signs in the short term is also not a clear indication that the tendency of the major index crimes to rise and fall together has ended. With all the variations over the short term so close to zero, the differences between small increases and small decreases are not strong evidence that any separate categories are breaking away from the generally flat trend in crime. Only the decline in assault is at all suggestive of a real downward movement when other types of crime remain stable.

A One-Way Street

The data for the first years of the new century show clear indications that the significant declines of the 1990s ended just at the turn of the century, but the stability of crime since 2000 is not strong evidence that stability over a long period will be the successor trend to the 1990s decline. Each of these conclusions deserves some unpacking.

The reason that even a three- or four-year period of stability marks the end of the 1990s pattern of decline lies in the sustained nature of the earlier decline. After 1991, there was no single year of nondecline in the

United States, and there was only one nondecline year in Canada. What makes recent trends definitively not in the pattern of the previous decline was the sharpness of that decline rather than any distinctive features of the recent past. It is much easier to conclude that the trends since year 2000 are not those of the 1990s than it is to determine what the recent numbers might signal for the immediate future.

The Great American Crime Decline has been interrupted by a period of stability. How long it might continue and what might happen next are not obvious from the flat trajectory of the short term. In this sense, the shift to date in crime is a one-way street—a clear indication that the uninterrupted series of crime drops has ended but no firm indication of what will happen next.

Leading Indicators?

One method of predicting crime trends, at least in principle, would be to track the changes over time in those social, economic, and criminal justice variables that are thought to influence crime. To the extent that the magnitude of the influences of factors like imprisonment and policing is known, trends in the predictor variables should be leading indicators of trends in crime. The problem with this strategy is that the magnitude of crime effects for all the predictors discussed in chapters 3 and 4 is very much in dispute (and should be in doubt). So the value of knowledge about any predictor variables as an indicator of crime rates in the future is modest at best. In fact, the relationship between trends in factors like police, imprisonment, or employment and future levels of crime may be of more value as a method of testing for the effects of predictors on crime rather than using assumptions about the impact of such variables on crime to confidently forecast crime trends.

But is it worth surveying the current status of crime predictors as one method of generating hypotheses about the direction and magnitude of future crime? Probably. For most of the criminal justice factors, the current policies and resources are relatively stable, but at levels quite close to historic highs. The rate of imprisonment is within 1% of its all-time high per 100,000. The numerical growth in prisoners each year since 2000 was small by recent standards, but the total incarcerated population is the largest ever, and that is the best measure of aggregate incapacitation.

The level of incarceration should produce approximately the same amount of crime prevention in 2006 as in 2000, perhaps with some falloff to the extent that longer prison sentences produce less avoided crime as the offender's time in custody is further removed from his street career as an active offender.

If the level of incarceration stays stable at the high levels of recent times, this might produce increased deterrence (to the extent that declining crime in the late 1990s was the result of increasing levels of general deterrence). But so little is known of the deterrent influence of marginal increase in incarceration in the 1990s, or any other time, that any deterrence assumptions are speculations. So break-even levels of incapacitation with speculative levels of deterrence are the best guess about punishment.

The current and near future demography of the U.S. population is reliably reported by the Census Bureau, and the news is relatively encouraging. Figure 7.2 continues the five-year reports of the proportion of the population who are aged 15–24 and 15–29 from 1980 until 2015.

The proportion of the population aged 15–29 hits its modern low in 2005 at 20.7% and stays close to that, rising to 20.9% in 2010 and then declining to 20.4% in 2015. Almost all of the decline in youth share observed after 1980 is maintained through 2010, and 2015 will have the smallest percentage of youth and young adults in the series. For the very youngest segment of the high-risk age group, the share of total population increased by 0.4% the five years after 2000 and will hold at that rate (14.3% of total population) through 2010. This level is a 24% decline from the 1980 pro-

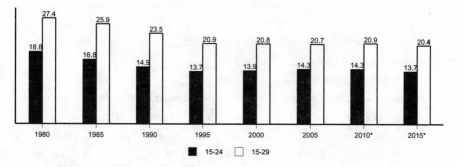

Figure 7.2. High-risk age groups as percentage of U.S. population, 1980–2010. Note: Census projection. Source: U.S. Department of Commerce. Bureau of the Census. International Data Base (IDB). Available at the website of the Census Bureau: www.census.gov/ipc/www/idbnew.html.

portion and just under a 4% increase from the 2000 total. But then the total percentage of the population 15–29 turns lower by 2015 than even in 2000.

The net impact of recent demographic shifts would appear to be quite small on crime rates. In context, however, this lack of additional impact is a result of demographic proportions holding at very favorable levels. The news couldn't have gotten much better than during the 1990s. More important, things didn't get measurably worse at any time after 2000 and will persist at good-news levels through 2015.

So the demographic news relating to the age structure of the population is good as far as the eye can see, and demographic projections are reliable for long periods into the future. The only problem is that demographic projections have not been a good basis for predicting crime trends with any consistency. Favorable demographics were associated with a steep rise in youth violence after 1985 in the United States, as well as with the major declines of the middle and late 1990s. So this is an encouraging indication for the future, but not a strong one.

What is astonishing about the long-term trends in age structure is the contrast between statistics and sentiment. Since 1980, the proportion of the population in high-risk ages has been declining or stable at historically low rates (see figure 7.2). But the views in the mid-1990s used these statistics to project unfavorable crime futures. There can be few more dramatic examples of the triumph of mood over data than the moral panic about the future of youth crime in the mid-1990s.

Most of the other crime-related indicators discussed in chapters 3 and 4 have varied within relatively narrow limits over the first years of the new century. Unemployment and economic growth did not sustain the 1990s boom statistics, but the slowdown in 2001 was relatively mild and brief.

Police employment is only available after 2001 for the UCRs sample of reporting agencies. Using that measure, the number of officers per 100,000 peaked in 1999, at 246 per 100,000, and fell in every year after that, reaching 230 per 100,000 in 2003, an 8% decline. This is the one clear negative leading indicator. More reliable data on police employment will come from BJS. The currently available data from BJS show increases in 2000 and 2001, when the UCRs show declines.

If abortion availability had any impact on crime rates after 2000, that would be observed as a gradual reduction in crime as the post–Roe v.

Wade population ages into its middle years. A "crime dividend" that should have been confined to people under 26 in 2000 should extend to all native-born populations under 36 by 2010.

Good News and Bad News

The known facts about plausible leading indicators for crime rates in the immediate future fit the structure of the "good news/bad news" jokes that were popular in the recent past. The good news is that all the external indications of future crime, except possibly police numbers, are consistent with either stability or even modest decreases in crime rates. Crime levels are quite low by recent historical standards, and there is no obvious reason to expect any large increases any time soon.

The bad news is that leading indicators for crime trends in the United States have little predictive value. All the trends in imprisonment, demographics, and economics in the United States of the mid-1980s were somewhat more sanguine than in recent times, but crime rates turned up sharply. There is no reason in reading the numbers to expect any upward movement in American crime rates. But given our proven vulnerability to crime rate surprises, it would not be prudent to make big bets on any tightly defined future for levels of crime and violence.

How Low Can Crime Go?

It is one thing to note that the crime decline of the 1990s has apparently ended and quite another to conclude that crime rates in the United States have declined as much as they are likely to in the proximate American future. This section shifts the subject from recent crime trends in the United States to the rather more speculative issue of how far crime rates might fall from current levels absent major structural or population changes. Is there a lower limit to rates of crime and lethal violence in the United States absent radical change? What sorts of information can we use to inform an analysis of this issue?

As a preliminary matter, it is prudent to note that any position one takes on the potential for further crime decline rests on implicit assumptions about causes of crime and the susceptibility of different types of crime to instrumental interventions. This makes the analysis of the capacity for further decline an interesting issue in its own right, but also a window into assumptions about broader questions. But the downside potential for crime from current levels is an issue that has not yet been explored in scholarly writing. I hope in this section to start a conversation rather than come to definitive conclusions.

Where does one look to gain any real historical comparative perspective on the potential room for decline in our current crime experience? I have found no precedent for a review of this question, and few obviously accurate empirical indications of the downside potential of U.S. crime and violence. There are three types of evidence—each imperfect—that deserve analysis as downside indicators: the variations over time in homicide rate during the twentieth century; the large cross-sectional variations in rates of crime and violence in the United States; and the historical trends in individual settings (like New York City, as discussed in chapter 6) that have shown greater variation than the average. There is a fourth possible approach that depends on estimating the potential contribution of particular types of crime prevention that have not yet been a major influence in most U.S. cities (e.g., estimating what will happen in Los Angeles when it adopts New York policing changes), but this approach tends to rely on the particular historical records mentioned as the third option, so I will treat this fourth possibility as part of my analysis of the third.

National Patterns

Figure 7.3 shows trends in U.S. homicide rates from 1950 until 2002.

Homicide is the best choice for this type of historical record because good data has been available for much longer than has data for crime (where nobody puts much trust in FBI UCRs estimates until after 1970), and the margin of error in official statistics is much smaller for homicide than for other types of crime. In the years after 1990, national homicide rates are in the range of from just under 5 per 100,000 to just over 10 per 100,000, with the high values almost exactly twice the low value. If this historical record provides any real evidence of the lower boundary of variations in homicide rates, the recent rate of U.S. homicide has not yet fallen to its lowest previous level, but the homicide levels of early in the twenty-first century are within 25% of that previous low.

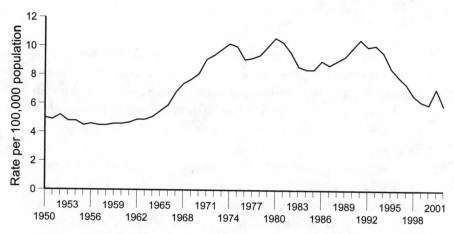

Figure 7.3. Homicide rate (NVSS), United States, 1950–2002. Source: National Center for Health Statistics. 2005. *Health, United States, 2005.* Hyattsville, Md.: U.S. National Center for Health Statistics.

But why should the previously established low level of homicide be regarded as a lower boundary to possible fluctuations? If the variations portrayed in figure 7.3 were regarded as cyclical movements in rate that could not be linked to any known instrumental causes, there would be some reason to regard the previous low point in the series as a potential natural boundary.

To the extent that cyclical influences are a significant influence, the historical record provides two relevant suggestions. The first is that some further decline has historical precedent. Unless some structural features of the nation have changed since the early 1960s, the national homicide rate has at least a 25% margin for further decline.

A second indication is that there is no twentieth-century precedent for declines in homicide under a rate of 4.8 per 100,000. To the extent that cyclical limits are important, this observation makes declines to under that previous low a more difficult prospect than the 25% marginal decline that is documented history. One final point about historical precedents and limits is that historical precedent might have some probative value even if historical limits do not. There is no logical reason why accepting the predictive value of previous low points as providing a range of achievable future rates requires the observer to also accept the lack of historical precedent as a firm limit on future decline.

Cross-Sectional Variation

If U.S. history provides one window into the possibilities and limits of crime reduction, can observers also learn from the enormous variations between places in the United States about how much lower crime rates can fall? Figure 7.4 demonstrates the magnitude of differences between cities in homicide by showing the rates of killing per 100,000 population of the 20 largest cities in the United States in 2000.

The range in death rates, even among major cities, is huge. Detroit and Baltimore, at the high extreme, have homicide rates almost 20 times those of Honolulu and San Jose at the low extreme of the distribution, and the magnitude of difference is not explained by two or three extreme cases. The average homicide rate in 2000 for the five highest rate cities was 29.4 per 100,000, as against a rate of 4.2 per 100,000 for the five lowest rate cities—a 7-to-1 difference in rate.

The important question for present purposes is whether that huge variation provides evidence that big-city homicide rates can drop significantly without major changes in U.S. cities. Certainly if Detroit and Baltimore could achieve the homicide levels of Honolulu and San Jose, the potential for decline in aggregate national homicide rates would be more than substantial.

The problem, of course, is that the cities arrayed on the continuum of figure 7.4 differ from each other in many respects; indeed, 20-to-1 differences in homicide rates are a strong signal that demographic and social structural differences are in place to constrain potential crime reduction.

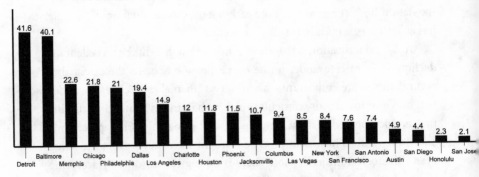

Figure 7.4. Variation in homicide rates per 100,000 among the 20 largest U.S. cities, 2000. Note: In declining order. Source: U.S. Department of Justice. Federal Bureau of Investigation. *Uniform Crime Report*. Washington, D.C.: Government Printing Office.

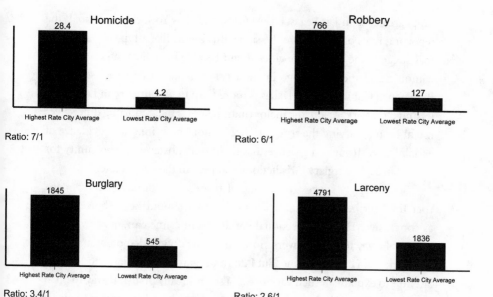

Figure 7.5. Variability of four offense rates among 20 largest U.S. cities, 2000, top quartile versus bottom quartile. Note: Rates per 100,000. Source: U.S. Department of Justice, Federal Bureau of Investigation, *Uniform Crime Report* (2000), Washington, D.C.: Government Printing Office.

Why should we compare Baltimore with Honolulu? Why not with Toronto or Paris? What can cross-sectional differences add to any analysis of potential for crime reduction other than the fact that some large cities subsist on levels of criminal homicide that are a small fraction of the highest rate cities? What other than a sense of human possibility should one take from such comparisons?

Figure 7.5 expands the statistical comparison of big-city crime to four offenses—homicide, robbery, burglary, and larceny. The two offenses of violence show the most variance with rates among the highest rate quartile of the 20 largest cities at least six times as high as average rates for the lowest rate quartile of cities. But the variance for even property crime is quite high—almost 4 to 1 for burglary and 2.6 to 1 for larceny. Why is that?

While large differences in crime rates can be signals of important differences between cities in demographic and environmental features, the distribution of cities in reported rates of larceny and burglary are not obviously linked to demographic or environmental differences between cities. San Antonio, Texas, and Columbus, Ohio, have reported larceny two and a half

What Happens Next?

times greater than Las Vegas, Los Angeles, and New York City in 2000. If the reporting rates of larceny are the same, this seems like a type of variability that suggests the higher rate cities might be able to reduce rates of larceny without fundamental change in the city's population or social structure. Burglary in Columbus and Dallas is more than twice burglary in Los Angeles and New York. Again, the major caution here is that reporting differences might be magnifying the true variance. If not, the prima facie evidence of variability is strongly suggestive that there is a substantial opportunity for decline in high-burglary jurisdictions and thus in the overall rate.

But "strongly suggestive" is one of those artful phrases lawyers concoct to describe circumstantial evidence that should never be regarded as conclusive. The cross-sectional variations in crime can, in my view, be a valuable way to start conversations about the downside potential of current American crime volume. But I do not regard multivariate models that attempt to explain all such variance as a scientifically plausible way to push forward in the analysis of the downside potential for U.S. crime. I believe that historical changes are far better evidence of downside potential than cross-sectional variations.

New York City as a Leading Indicator

The strongest evidence I have seen that larger drops can come in national crime numbers is the double dose of decline that was documented in New York City during the 1990s and has continued in the first years of the new century. What makes the declines observed in New York City a better measure of the downside potential for crime in other places than the differences between cities is the absence of major changes in New York before and after its crime decline. The city's population, economy, housing, and education systems all changed marginally. The problem with trying to imagine Detroit achieving San Jose's homicide rate is the world of differences between them. The New York story is a much more plausible account of the potential that many places might have to reduce crime.

And when the declines in New York City are compared to most other places, the amount of additional room to decline that one estimates using the extra crime reduction in New York is both substantial and open-ended. For starters, the decline in New York during the 1990s was about twice the national average. On that basis alone, we could guess that a further potential decline equal to what the nation outside New York achieved in the 1990s. This alone is more than twice the cyclical room estimated from national homicide patterns.

But New York City has also continued its crime decline into the twenty-first century. Figure 7.6 shows the drops in recorded crime for the seven traditional index offenses in the city from 2000 to 2004 (New York was the only city with declines in all categories for this period).

The recorded crime drop in New York after 2000 was in double digits for all offenses, with the average offense rate dropping about 26% in four years. This increases the total amount of additional room to decline we might estimate for other areas by the additional volume of decline already on record. And it makes the potential for further decline in other places open-ended as well, because the decrease in New York crime does not appear to have stopped.

There are important cautions necessary before using New York City numbers as an expectation for potential crime reduction in the rest of the nation. First, the use of reported crime as a measure of actual crime reduction assumes that nobody is cooking the books and that reports are a good measure of actual crime volume. There is more than a modest margin of error in these assumptions. Second, as discussed in chapter 6, New York's crime density may have been higher and at an artificial peak in 1990s, so that the gross decline in New York may be an overestimate in the room to decline from more modest base rates for other places. Yet the drops in crime after 2000—when the city's rates were already quite low—suggest that much more than regression from peak rates sets New York apart from

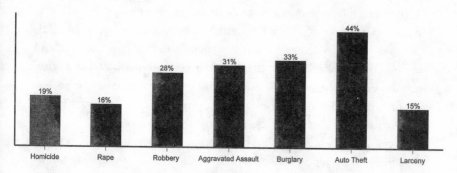

Figure 7.6. Crime declines in New York City, 2000–2004. Note: Rate per 100,000, percentage change. Source: U.S. Department of Justice. Federal Bureau of Investigation. *Uniform Crime Report.* Washington, D.C.: Government Printing Office.

What Happens Next?

its sister cities. And these further low rates are strong indications as room to decline elsewhere.

The Limits of Potential for Decline

The third important reservation that limits the predictive power of this exercise is the fact that even if the potential for decline exists in most U.S. jurisdictions, that is no guarantee that any further reductions in crime will actually happen. Whatever the mix of policies and cycles that produces changes in crime rates over time, there is no logical or empirical necessity that the crime rate will ever fall to levels that are potentially within reach.

The weak science that supports particular crime prevention strategies means that cost-effective mechanisms for crime prevention are difficult to identify in advance. Even with pretty clear indications that police effects deserve major credit for New York City's exemplary performance since 1990, only the feckless would attempt to attach clear benefits to 10,000 more police, or even to aggressive street intervention. There are no money-back guarantees in the design of crime prevention initiatives. Is there any value, then, to the rather abstract notion of the potential for further decline?

Yes, there is. While no probability can be assigned to any jurisdiction reaching its downside potential, exploring the potential for crime decline has practical value, and if particular measures of potential decline can be validated, policy decisions can be better enhanced. Any realistic prospect that significant future crime decline is possible without fundamental change can motivate investments in strategies of reduction. Whether or not the extra crime decline observed in New York can be directly tied to either more police or the method of their deployment, the fact that offenses levels can be pushed continually downward can inspire a variety of prevention experiments, involving police and other approaches. The historical precedent helps define the size of the payoff, even if it doesn't clearly point to a mechanism to achieve the result.

And a variety of indications suggest that life-threatening violence is as responsive to prevention efforts as nonviolent offenses, and may in fact be more responsive to successful interventions than more numerous and less frightening property offenses. The strongest evidence for equivalent susceptibility is the record in New York City, where the fear crimes of homicide and robbery dropped as quickly during the 1990s as burglary. The somewhat weaker evidence from cross-sectional comparisons suggest that high-violence cities in the United States have rates of homicide and robbery six and seven times as great as low-violence cities, while the comparative multiple is about half that high for burglary and larceny. Even without assuming that there are methods of transforming Detroit into San Jose, there is at least a suggestion of a larger variability in violence than in property offenses.

So the exercise of trying to estimate the potential for further reduction in crime gives us a measure of the potential value of crime reduction efforts, even if we can't identify mechanisms of prevention or costs. And it promises progress with fear crimes like homicide and robbery. Even without further detail, this seems sufficient to inspire sustained effort to experiment and evaluate in search of more specific knowledge.

The Next Five Years: Some Open Questions

The second five years of the twenty-first century carry double-barreled importance for observers interested in assessing the long-range effects of the crime decline of the 1990s. Five more years of experience will provide much stronger indications of the shape of crime in the aftermath of the 1990s. And five more years of postdecline experience from 2006–10 will reveal much about the effects of lower crime on social and economic processes and on crime policy. By 2010, the nation will have had twice as much time to adjust to the lower crime conditions produced by the 1990s, and twice as much time to search for the effects of changing crime patterns on society and government. This concluding section will identify some open questions about crime, social reactions to crime rate changes, and policy effects of lower crime rates that five more years of experience should clarify.

Emerging Patterns of Post-Decline Crime

The first four years of the new century marked a clear break with the sharp decline in crime of the 1990s, but what is not clear is what shape the crime trends are taking in the aftermath of the drop. The best description for crime trends early in the present decade is flatness, but that type of trendlessness is not uncommon in three- and four-year spans, as pointed out in the first section of this chapter. Even when we double the time period from the earlier three years to six years, relatively small changes are anything but rare. Over the 44 six-year spans between 1950 and 1999, the average change in homicide rates was 14% and in burglary rates was 28%. But the total change over six years was less than 5% in 11% of the six-year periods for burglary and in 14% of the six-year periods for homicide. So four or even six years of flat crime rates is not a good foundation for proclaiming the end of cyclical variation in crime in the United States. But 10 years of modest and trendless movement in aggregate crime rates would be a long enough period so that flatness itself could be seen as a discrete trend. The first years of the new century are an indeterminate era for crime, in part because it is difficult to prove a negative in crime trends. In retrospect, the early years of the century may nicely fit into a new flat crime era, but a decade's perspective will be necessary before any firm conclusions are prudent.

There are two further crime pattern questions where another five years of experience can provide a helpful test. As previously discussed, the total variation in crime rates from auto theft (up 6%) to aggravated assault (down 9%) is too small to suggest that some categories of crime might have started to diverge from the general joint fluctuation of very different types of crime over time. Another five years of experience may double or triple the gap between different types of crime in the national aggregates. The diverse categories of crime have been jointly trending for more than a generation in the United States, with changes in burglary predicting changes in homicide, and vice versa. This is not common in many other developed nations (Zimring and Hawkins 1997, ch. 2). The century's first decade will be an interesting test of the persistence of linked trends.

One further issue that data from the next five years can clarify is the beginning of a shift upward in age of offenders arrested in the United States in the late 1990s. The FBI reports age of arrest by year through age 24 and then by age group (e.g. 25–29) for older offenders. Table 7.3 shows the median age of arrest for the seven traditional index crimes in 1990 and 2003.

The median age of arrest is stable for four crimes (rape, assault, burglary, and larceny) and decreases for robbery. For three offenses, the median age at arrest increases. Homicide shifts from age 24 in 1990 to early in the 25–29 category in 2003. Auto theft shifts from 18 to 21. The arrest pattern for burglary shows some shift toward older offenders, but the median age doesn't increase.

Table 7.3

Median age or age group of arrest, United States, 1990 versus 2003, seven index crimes.

	Median age of arrest	
	1990	2003
Homicide	24	25–29
Rape	25–29	25–29
Robbery	22	21
Aggravated assault	25–29	25–29
Burglary	21	21
Larceny	22	22
Auto theft	18	21

Source: U.S. Department of Justice. Federal Bureau of Investigation. *Uniform Crime Report.* Washington, D.C.: U.S. Government Printing Office.

There are two reasons why ages at arrest might have increased in the late 1990s. The first is that youth homicide shot up in the late 1980s and early 1990s and then dropped even more than adult arrests in the middle and late 1990s. But a second reason that youth should be a declining proportion of arrests is that nonrecidivists may have larger than aggregate drops in participation in major crime (see chapter 6). If the age of arrested offenders continues to creep up in the coming years, this second explanation will be the most obvious reason. Over the long run, a decline in the crime share of young offenders should be a leading indicator of further declines in rates of total crime. If the total arrests for the under-30 population goes any lower in the middle of the current decade, crime rates in the last part of the decade should go down, if all other things are equal. But "all other things" are, of course, in a constant state of flux.

The Cumulative Social and Economic Effects of Crime Declines

If crime rates stay stable during the rest of the first decade of the twenty-first century, or if they decline, the period after 2006 will provide a better opportunity to test for some long-range social and economic impacts of lower crime than the first half of the current decade. Many important social impacts of a crime decline will have long gestation periods. Consider first how to test theories of the effect when an entire generation of high-risk kids passes through adolescence and into adulthood in a lower crime environment. That is not a quick study, because those who were turning 13 in 1998 will only turn 23 in 2008.

A second reason for long periods of lower crime being the best environment for testing social effects is that it is not so much crime rates themselves but a population's expectation of future crime rates that will influence attitudes, residential preferences, and use of public spaces. And expectations of lower crime may take time to generate, particularly when it is expectations for the long term that are important when people make decisions about cities and neighborhoods. The final reason that research on the effects of less crime will have to wait for the second half of the decade is the failure of social scientists to launch such studies earlier. The time to start is more than ripe.

Because the largest impacts of serious crime are on the least advantaged segments of a population and the least protected parts of cities, those sectors and areas should be the primary beneficiaries of lower crime and the shift in public expectations for lower crime in the future. Boys in high-poverty and formerly high-crime neighborhoods who enter adolescence at the turn of the century will have much lower rates of arrest for serious index felonies. Whether this means they will also have fewer arrests or lesser levels of the school and job market problems associated with serious criminal justice involvement is an open question, but one that straightforward empirical research can answer without difficulty. One natural place to study this process is New York City, because of the size of its crime decline. But other cities with smaller crime declines should also be studied because New York City's police proactivity during the 1990s may have impacts on high-risk youth that other cities with crime declines do not experience.

Not only should the expectation of less crime make cities more attractive potential places of residence as opposed to suburbs but also the formerly high-crime areas within cities should benefit the most from expectations of less crime. And cities with larger declines in violent crime should show more substantial benefits in housing appreciation, net population migration, and other manifestations of citizen preference than cities with smaller crime decline histories.

The statistical comparisons that can be made cross-sectionally and over time are not powerful science, and I suspect that following youth cohorts is more likely to yield conclusive results about the effects of crime reduction. Yet it seems plausible that sharp declines in violent crime are some of the greatest friends that urban gentrification can ever have, and that the largest gains in residential credibility should come in those areas where fear had been most important as a residential deterrent. Looking over the two decades after 1990 should teach us plenty about how important fear of crime has or hasn't been in the previous half-century as an influence on population movements.

There are also a wide variety of ways that expectations of lower crime rates can influence attitudes and actions regarding intergroup relationships in the United States. Does reduced fear of crime lead white Anglos who live in cities to have less hostile attitudes toward African American and Hispanic minorities? If so, such improvements should be more evident over time in cities where crime has declined the most. At the same time, the expectation of lower crime might make minority families in primarily minority areas of the cities less anxious to relocate to suburbs. It is at least possible, then, that lower crime rates reduce both the resistance to minority migration out of predominately minority areas and the desire of minority families to undertake such migration. But this assumes that crime fear has really been the primary motive that white respondents have reported rather than a cover story for other antiminority feelings less amenable to change. And the incentive for minorities to move from center-city areas may also turn out to have more to do with educational opportunities than with crime. It is much easier to compile a list of significant questions to ask about the manifest and latent impacts of expectations of lower crime rates in cities than it is to be confident of the answers.

Lower Crime Rates and Crime Policy

What should the impact of lower crime rates be on the priority citizens give to crime prevention and control as a government activity and on the type of crime policy that citizens prefer? There is not much detailed analysis on the links between crime rates and crime policy, and most writing discusses the link between rising crime rates in the 1960s and 1970s and the demand for repressive crime policy in the United States (e.g. LaFree 2002). Two separate effects might be plausible products of increasing crime. First, increasing crime might make government efforts to control crime a more salient issue—increasing the priority of crime as a political issue and increasing the resources citizens are willing to invest in its control. Second, increasing crime might push citizens toward support of more punitive types of crime-control policy, with an emphasis on punishment by imprisonment and greater expression of hostility toward criminal offenders.

Certainly both a higher salience of crime as a political question and more punitive policies were produced in the 1970s, the 1980s, and especially in the early 1990s. This is far from establishing a causal relationship between crime rates and these two dimensions of policy, but the popular wisdom of the mid-1990s accepted that causal account.

Does this mean that the expectation of lower crime rates will make crime policy a less salient issue and push citizens toward nonpunitive crime-control measures? Is there symmetry in the relationship between crime rates and policy demands?

It does seem clear that over the decade after the early 1990s, with the federal crime-control act of 1994 and "three strikes and you're out" legislation in half of all states as a high-water mark, crime control has become a less important political issue in federal and state government. What is less clear is how important declining crime has been as the cause of the moderation of the political frenzy about crime. The political significance of crime may have been at a post–World War II high in the United States in 1994, even though homicide rates were higher in 1974 and 1980. Certainly some of the lower pressure in the late 1990s and beyond was a regression to more normal historical levels of political priority.

But the substantial reduction in crime rates almost certainly contributed to the decline of crime policy as a political priority. The exact portion of the relaxation in pressure that can be attributed to lower expectation of crime producing lower fear cannot be determined on the basis of present evidence or perhaps ever. But a major reason why crime is a lesser worry in the United States is the fact and expectation of less crime.

Does this mean that relaxed anxieties have produced diminished public readiness to spend on crime control? Might there be an optimum level of crime spending fixed by some equilibrium point where the public willingness to spend to prevent crime moves up and down with the crime rate the public expects? Probably not, because even though falling crime rates reduce public fear, a compensating vector may obtain—because declining crime increases public confidence in the government's ability to control crime through official responses. A willingness to believe that "everything works" may lead citizens to tolerate higher levels of expenditure for crime control. So while the decreased fear might reduce demand for control, the increased confidence in effectiveness could push in the opposite direction.

Does reducing the level of expected crime shift citizens' sentiments toward the proper treatment of criminal offenders? For a variety of reasons, this may not be true for individual sentiments, but the political environment for executing crime policy may become more flexible even if public attitudes about punishment are relatively fixed. Burglars and robbers are never going to win popularity contests with citizens or legislators. And other things besides fear of crime support hostility toward offenders and enthusiasm for punitive responses to crime. So the substantive content of public attitudes may not change quickly, if at all, in scenarios where sustained lower crime rates reduce crime expectations . But the emotional intensity of negative sentiments can change (this is a manifestation of what has been termed the "salience" of the crime issue), and this might create more willingness to delegate authority on crime-control decisions to government and flexibility about the means chosen by policy-makers (Zimring and Johnson 2006).

The next five years will be a particularly good time to carefully track crime rates and begin to seriously study their consequences. Even before we can know how much more potential for declining crime exists, there are ample reasons to trade this chapter's abundance of suppositions about the effects of lower crime rates on urban life and criminal justice policy for the more attractive hard currency of facts.

Seven Lessons from
the 1990s

8

The Elusive Bottom Line

The natural appetite for explaining events like the 1990s is for a single sound bite—a bottom line that isolates a particular cause and identifies the key element that will determine the shape and volume of crime in the future. This is a book without a bottom line, for both encouraging and discouraging reasons. First, the discouraging news: there was no single cause or even an evident leading cause for the nine years of declining crime at the national level, and there is no short list of leading indicators that provide clear views of the future. The lack of clarity in the view from 2006 comes in almost equal measure from what criminologists do know about the 1990s and from what they don't know. Further, the knowledge gap in current social science understanding comes almost equally from the unavoidable weakness of a nonexperimental discipline and from avoidable provincialism and ideological blinders. That is my list of the discouraging reasons why a book like this doesn't boil down to a single bottom line.

The happy news is that there are a great many important things already known and soon to be learned from the 1990s and their aftermath. After the growth of serious crime between the mid-1960s and the mid-1970s and fluctuations in a narrow band during the late 1970s and 1980s, the experience of the 1990s teaches us about not only the causes of downward crime fluctuations but also their effects. So it is not merely that the lessons of the 1990s are too ambiguous for a single punch line; they are too rich as well. There is much to be learned about crime and its causes, about the insights and limits of crime scholarship, about the linkage between social structural features and the rates of various types of crime, about the effects of increases or decreases in crime on the social and political environment, and about the potential for further crime declines in the American future.

But how to write a last chapter about this embarrassment of partially uncovered treasures? This conclusion amounts to a long-winded executive summary. I will isolate seven important lessons that can be derived from the known facts of the 1990s and to provide a brief summary of the evidence for each.

Lesson 1

The crime decline was real, was national in scope,
and was larger and longer than any documented decline in the
twentieth century.

In the nine years after 1991, the rates of all seven major common crimes declined steadily all over the United States. For most of the "index crimes," the decline was between 35 and 40%, with only the residual offense of larceny and the heterogeneous crime of aggravated assault showing significantly smaller reductions. Crime declined in cities, suburbs, towns, and rural areas; crime declined in all regions; and crime declined (after 1993) among offenders and victims of all age groups.

Because officially reported crime statistics depend on the discretion and classification skill of local police, one natural question is the extent to which an epidemic of good news like the 1990s crime decline was a function of imperfect or changing police reporting. This didn't happen in the 1990s. The two offenses with the best statistical reports and controls independent of police statistics in the United States are homicide (where medical examiners and vital statistics operate) and auto theft (where almost ubiquitous theft insurance generates high rates of official reports). These two offenses declined as much as most other index offenses. Indeed, changing standards of police priority for two offenses—forcible rape and aggravated assault—make it likely that new criteria for police reporting might have increased reported cases and thus understated the true decline of these crimes in the 1990s.

What set the decline during the 1990s apart from other modern crime dips was its length rather than its intensity. To drop nine years in a row was a new postwar decline record for most index offense rates. The size of the decline was more a function of its length than of sudden or sharp drops.

The broad and sustained crime decline in the United States was not typical of other advanced, developed nations during the 1990s, with one important exception. While other G-7 nations had declines in some categories of offenses, only one other nation reported a broad decline close in duration and magnitude to that of the United States. That nation was Canada. This common pattern for the two contiguous nations has received some scholarly attention (from Canadian scholars) but has not yet spawned a comparative study or entered into the academic discourse on the U.S. decline.

Lesson 2

The crime decline of the 1990s was a classic example of multiple causation, with none of the many contributing causes playing a dominant role.

In retrospect, the 1990s seems like a conspiracy of glad tidings for crime control. The social and economic conditions that had long been regarded as favorable for declining crime were abundantly present in the 1980s and the 1990s. The percentage of the population in the high-risk ages of 15–29 dropped from 27.4% of the U.S. population in 1980 to 20.9%—in 2000, a major decline. The economy expanded consistently after 1992—and this longest consecutive postwar economic expansion tracks the crime decline almost exactly. The boom years of the late 1990s reduced the percentage of 16- and 17-year-olds who were neither working nor in school by one-third, a measure of activity that is plausibly related to crime commission rates.

Criminal justice efforts paralleled the good economic and demographic news. The rate of incarceration grew quite substantially during the

1990s even as crime rates fell, and the total population incapacitated reached an all-time high. There were also significant additions to police forces during the 1990s, although the net increase in police is difficult to measure precisely.

With all these traditional vectors of crime prevention coalescing during a single period, there are two linked mysteries about the behavior of crime experts. One is that there is now no consensus on how much impact any one of the glad tidings of the 1990s had on the crime rate! Many minimized the reduction in the youth and young adult population (see Levitt 1999), but the parallel decline of crime in Canada, where none of the prison and police trends occurred and the economic cycles were not in sync with those of the United States, makes it more likely that the one trend that the Canadian and U.S. populations shared—a reduction in the relative size of the youth population—probably had more impact than the criminological cognoscenti in the United States were prepared to admit.

The imprisonment, police, and economic booms, which didn't happen in Canada, seem for that reason much less likely to have played a dominant role in the United States decline. But the reason that police, imprisonment, employment, and population figures don't produce precision and certainty in estimates of their impact on the crime rate is that we really don't know very much about the unconditional impact of any of these factors on rates of crime. The statistical tools available to produce estimates are not strong, and the estimates that can be produced vary substantially. So much for the hardy perennials of the crime-control debate discussed in chapter 3.

The knowledge gap about new theories of crime reduction that were spawned in the 1990s is even worse. Estimating the contribution of new factors that were proposed as crime prevention mostly because they fit with the timing of the 1990s crime decline are even more problematic. The abatement of crack cocaine and the diminishment of unwanted births in the wake of elective abortion laws may have played a role in declining crime in the 1990s, but evidence on these theories must come from other places and other times to be persuasive.

This lack of certainty about the causes of fluctuations in crime is the only explanation for the failure of crime and criminal justice specialists to see some crime decline on the horizon in the 1990s. The population and imprisonment trends of the 1990s were well known by 1995, but nobody was predicting that a crime decline was just around the corner, even after it had begun! Liberals and conservatives seemed united in pessimism about the period after 1995, even when an economic boom joined the prison and demographic trends.

The reason for this was the 1980s. Between 1985 and 1990, the prison population grew at the greatest rate in history, the youth population declined, the economy boomed, and life-threatening crime in the United States went up. Since all those macro-trends had failed to predict even the direction of the crime rate in the late 1980s, it did not seem prudent to rely in the 1990s on a set of leading indicators that hadn't led anywhere a decade earlier. The lack of predictions of glad tidings in the mid-1990s could well have been a case of "Once bitten, twice shy."

But maybe not "three times shy." And that, too, could be a problem. There is reason to fear that many of the professional observers who were embarrassed by failing to predict the crime declines of the 1990s are now prone to overestimating the predictive powers that might seem to have been conferred on the profession by good news. Sustained crime declines encourage people to believe they know what drives crime trends, just as stock market booms convince investors that they are financial wizards. In both investment and government, doing well is too easily confused with knowing what you are doing.

Increments of knowledge are available from the 1990s on a number of questions. But the stubborn refusal of crime rates to go down in the late 1980s is a cautionary tale we should not easily forget. Our capacity to estimate the effects of social and criminal justice factors on crime rates is quite modest in 2006. But modesty is a difficult posture to sustain when surrounded by good news.

Lesson 3

It will not be possible to comprehend what caused declining crime in the United States until more is known about the parallel crime decline in Canada.

The broad decline in Canadian crime that is almost perfectly matched to the timing of the United States decline and about 70% of its relative magnitude is a challenge to the instrumental explanations of decline that have been common in the United States. It is also an indication that cyclical influences not tied to economic fluctuations or criminal justice policy may have played a major part in the crime decline in both nations.

The crime decline in Canada started in 1991 and involved 9 of the next 10 years, a perfect temporal fit with trends in the United States. The decline was almost as broad as the U.S. one (six of seven index crimes versus seven of seven) and almost as substantial in relative magnitude. Many of the factors believed to be important in the U.S. decline—a decade-long economic boom, an explosive expansion of incarceration, added police—didn't happen in Canada. Even when Canada had a history similar to that of the United States as with abortion liberalization, the decline in homicide arrests that Canada experienced did not get concentrated on the younger offenders, so no plausible case can be made that the limited abortion rights that obtained in Canada prior to 1989 paid any visible dividend on homicide.

The Country That Didn't Brush with Crest

Canada functions almost as a control group for the U.S. experience during the 1990s. It was a nation that didn't hire police, didn't increase imprisonment, and didn't grow its economy over nine years in a row, yet it had a crime decline at the same time and close to the same magnitude as that in the United States. I have already suggested that the parallel experience of the two countries demands a second look at their one shared crime related characteristic: the decline in the proportion of the population aged 15–29.

But there is also, in two eras of parallel crime movement in the history of the United States and Canada, a suggestion of cyclical influences not tied to known instrumental causes. The explosive growth in crime and violence that happened in the United States from 1965 to 1974 was neatly paralleled in Canada by 10 years of increasing crime that began one year later. At other times, notably when crime fell in the United States after 1980, there was no parallel movement in Canada. But it is well beyond coincidence that the two major crime movements of the last half of the twentieth century were almost perfectly synchronized in these two contiguous countries.

Further, both Canada and the United States had demographic shifts in the late 1980s that were consistent with expecting a crime reduction, but no such reduction occurred. In the United States, the onset of crack cocaine was the usual explanation for this missing demographic dividend, but Canada didn't have a crack problem at that time. In the short run, careful comparative study of the United States and Canada may widen the list of mysteries before it resolves them. But it would not be wise for any serious student of crime in the United States to neglect comparisons with Canada when analyzing crime trends.

Lesson 4

New York, the nation's largest city, had a crime decline during the 1990s almost twice the national average, and the city's downtrend has continued through 2004, making it a natural laboratory for studying the effects of a lower crime environment on urban life.

The crime drop in New York City is the largest and longest documented general decline in crime in American history, averaging close to a 75% drop from peak rates in the 1990s and still dropping in the middle of the next decade. The New York City pattern is of historic importance in a number of respects. While the half of New York's 1990s decline that reflects the national pattern probably reflects the same mix of multiple causes that apply nationally, much of the other half of the city's decline is almost certainly the result of three major changes in the city's police department. If the combination of more cops, more aggressive policing, and management reforms did account for as much as a 35% crime decrease (half the total), it would be by far the biggest crime prevention achievement in the recorded history of metropolitan policing.

But even more important than documenting the particular causes of the city's crime decline will be learning about the effects of declining crime in a megacity that has sustained a three-quarters drop in life-threatening violence. Crime rates probably affect a wide range of aspects of urban life—opportunities for minority youth, real estate values, intergroup relations and Anglo whites' attitudes toward minorities, the distribution of crime, rates of violence by police, and violence directed toward them. New York City is now the obvious laboratory for studying the effects of significant crime reduction on the social, economic, and political life of cities.

Unless the recidivism rates of offenders released from prison for crimes like robbery and burglary went down by 70% in 10 years, the rate of serious offenses by youth went down even more than the general crime rate in

New York City. What effect has this had on the arrest rates of minority youth, on youth transitions from school to work? Now that neighborhoods formerly impacted by violent crime are at lower risk, how does that affect who lives in these areas and who wants to live there? What is the impact of lower crime rates on the civic reputation of the city in the suburbs? How does this affect the attitudes toward minorities that are expressed by white people in Scarsdale and in Syracuse? How does a lower crime environment influence the residential desires of youth and young adults in New York City? Of senior citizens? These are among the multitude of important questions waiting to be asked and answered in New York City.

Lesson 5

Two kinds of parochialism have hampered the effort to under-
stand the effects that social and criminal justice factors have on
crime rates: (1) the failure by many investigators to consider
data and insights outside their narrow disciplinary perspective,
and (2) the failure to consider events outside the United States.

The inherent limits to the statistical procedures used to estimate the impact of policies or of changed social circumstances on crime rates are substantial, to say the least. The comparisons over time or between different places with different characteristics often attempt to control for all the factors other than what is being studied by creating multivariate statistical models that attempt to comprehensively measure all the influences on crime rates. The problem, of course, is that there are no standard models of the determinants of crime over time or cross-sectionally.

The lack of a good standard model of crime causation doesn't prevent regression manipulations from producing estimates of effectiveness—for the number of police, or for adding to a prison population, or for laws mandating that most adults can qualify for concealed weapons permits. Exactly the opposite. The ad hoc statistical controls for crime used in the cottage industry of regression studies can produce a wide variety of different crime models and a very wide variety of different estimates of effects.

This is true with both cross-sectional and time studies. Often, simple comparisons of new policies over time without elaborate statistical controls turns out to be a more credible strategy of assessing the impact of changes than trying to control for all other influences, although so many things can change over time that even the uncomplicated observation of natural experiments carries its own risks of erroneous inference. All of the methods that are used in current research are imperfect, and the best hope for increasing knowledge is the use of a number of differently imperfect methods to produce similar estimates of effect. Without real hope of controlled experiments to assess many important crime causation questions, a cumulative research strategy called "triangulation of proof" is a best hope for increasing knowledge. Hans Zeisel described this approach with admirable simplicity 20 years ago:

> Most efforts of scientific proof suffer from one shortcoming or another. Because of physical, social and conceptual limitations, our research efforts are forever imperfect . . . some of these uncertainties are reduced by . . . the confluence of evidence from two or more independent research approaches, a constellation for which the term triangulation has been receiving some acceptance. (Zeisel 1985, p. 253)

The central notion is that two or more imperfect methods, if they are imperfect for different reasons, can reduce the margin of error by locating estimates of measured effects in a particular region of outcomes. The metaphor comes from an error-narrowing technique used by surveyors.

The entire discourse of social and behavioral science can be imagined as a collective enterprise of triangulation of proof in which a wide variety of different methods and perspectives produce successively more accurate approximations of the relationship between elements that are believed to influence crime rates and crime.

If that is the model of social science progress, the reality of the process has fallen short in several respects. One problem I mentioned in chapter 3 is what has been called "the cross-sterilization of the social sciences." Researchers in one social science operate without paying attention to the research results or research perspectives of other disciplines. The chief offenders in the recent history of crime decline research have been economists, though this may be a function of the wide range of published research on the topic from economists. The failure of an economist to consider published research by noneconomists on the effect of variations in police on crime rates has produced estimates that ignore the majority of published reports and has biased the results toward positive findings.

The failure of economists to examine demographic literature when discussing the impact of abortion on fertility has meant that they have not considered the dramatic impact of other birth control change on fertility. This narrowness of vision is common. The margin of error in crime studies will be high in any event, but the artificial narrowing of perspective makes a bad situation much worse.

A second effect of narrow disciplinary isolation on crime-related topics is the Balkanization of crime scholarship into subunits that share beliefs about questions where there is crossdisciplinary disagreement. On questions like deterrence, where economists are predisposed to think of variations of threatened punishments as a species of raising the price of crime commission, the assumption of effectiveness is strong, and very weak statistical evidence is welcomed. Other social scientists are more skeptical. (Compare Berk 2005 with Levitt 2004 on recent death penalty research; compare Blumstein, Cohen, and Nagin 1978 with Ehrlich 1976 for an earlier example of the same gap.) As long as sectarian groups preach only to their converted believers, the opposite of triangulation of proof is the result. Sadly, as of 2006, very little research and research analysis on the crime decline has been interdisciplinary in either scope or perspective.

The second destructive provincialism that has constrained the quality of research on the crime decline in the United States is the failure to consider the experience of other nations. Exhibit A of both the provincialism of U.S. social science on the crime decline and on its destructive impact is the failure to consider or learn from the parallel experience of Canada. The substantive implications of the parallel Canadian experience were discussed in chapter 5 and touched on earlier in this chapter. How researchers can persist in single-country isolation when scholarly work is published and discussed on Canada is a cautionary tale worth telling.

The first installment of how Canadian data should have entered into U.S. discourse begins at the annual meeting of the American Society of Criminology in November 2000, an organization with many Canadian and U.S. criminologists and other subject matter specialists. In his review of the Blumstein and Wallman book on the crime drop in America in the American Journal of Sociology (Blumstein and Wallman, eds., 2000), John Laub reported the following about a session at the meetings devoted to discussing the book.

> In fact, an exclusive focus on the United States may limit our
> understanding of trends in violence. At a recent meeting of the

American Society of Criminology, Rosemary Gartner, a sociologist at the University of Toronto, pointed out that while homicides in Canada have fallen markedly during the 1990s, there has been little change in drug demand or drug markets, incarceration rates have fallen, police practices have not changed in any systematic way, and overall the Canadian economy has not been particularly robust during this time period. This suggests that there is much that can be learned from a comparative study of crime trends in the United States, Canada, and Europe. (2001, p. 1821)

This account entered the scholarly literature on the topic only because Laub told the story of Professor Gartner's intervention in his review.

Professor Laub's published report of Canadian developments was followed by the publication in 2002 of a detailed analysis of Canadian homicide patterns in Homicide Studies, an American journal with a principally sociological audience (Sprott and Cesaroni 2002). This was followed by the publication (in French) of a longer, multicrime analysis of the Canadian crime decline (Ouimet 2004).

What happened next is that nothing happened. The discouraging element on the story is the failure of scholarship on the U.S. decline to take account of the Canadian data and their potential implications for several years (see e.g. Rosenfeld 2004; Levitt 2004). More than disciplinary and national boundaries might be at work here. The Canadian experience complicates matters without providing any substitute sound bite to summarize the crime decline.

In the long run, of course, empirical data of such obvious relevance to the crime decline in the United States must be acknowledged. But most of the research generated by the crime decline or any other hot topic is conducted shortly after the topic arises. The waste of human effort that occurs when comparative data is ignored is almost as discouraging as the unjustified conclusions about causes that may crop up as a result of comparative ignorance.

Lesson 6

Since the national crime decline ended, almost as if on cue, in
2000, rates have stayed near the lowest levels of the 1990s.
But there are indications that crime rates could drop further,

perhaps much further, without major changes in the American
social framework.

There are several indications in the statistical portrait of crime in the United States that substantial declines in crime could happen without fundamental change in social or economic structure. Historically, crime rates have been somewhat lower at the national level then they are in 2006, although this occurred last in the 1960s. The wide gap between big cities in rates of offenses such as larceny and burglary suggests that cities on the high end of that distribution could experience substantial drops in many offenses. Whether that logic carries over to a variety of violent offenses is an open question.

The most persuasive evidence that U.S. crime levels could fall further is the size and character of the recent crime decline in New York City, and several other places (see appendix 4). The gap in recent declines between New York—with a crime rate still declining in 2005—and the rest of the 15 largest cities in the United States leaves sufficient room for rates of homicide, robbery, and auto theft to fall by almost half from current rates in most large cities just to catch up with New York.

This type of historical pattern is more persuasive evidence of the potential for change than cross-sectional variation, because it is change that has happened without any large variation in the city's population, economy, or ecology. If there are any natural limits to reductions of crime rate under current social conditions, they have not yet been encountered in New York. This suggests that most other cities have substantial downside potential in crime levels before the nature of modern urban living imposes constraints on the capacity to control crime.

And that brings us to the last and most important lesson of the 1990s for students of crime and society in the United States.

Lesson 7

Whatever else is now known about crime in America, the most
important lesson of the 1990s was that major changes in rates of
crime can happen without major changes in the social fabric.

The crime decline in New York City was a substantial departure from not only the peak rates the city had experienced during 1990 but also from long-term trends. During the 1980s, the mean annual homicide rate in New York City was 22.7 per 100,000; in 2003, the homicide rate was 7.4, a decline of 74% from the 1990 high point but also a drop of more than two-thirds from the 1980s average. The drop in some other offenses from long-term averages was just as substantial: robbery, 67%, burglary 77%, auto theft 67%. Several other cities have very large crime drops from long-term trends as well (see appendix 4).

The most remarkable part of this story is not what changed in New York City over the 1990s but what did not change, which was most of the city of New York. There were clever programs to stop fare avoidance in the subway system (so that even prospective criminals were charged admission), but the subways didn't change, nor did the schools, the streets and surface transportation system, the population, or the economy. The celebrated makeover of Forty-second Street during the 1990s from sleaze district to theme park was the exception that proved the rule. New York is, in most important respects, the same city in 2006 that it was in 1990, with a similar population, economy, and physical environment. The very substantial drop in crime was most important not for its testament to particular causes but as evidence that crime propensities are not inherent characteristics of either a population or an urban setting but rather are highly variable aspects of an urban environment. The same city can have radically different rates of crime if only relatively superficial environmental conditions change.

The highly variable character of urban crime contradicts most of the major ideologies of crime that were in play during the 1990s. For those political conservatives who are wedded to hard-line penal responses, the mid-1990s fashion had become a demographic determinism whereby the "moral poverty" of broken families foretold "coming waves of juvenile violence" and future cohorts of "juvenile superpredators." In this approach, it was assumed that criminal propensities were hardwired into populations, so that the expected crime rate from a high-risk group at liberty should not vary much over time. Those who espoused this worldview were convinced that crime rates were highly predictable 10 and 15 years into the future. And we were told in the mid-1990s that crime rates were headed up. That was the hard right newscast as late as 1996. It would be difficult to imagine a more complete disproof of crime rate predictions than that which confronted the chorus of crime rate determinists by the late 1990s.

But the sharp drop in crime across the nation was also a surprise to the "no peace without justice" group of liberal social scientists, and the crime drop of the 1990s casts a broad shadow across a whole series of theories that posit direct links between particular cultures or values and persistently high rates of crime and violence. The cultural values in New York City's ghetto and barrio neighborhoods certainly didn't change at the same pace as the homicide rate. While the economic conditions for entry-level workers improved during the late 1990s, that was not sustained in the city after the attacks of September 11, 2001. The use of hard narcotics in New York City may have abated slightly during the 1990s, but the drug tests of arrested persons continued to reflect extensive use of cocaine and no major decrease in heroin. New York City probably continued to be the hard-drug-use capital of the United States, but crime dropped anyway. The physical, social, and economic character of the city did not change much at all, but the crime rate did.

Nature versus Nurture versus Neither

The sharp decline in crime that happened to New York City is thus of no comfort to either side in the endless debate about human nature versus social environment as an explanation for crime in the United States. There was very little change in either the population of the city or in the social and economic structure of life in the city to explain very large movements in the volume of crime. But the consequences of the crime drop for personal theories of crime volume are more problematic than for the environmental approach. The people who live in New York City in 2006 are quite similar to those who were expected to be there when dire predictions about future crime rates were being made. The population at risk was near constant and crime dropped by more than 70%. If "crime is caused by criminals," where did all the criminals go?

The dramatic reduction in crime doesn't contradict the power of social environments acting on crime rates, but the big drops we have witnessed do contradict the environmental determinism of recent social theory. The assumption of environmentalists (including this one) was that basic and substantial changes in urban environments would be necessary before big declines in life-threatening crime could be expected. The environmental surprise of the 1990s was that small changes could produce large effects. The major social, educational, and economic problems remained yet crime went down.

Does this mean that individual and large environmental theories of crime causation are obsolete? No, it doesn't. But it may mean that theories which do a good job of predicting how crime gets distributed in a city may be much less important in predicting the level of crime at any given time. Crime rates among low-opportunity youth may be much higher than among young persons with better education and economic opportunity, but this distributional feature of crime doesn't mean that crime levels can only decline if schools improve (Zimring and Hawkins 1997, pp. 217–218). Individual and social risk factors may tell us who is at greater versus lesser risk of involvement in crime without being useful indicators of how much crime will happen or what kinds of crime will be committed.

There is one further aspect of the competition between individual and environmental explanations of crime worth special emphasis when considering the crime decline of the 1990s. Much of the decline noted in both Canada and the United States may not be explained by either individual or environmental factors. With the strong circumstantial evidence of cyclical effects present, it is not prudent to assume that any significant measure of happy news on the crime front can be easily assigned to discernable causes.

But even the most skeptical observers should learn an important and hopeful lesson from our recent adventures with declining crime.

The largest lesson of the 1990s, in New York and elsewhere, is that crime rates of the magnitude and seriousness of the preceding generation are not hardwired into the ecology of modern life or the cultural values of high-risk youth. Far more than we thought, serious crime is a highly variable component of modern urban life. The best methods of crime prevention and reduction have yet to be determined. Whether various preventive outcomes are worth their costs is a separate set of concerns. But we do know this: we don't have to change the world to change the crime rate. Very high rates of life-threatening crime are not an inevitable feature of the American social structure, now or in the future.

Appendix 1

Crime and Abortion Policy in Europe, Canada, and Australia

The variation in abortion policy that existed in Europe makes some comparative crime analysis possible over time. Unfortunately, there is no audited general crime statistics authority in western Europe, nor are there common definitions of offenses. The World Health Organization does have a carefully defined category of willful homicide that can be used for international comparisons.

I report on six European countries that have three different patterns of formal legal regulation of abortion during the last third of the twentieth century. Two nations—Spain and Ireland—entered the most recent era with tight restrictions on abortion and did not reform their laws. These are places where no crime reductions from legal change could be expected, although the availability of abortion in other nations might promote travel and increase the abortion rate of Spanish and Irish citizens in the 1970s and beyond. A second group of nations had liberalized access to abortion long before the 1970s but increased access during the 1970s. Sweden had long provided medically rationed abortions, and the United Kingdom had provided medical practitioners with a defense to criminal prosecution since King v. Bourne in 1939. The reforms in the mid-1970s made abortion more accessible, but the change in availability should be less dramatic than in countries that changed from no legal abortion to no restriction.

Two countries are candidates for sharper shifts, although each particular history is qualified. France shifted to elective abortion in 1975, but
some medical abortion was available in earlier years. Italy had no legal
abortion until 1978 and then instituted elective abortion, but this happened five years later than in the United States, so the impact on crime
should be that much later.

Table A1.1 summarizes the trend in willful homicide for these six nations using World Health Organization statistics.

Four of the six nations report modest declines in homicide, ranging
from 10% in Spain to 23% in the United Kingdom. Ireland has a modest
increase, and Italy reports a drop in homicide to half the 1980 rate. The total homicide rates in all six nations in 2000 are separated by only 0.28 per
100,000 from lowest to highest. How might these trends be linked to shifts
in abortion?

Figure A1.1 shows the record of officially known abortions for the six
nations in the European sample by year as a rate per 1,000 women aged
15–49. The data in this figure are limited, as are the U.S. data, because only
lawful abortions are counted. This will underestimate the total abortion
rate, particularly during periods when legal restrictions exist. This "legal
only" bias will also overestimate the increase in abortion rate as policy is
liberalized, because a greater percentage of total abortions get counted.

Table A1.1

**Change in homicide rate per 100,000 in six European
countries, 1990–2000 and year 2000 rate.**

	1990–2000	2000
Ireland	+21%	1.04
Spain	−10%	.96
United Kingdom	−23%	.76[a]
Sweden	−16%[b]	1.02
France	−16%	.85
Italy	−52%	.92

Source: World Health Organization Regional Office for Europe.
2005, June. European Health For All Database (HFA-DB).
Available at the website of the World Health Organization
Regional Office for Europe: http://data.euro.who.int/hfadb/.
[a]1999 is last year available.
[b]Based on 1987 beginning rate of 1.22.

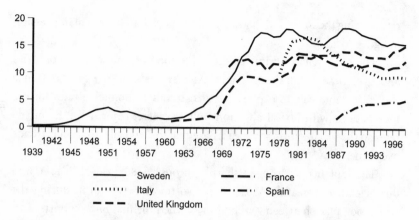

Figure A1.1. Abortion rate (per 1,000 women aged 15–49) by country and year, 1939–98. Source: U.S. Department of Commerce. Bureau of the Census. International Data Base (IDB). Available at the website of the Census Bureau: www.census.gov/ipc/www/idbnew.html.; www.johnsonsarchive.net/policy/abortion/#st.

Sweden and the United Kingdom have significant numbers of legal abortions earlier than the other nations reporting, and the Swedish abortion rate is higher throughout the period than those of the other countries. The second largest aggregate abortion experience is the United Kingdom, with France a close third place. During the 1970s, however, the French abortion rate was higher than the U.K. rate. The Italians begin legal abortion only in 1978 but soon had a rate equal to Sweden in the early 1980s, which then declined substantially in the mid-1980s.

The impact of abortion legalization in Italy on cohorts old enough to be committing crime by 2000 is much smaller than those in the other reform nations because the first postliberalization children were born in 1979, and the total rate of terminated pregnancies by this measure is less than half the U.K. and Swedish rates and somewhat lower than the French rates. For the aggregate impact on crime in the 1990s, that is the ranking one would theorize. But Italy should have a particular drop in very young offenders, given its late entry in to the elective abortion category. Spain and Ireland have no legal abortions during the years that children born might contribute to crime in the late 1990s. They are, in this sense, control countries, although obviously Spanish and Irish women with the requisite financial resources could obtain lawful foreign abortions in the 1970s and 1980s, and this is not measured in the figure. So the true contrast in abortion rates during the 1970s and 1980s is certainly less than the visual impression in figure A1.1.

The most reliable crime category for comparison between countries and over time is homicide. Figure A1.2 expands on the 19-year trends shown in table A1.1 to explore detailed trends in homicide rates for the four nations with liberal abortion policies. Here, I normalize homicide rates so that each nation's 1980 start is equal to 1 and all variation is trends over time.

The Italian rate dropped sharply through 1986, peaked in 1991, and downtrended thereafter. More than two-thirds of the drop during the 1990s took place between 1991 and 1995, when the first birth cohorts after the abortion reform turned 16 years old.

Figure A1.3 adds trends in reported homicide for the two "control" nations, again starting the two nations at their 1980 start equal to one.

Over the entire two decades, trends in homicide for five of the six countries are remarkably flat, and even the rate of homicide in these very different nations is quite close (see table A1.1). All during the 1980s and 1990s, the homicide rate in Sweden, the United Kingdom, France, Ireland, and Spain stays quite close to 1 per 100,000 per year. The very few exceptions to this pattern are a one-year jump in Ireland (the least populous

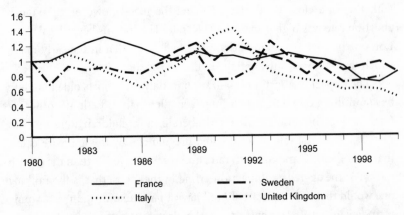

Figure A1.2. Homicide rate by country and year, 1980–2000. Sources: World Health Organization Regional Office for Europe. 2005, June. European Health For All Database (HFA-DB). Available at the website of the World Health Organization Regional Office for Europe: http://data.euro.who.int/hfadb/. U.S. Department of Commerce. Bureau of the Census. International Data Base (IDB). Available at the website of the Census Bureau: www.census.gov/ipc/www/idbnew.html.

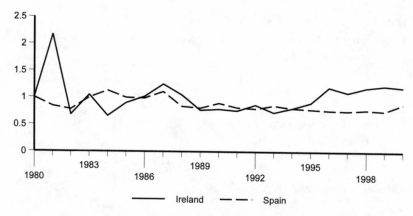

Figure A1.3. Homicide rate by country and year, 1980–2000. Sources: World Health Organization Regional Office for Europe. 2005, June. European Health For All Database (HFA-DB). Available at the website of the World Health Organization Regional Office for Europe: http://data.euro.who.int/hfadb/. U.S. Department of Commerce. Bureau of the Census. International Data Base (IDB). Available at the website of the Census Bureau: www.census.gov/ipc/www/idbnew.html.

nation) in the early 1980s and some fluctuations in the late 1980s in Sweden (the second least populous nation).

The exception to this pattern is Italy, a large nation that nonetheless had a series of peaks and valleys in homicide rates throughout the two decades, with the highest rates in the early 1980s and early 1990s and lower rates in 1987 and again after 1994. The nature of the cyclical pattern is one reason for caution in seeing the late-1990s decline as a product of abortion policy. A second reason for caution is that Italy had the lowest expected crime impact from its abortion policy because the legal abortions started so late.

Still, the large drop in Italian homicide during the 1990s invites further analysis, and the obvious technique for this is to compare trends in homicide arrests in Italy for age. I obtained published data from Italy and France for 1990 and 2000 comparing criminal convictions during those two periods by age. The search here is for the distinctive fingerprint found in the U.S. data by Donohue and Levitt: a decline in homicide arrests for younger more than older offenders.

Table A1.2 tells the story for homicide convictions for Italy, the only national statistics I could find. The table reports trends for total homicide convictions and also for all grades of homicide (including attempted murder).

Table A1.2

Trends in homicide convictions for ages 15–24 and 25–44, Italy, 1990–2000 (rates per 100,000).

	1990	2000	Percentage change
Total homicide (including attempted murder)			
15–24	16.6	16.8	+2
25–44	14.8	12.2	−18
All homicide except "culpable homicide"			
15–24	1.98	3.45	+74
25–44	1.34	3.0	+123

Source: (Convictions) Instituto Nazionale di Statistics Annuario 1990, 2000, Rome. (Population) Department of Commerce. U.S. Bureau of the Census. International Data Base (IDB). Available at the website of the Census Bureau: www.census.gov/ipc/www/idbnew .html.

The pattern for total homicide convictions is the reverse of what abortion liberalization would produce, with a slight increase for the youth segment and a modest decrease for ages 25–44. When the lowest grade of conviction is removed, both age groups show an increase in other homicide convictions, but the youth group has a smaller increase. The total homicide conviction pattern seems to be the better selection for age-specific trends.

The national-level data that are available for France also concerns criminal convictions rather than arrests. Conviction statistics are, in one sense, more reliable than arrest statistics, but the level of convictions is also much more sensitive to variations in policy over time. The data from France use rates per 100,000, as reported by Laurent Muccheilli (2004). I measured variations in rates of conviction for offenses of theft and offenses of violence between 1990 and 2000. The 2000 totals involve four age groups born after 1975 and three older age categories from before 1975. The Donohue/Levitt theory would predict a larger decline or smaller increase for the younger group. Table A1.3 provides mean changes in rates per 100,000 for the younger versus older age groups.

The average theft convictions decline by 14%, for both younger and older age groups between 1990 and 2000, with no net advantage to the younger group. For offenses of violence, conviction rates increase for both

Table A1.3

Average changes in conviction rates for younger and older age groups, France, 1990–2000.

	Theft offenses	
−14%	*−14%*	—
Under 25 (four age groups)	Over 25 (three age groups)	Difference, younger versus older
	Violence offenses	
+150%	*+60%*	*+90%*
Under 25 (four age categories)	Over 25 (three age categories)	Difference, younger versus older

Source: Laurent Mucchielli. 2004. "L'Evolution de ladelinquance juvenile en France (1980–2000)." *Societes Contemporaines* 53 (1): 101–134, p. 109.

younger and older age groups, but the increase is more than twice as high for the younger groups that are candidates for the abortion impact. Neither category provides any indication of the age-specific effects that abortion impact would produce.

The search for English data on arrests and charges by age was also only partially successful. The Home Office does not maintain any national-level data on arrests by age but does record, for homicide offenses, the ages of persons charged with different grades of homicide in court. This is a much earlier stage in the legal process than the convictions reported for Italy in table A1.2 but is a later stage than the arrests reported for the United States. The later in the process a count happens, the more that count can be influenced by changing patterns of discretion by police, prosecutors, and judges.

Figure A1.4 shows the trend in homicide charges per 100,000 population in each age group for the major age groups at risk in England and Wales in 1990 and 2000.

As was the case for Italy, the trend in charges over the decade was up for all age groups, even though the homicide rate reported at the beginning of the decade was higher than at the end. The important issue for testing whether the postliberalization cohorts were a major source of the lower homicide rates is whether the two youngest groups show larger drops (or smaller increases) over time. The answer in figure A1.4 is no.

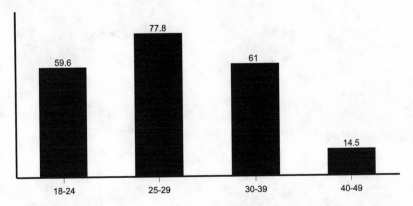

Figure A1.4. Percentage increase in homicide charges per capita by age, England and Wales, 1989–90 to 1999 (1 April) to 2001 (31 March). Sources: U.K. Home Office. U.K. Census.

Testing Claims for Canada and Australia

There are two other settings in which statistics on crime over time have been publicly mentioned as evidence of abortion legislation effects: Australia and Canada (see Levitt and Dubner 2005, p. 141). Detailed Australian data were not available in published sources, but the Canadian statistics are accessible. Anindya Sen, of the University of Waterloo, generated a time-series study (Sen 2005) that implies that the first wave of Canadian abortion reform reduced violent crime. Data on arrests by age are only available for the crime of homicide from Canada, and Jane Sprott and Carla Cesaroni (2002) show no differential reduction in the homicide arrests of younger offenders, so it is difficult to infer any abortion effects from the 1990s homicide decline in Canada.

The Australia economists who announced results consistent with abortion liberalization effects did not break out trends over time in arrests to replicate the U.S. analysis. Indeed, the only data available at the national level in Australia on crime by any age category is for homicide charges. Table A1.4 shows trends in homicide charges for Australia by age group for 1990 and 2000.

The homicide trends in Australia were consistent with abortion legalization effects to some extent, because the rates went down for the youngest groups but went up for the population who were aged 30–39 and

40–49. The only inconsistent pattern in table A1.4 appears for the two age groups over age 50, where the rates were very low but the trends turned down.

But the pattern in table A.1.4 would not produce much total homicide reduction due to age differences in rate, and the largest percentage reduction was for ages 50–59. Still, there was some hint of age effects in the homicide totals, so I requested age-specific data from New South Wales on a series of other crimes over the same time period.

New South Wales had a population in 2000 of 6.8 million, just under 40% of the national population total, and the state contains Sydney, which is nearly as large as Los Angeles and is the largest city in Australia (see Zimring and Hawkins 1997, ch. 1). Table A1.5 shows trends in criminal charges per 1,000 population for six offenses in the state. Excluded are those aged under 15 (less than 0.1%) and over 50 (where the arrests are spread across populations with greatly different crime involvement risks).

When aggregate rates of charges for the six offenses listed in table A1.5 are computed, two of the three youngest population groups show arrest trends indistinguishable from those of ages 30–39. Ages 15–19, 25–29, and 30–39 produced increased charge rates of 17%, 18%, and 21%, respectively. The only youth segment with low growth was the 20–24 age group, with by far the highest arrest rate in 1990 but only 5.3% growth from that base. The over-40 age group, low in 1990, was also the only group where the charge rate declined over the 1990s, but it was a 23% decline in theft arrests that pushed the aggregate charge total lower.

Table A1.4
Homicide charges by age groups, Australia, 1990 and 2000 (rates per 100,000).

Ages	1990	2000	Percentage difference
Under 20	1.16	.945	−19%
20–29	4.89	4.02	−17%
30–39	2.74	3.29	+20%
40–49	1.56	1.83	+17%
50–59	1.1	.63	−43%
60 and above	.338	.314	−7%

Sources: Homicide charges: data provided from Australia Institute of Criminology. Population: Australia. Bureau of the Census.

Table A1.5

Trends in criminal charges by age group, New South Wales, 1990–2000 (rates per 1,000).

Age	Aggravated robbery (%)	Robbery (%)	Aggravated assault (%)	Assault (%)	Breaking and entering (%)	Car theft (%)	All charges (%)
15–19	—	+557	+9	+24	−6	−2	+17
20–24	+43	+505	−19	+2	−3	−17	+5.3
25–29	+7	+472	−10	+18	+11	+25	+18
30–39	−3	+568	−10	+35	+52	+70	+21
40–49	+17	a	−17	+13	+81	+102	−1.6

Sources: Charge data: Provided to Franklin Zimring by New South Wales. Bureau of Criminal Statistics and Research. Population: Australia. Bureau of the Census.

[a] Less than five cases in 1990.

The New South Wales offense trends do not produce a clear difference in charge trend by age. Lacking this confirmation, the evidence of abortion liberalization impacts on Australia crime are not compelling.

Some Missing Links

The data collected on arrests or criminal charges by age from Europe, Canada, and Australia fall far short of a definitive test of the effects of abortion liberalization on crime rates. Information was only available on criminal charges (England, Wales, Canada, and Australia) or conviction (Italy and France) and frequently only for homicide. Data for a variety of other crimes was only available for the state of New South Wales in Australia. Further, the only time trend I explored was between 1990 and 2000, the same decade Donohue and Levitt used in the United States but by no means the only potential cut line one could use to test age specific patterns in crime over time. National-level data on the European continent and in Canada and Australia will be hard to find, but rich data from smaller subunits of these countries can no doubt be found.

But unless different (and substantially plausible) time comparisons produce very specific patterns by age, the miscellaneous indicators assembled in this appendix provide little reason to suppose that the United States–style age-specific arrest pattern will generalize to other nations that produced similar timing for abortion liberalization in the mid- and the late 1970s. And without that distinctive "fingerprint," the search for abortion impacts on crime of any magnitude will be mired in ambiguity.

Appendix 2

Supplementary Statistics on Crime Trends in Canada during the 1990s

This appendix provides data on three statistical analyses referred to in chapter 5, data on sex crime killings, data on car insurance claims in several Canadian provinces, and data on trends in annual offenses in major Canadian cities.

Rape Killings

One test of trends in serious sex crimes is trends in homicides that the police believe were the result of sexual assaults. A detailed count of such cases has been reported only since 1992, and figure A2.1 shows the trend in homicide listed as involving sexual offenses over the period 1992–2000.

The drop in apparent sex offense homicides is sustained throughout the decade after a suspiciously large decline for a new reporting category between year 1 and year 2. By 2000, the sex offense homicide total is less than a quarter of its 1992 volume, a drop that is more consistent with the steep drops in aggravated sex assault than with the more modest drop in the general sex assault category.

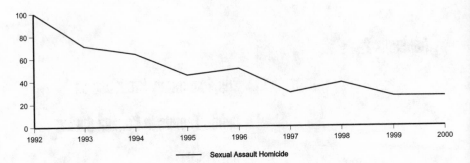

Figure A2.1. 1998 = 38 Killings. Percentage change for rates of homicide involving sexual assault for Canada, 1992–2000. Source: Statistics Canada. Integrated Meta Data Base (IMDB). Ottawa.

Auto Theft Insurance Claims

No national-level data is available in Canada for insurance claims, but data on total theft claims experience by year is available for the six areas where private insurance companies provide coverage. I obtained this data for the 1990s and reproduce it in figure A2.2.

What the figure reports is changes in the total number occurring in each year of theft claims reported to the insurance company within

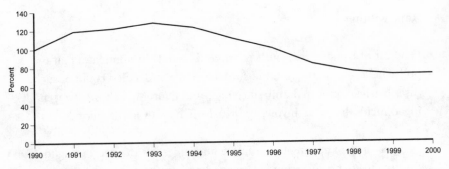

Figure A2.2. Percentage change in incurred number of theft claims (private passenger vehicles) for Ontario, Alberta, Atlantic Provinces, Yukon, Nunavut, and North West Territories, Canada, 1990–2000. Source: Insurance Bureau of Canada. Private Passenger Automobiles Excluding Farmers. (Data for 42 months following accident year.)

40 months of the occurrence. This figure is not adjusted upward for either changes in the number of citizens or changes in the number of insured cars and trucks, so the trends in rate per 100,000 persons will be lower as the population expands.

I was able to obtain loss claims for Quebec from one of the public insurance systems, and that data is shown in figure A2.3.

The gross volume of theft claims decreased by more than a third over the decade, again more consistent with lower instead of higher theft levels. Again, however, there are no controls for the extent of insurance and rates of claim per 100 thefts.

The total rate of claims jumps 20% between 1990 and 1991, stays over 120 through 1994, and then drops steadily for the remainder of the 1990s to 72% of the 1990 total by year 2000. The independent measure from insurance records confirms exactly the jump in theft between 1990 and 1991, but it is in the later part of the decade where the two measures part company. When the population total increase of 12.8% is added to the 2000 rate of incurred claims, the total decline per 100,000 population in the six provinces from 1990 to 2000 is 32%. The gap between this estimated decline and the official national estimate of a 26% increase is substantial. A 32% decline in auto theft is quite close to the national decline reported for the 1990s in the United States—37% in the FBI totals reported in figure 5.1.

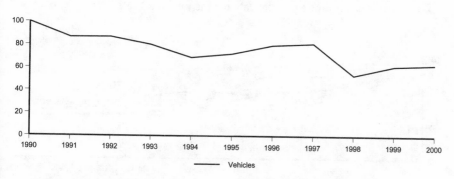

Figure A2.3. Number of stolen vehicles, Quebec, 1990–2000. Note: Year 1990 = 100. There were 50,192 auto thefts in Quebec in 1990. Source: Société de l'Assurance Automobile du Québec.

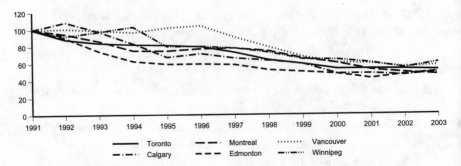

Figure A2.4. Percentage change in breaking-and-entering rates in six cities, Canada, between 1991 and 2003. Source: Statistics Canada. Integrated Meta Data Base (IMDB). Ottawa.

Crime Trends in Major Cities

City-Level Declines

Data were available for the city level for six of the seven largest metropolitan areas in Canada (except Ottawa). Figure A2.4 shows the pattern for each city in break-and-enter rates over the 1990s; in each case, a city's 1990 rate is expressed as 100 and each later year as a percentage of the 1990 rate.

All of the metropolitan areas experienced substantial declines, averaging 45%, but the range in declines between the cities over the decade was fairly narrow, from 36% to 53%.

Figure A2.5 shows parallel data for the total theft rate.

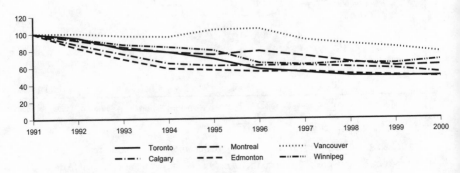

Figure A2.5. Theft trend for six Canadian cities. Source: Statistics Canada. Integrated Meta Data Base (IMDB). Ottawa.

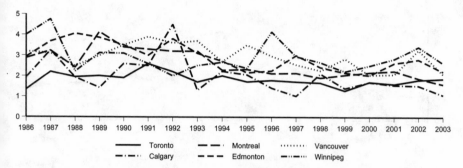

Figure A2.6. Canadian census metropolitan area homicide rates per 100,000, 1986–2003. Source: Statistics Canada. Integrated Meta Data Base (IMDB). Ottawa.

All of the cities show declines for the decade, and all but Vancouver show steady declines throughout the decade. In 2000, the range in total declines for the five cities other than Vancouver is again narrow, from 32% to 52%, but Vancouver reports a total decline of 24%, half the decline reported in Edmonton, Calgary, and Toronto.

Figure A2.6 shows year-by-year rates in the six metropolitan areas for homicide, a much lower frequency crime with more year-to-year volatility.

All of the metropolitan areas show declines over the decade, with an average of 37%. All the cities, except Toronto, report declines between 33% and 52%, while Toronto has only an 11% decline.

For the three offenses, the decline is widespread, and there is no New York City–style "outlier" jurisdiction where the decline is double the average. Edmonton has a slightly higher level of decline (about 10% higher than the average).

A 40-Year Perspective

To further test the magnitude and duration of crime trends in Canada, data on rates of two offenses were analyzed over the period from 1962, when the national statistical reporting system was put in place. The two crimes selected were homicide and breaking and entering. Each is a discrete offense without major reclassifications over the time period (as happened with larceny and sexual assault) and not subject to major swings

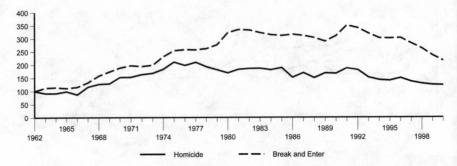

Figure A2.7. Percentage change in homicide and breaking and entering rates for Canada, 1962–2000. Source: Statistics Canada. Integrated Meta Data Base (IMDB). Ottawa.

when police shift thresholds, as happens with grades of assault. Figure A2.7 starts each offense at 100 in 1962 to emphasize trends over time.

This long-term snapshot shows two periods of sustained trends that involve both offenses. The longest downturn was the 1990s, and I discuss its length and magnitude in chapter 5. But this 1990s downtrend is matched in length and surpassed in size by increases in both offenses between the mid-1960s and the mid-1970s. The timing of the sustained Canadian crime increase closely corresponds to the more famous U.S. crime expansion from 1964 to 1974. While the relative magnitude of the homicide expansion in Canada is great, the base rates for this offense is much smaller than in the United States. The close parallel in timing of the two crime trends in 40 years provides powerful additional evidence of linkage between crime cycles in the two countries.

Appendix 3

This appendix reports on trends in unemployment, age structure of the population, incarceration and drug overdoses for the city of New York and the United States during the 1990s. The context for collecting these data was the search for alternative explanations to policing changes to explain the larger than normal crime declines that happened in the 1990s in New York City. The subject of the analysis in chapter 6 is not the totality of the crime in the city but rather the declines beyond the national average that happened in the city, the "half a loaf " strategy of seeking an explanation only for the city's extra decline. So the target of inquiry must be the search for extraordinary changes in the city during the 1990s—changes in policy, economy or population that are above and beyond national trends. Much of the trend data was reported and analyzed in Karman (2000).

Figure A3.1 reports on roles of unemployment for New York City and for the United States by month from 1980 to 2000. The general unemployment rate is reported because age-specific unemployment for youth was not available at the city levels.

The unemployment rate in the city starts higher in the 1980s than the national aggregate and stays higher until late in 1986. During the late 1980s, unemployment in the city turns lower in the city than national rates from late 1986 until late 1988 but then turns higher than the national average for

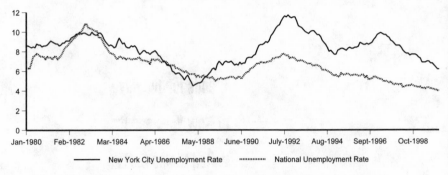

Figure A3.1. New York and U.S. unemployment rates (seasonally adjusted), 1980–2000. Source: U.S. Department of Labor, Bureau of Labor Statistics, Labor Force Statistics from the Current Population Survey. Available at: www.bls.gov/cps/cpsatabs.htm.

the rest of the 1980s and all of the 1990s. The gap between city and national jobless rates grew to 4% briefly in 1991 and stayed in the range of 2–3% in the middle and late 1990s as both the national and city economies improved. Throughout the late 1990s, there was no period when the city's unemployment rate was less than 50% higher than the national averages, so any theory of differential New York City economic advantage would seem strained. The improvement in the New York City economy over the late 1990s is a candidate for explaining part of the city's crime decline but not its distinctive status.

The demographic changes in New York during the 1990s are also not an obvious source of the extra crime decline for the city. There was some change in the age structure of New York City's population over the 1980s and 1990s, but the decline in the population share of younger groups was much smaller than in the nation as a whole. Figure A3.2 tells the New York story.

The proportion of city population aged 15–29 dropped from 25.4 to 22.4 over two decades, only about half as much as the decline in the nationwide age 15–29 population share, and the 1990s decline was slightly less than half of the 20-year pattern. So this relatively small shrinkage in the youth share of the population might have had some downward influence on crime rates in the city, but probably less downward influence in New York City than nationwide. So population composition holds no clues to why crime went down more in New York than in the rest of the nation. Since that is the issue, I regard the demographic trends as eliminated from consideration.

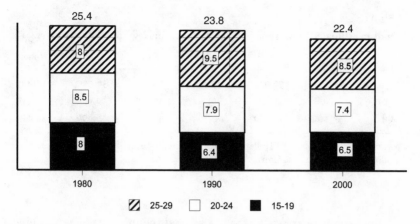

Figure A3.2. Proportion of New York City population in three young age groups, 1980, 1990, and 2000. Source: U.S. Department of Commerce. Bureau of the Census. International Data Base (IDB). Available at the website of the Census Bureau: www.census.gov/ipc/www/idbnew.html.

There are two complementary methods of tracing trends in secure confinement in New York City. The first is to track the prison population for the state of New York. This includes some non–New York City inmates, but the majority of commitments are from the city. Table A3.1 shows rates of imprisonment for New York state per 100,000 and for the nation as a whole.

Table A3.1
Imprisonment rate trends in the United States and New York, 1980–2000 (rate per 100,000).

	New York State	U.S. total
1980	120	136
1990	285	271
2000	331	486
Change 1980–1990	138%	99%
Change 1990–2000	22%	80%

Source: U.S. Department of Justice. Bureau of Justice Statistics. *Source Book of Criminal Justice Statistics*, 1990 and 2000. Washington, D.C.: U.S. Government Printing Office.

Table A3.2

Trends in estimated prison and jail commitments in New York City, six years.

	1985	1987	1990	1993	1997	1999
Jail	44,820	50,920	43,480	31,700	36,020	41,000
Prison	8,508	11,712	16,724	15,872	12,676	13,455
Total	53,328	62,632	60,204	47,572	48,696	54,455

Source: Fagan J., V. West, and J. Holland, "Neighborhood, Incarceration and Vote Dilution," Unpublished MS., Columbia University School of Law, 2006.

Imprisonment trends for New York and the other states were quite similar, but New York grew slightly faster in the 1980s (138% versus 99%), while the rest of the national closed that gap by growing much faster than New York during the 1990s (80% versus 22%). So imprisonment growth could have contributed to declining crime in New York, but there is no reason to suppose that increasing incarceration in the city could explain a New York decline that exceeded the national average during the 1990s when the New York state prison growth was less than one-third the national average.

Table A3.2 shows estimated commitments to jail and prison from New York City for six sample years between 1985 and 1999.

Prison commitments from the city peaked in 1987 and 1990 and stayed lower throughout the decade. Jail commitments peaked in 1987 and fell off by 20–40% during the 1990s. There are no directly comparable figures available for the rest of the United States, but the trend in new incapacitation in New York City was modestly downward during the 1990s, when the state prison population grew only 22%, while the national average was 80%.

The faster growth occurs in the 1980s in both commitments and total prison population. Then, after 1991, new prison commitments turn down but the total prison population continues to climb.

A variety of different drug use indicators are available for big cities. Figure A3.3 provides annual city-wide hospital discharge numbers for cocaine overdoses in the 1990s.

The pattern in figure A3.3 suggests high levels throughout the decade, with no clear tracking between crime rates and drug treatments until 1998. Overdose treatments jumped in 1991, stayed high through 1998, and then dropped to the approximate volume of 1990.

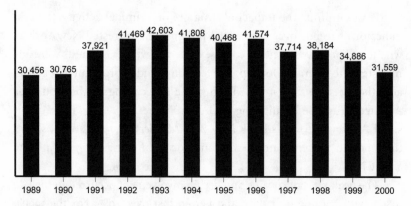

Figure A3.3. Cocaine overdose hospital discharges by year. Source: New York City, Department of Health.

Figure A3.4 traces deaths recorded by vital statistics as resulting from accidental injury from drug overdoses. The solid line traces deaths by all drugs (including alcohol and methyl alcohol), and the dotted line is for the drug category that includes heroin (which is only reported through 1998).

The total overdose deaths dropped during the first half of the decade and then fluctuated around 60 to 70 per year. The heroin deaths (only available through 1998) dropped from 61 in 1990 to 13 in 1991 and stayed close to that lower total through 1998.

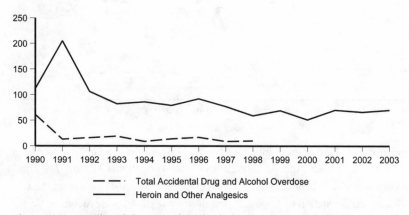

Figure A3.4. Accidental drug overdose deaths by year, 1990–2003, and heroin and other analgesics, New York, 1990–98. Source: New York City Health Department. Vital statistics data.

For examining the impact of drug use on criminal activity, the best indicator of trends over time is the percentage of arrested New Yorkers who tested positive for either cocaine or heroin when urine tests were administered to them in a lockup. The federally funded program that generated these tests was first called Drug Use Forecasting (DUF) and later Arrestee Drug Use Monitoring (ADAM). Figure A3.5, taken from graph 5.2 of Andrew Karman's book *New York Murder Mystery* (2000), shows the reported percentage of heroin and cocaine findings by year in New York City.

The peak rates of cocaine and heroin involvement occurred in the late 1980s, with cocaine near 80% and heroin just over 20%. For the 1990s, heroin tests dipped slightly in 1991 and were then stable throughout the 1990s. Cocaine positive results stayed at or above 60% for the first five years of the 1990s, dropped in 1996 to just over 50%, and remained near that figure through 1998. For those arrested in the city, the dominant pattern through the 1990s was both stable and, in the case of cocaine, high usage. Certainly, no decrease in drug use among those arrested paralleled the decline in crime during the 1990s, but of course the urine-testing program was limited, by definition, to persons with high levels of criminal involvement. The drug-to-crime connection was just as strong in New York City in the late 1990s as in earlier years.

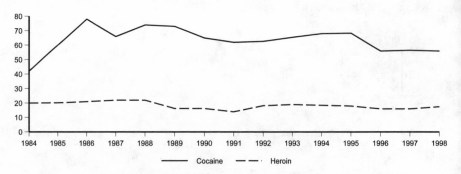

Figure A3.5. Percentage of inmates testing positive for drug use in New York City jails by year. Source: Andrew Karman. 2000. *New York Murder Mystery: The True Story behind the Crime Crash of the 1990s.* New York: New York University Press. Visual reconstruction of graph 5.2, "Trends in Drug Use by Male Arrestees, New York City, 1984–1998," p. 177. Original source: New York State OASAS, drawing on ADAM (formerly DUF) data, 1985–99.

A Process of Elimination

The issue that provoked the data analysis was whether, in the known facts about New York City, there were any major changes in society or government that might help explain the differential decline in crime. This was a search for plausible rival hypotheses to changes in police as a cause for New York's better than average crime drop. If the issue were whether other changes in the city might decrease crime levels, there would be a number of changes that might compete for credit, including economic prosperity, increased incarceration, and demographic shifts. But trends in all these variables were not as great as national averages, so the New York patterns would not be expected to cause any differential crime decline. All of these trends help us understand why crime in New York City dropped during the 1990s; none of these trends help us explain why New York City's crime dropped twice as much as the big-city and national averages.

What sets the police changes apart from the other changes reported in the city is that New York City's policing changes were much greater than those of other cities. So the police trends stand alone as a potential explanation of all the extra crime reduction that is the central concern of chapter 6.

Appendix 4

Measuring the Extent of Decline in Selected High-Decline Cities

This appendix uses some of the measurement strategies employed in chapter 6 to study the extent of decline in five cities that have been identified as high-decline cities. The candidates are the 4 that had the greatest declines out of the 15 largest cities, profiled in chapter 1—New York, San Jose, San Diego, and Houston—and one smaller city that was noted in the literature for a sharp decline, Boston. The analysis in this appendix parallels the treatment of New York City in the first section of chapter 6. The aim of this analysis is twofold: first, to test the distinctiveness of the New York City crime decline discussed in chapter 6, and second, to give non–New York City examples of extreme crime-decline histories that provide evidence for the potential of further decline in other cities. A second section discusses how much of New York City's decline is not part of the general drop.

Table A4.1 provides baseline long-term crime levels for the five cities by constructing mean rates of seven index offenses during the 1980s.

Using homicide as the measure, the mix of cities with large 1990s decreases included two with high homicide rates (New York and Houston), two with low rates for big cities (San Diego and San Jose), and one mid-level homicide city (Boston). For robbery, however, both New York and

Table A4.1

Rates per 100,000 for index crimes—1980s averages, five U.S. cities.

	Murder	Rape	Robbery	Aggravated assault	Burglary	Larceny	Auto theft
San Diego	10.3	41.9	326	362.5	1,774.1	3,971.3	1,287.7
San Jose	6.7	62.6	196.2	301.8	1,432.6	3,819.4	508.9
New York	23.4	50.4	1,235.6	742.3	2,070.2	3,764.3	1,402.7
Houston	28.7	76.8	598.4	308.1	2,640.0	3,918.5	1,780.0
Boston	16.1	84.8	1,130.9	882.5	2,14.9	4,721.8	3,301.8

Source: U.S. Department of Justice. Federal Bureau of Investigation. *Uniform Crime Report.* 1980–1989. Washington, D.C.: U.S. Government Printing Office.

Boston had much higher rates than Houston. For larceny, the four biggest cities had rates per 100,000 that varied less than 10%.

Table A4.2 presents the reported crime rates for the five high-decline cities in 2000.

Table A4.3 shows the percentage decline for each city in each offense when totals for 2000 are compared to the 1980s averages.

The first obvious point made by table A4.3 is the extensiveness of the decline in these cities preselected for their big crime drops. The second obvious pattern is the role of aggravated assault as the exception to the rule of extensive and general decline. The range for this offense goes from a decline of almost half in New York to a doubling of rate in Houston, with the median city in assault trend (San Diego) reporting a 9% increase.

Table A4.2

Rates per 100,000 for index crimes in 2000, five U.S. cities.

	Murder	Rape	Robbery	Aggravated assault	Burglary	Larceny	Auto theft
San Diego	4.3	27.6	140.3	393.3	530.5	1,817.7	747.7
San Jose	2.1	37.7	75.6	435.2	298.3	1,407.4	292.2
New York	7.4	19.9	320.9	385.9	349.4	1,541.7	291.8
Houston	12.0	42.3	429.9	634.9	1,210.9	3,494.3	1,034.4
Boston	6.6	55.2	416.0	765.0	687.6	2,924.3	1,233.8

Source: U.S. Department of Justice. Federal Bureau of Investigation. *Uniform Crime Report.* 2000. Washington, D.C.: U.S. Government Printing Office.

Table A4.3

Change in rates per 100,000 for index crimes between 1980s average and 2000,
Five U.S. cities.

	Murder	Rape	Robbery	Aggravated assault	Burglary	Larceny	Auto theft
San Diego	−58.4	−34.3	−57.0	8.5	−70.1	−54.2	−41.9
San Jose	−68.2	−39.9	−61.4	44.2	−79.2	−63.2	−42.6
New York	−68.5	−60.6	−74.0	−48.0	−83.1	−59.0	−79.2
Houston	−58.2	−44.9	−28.2	106.0	−54.1	−10.8	−41.9
Boston	−58.8	−35.0	−63.2	−13.3	−68.0	−38.1	−62.6

Source: U.S. Department of Justice. Federal Bureau of Investigation. *Uniform Crime Report.* 1990 and 2000. Washington, D.C.: U.S. Government Printing Office.

There are three separate ways of comparing the long-term trends in reporting crime for these high-decline cities.

Figure A4.1 provides each city with a grand mean representing the mean decline for all seven index crimes from their average 1980s level.

On this measure, New York is alone at the top and Houston is alone at the bottom with 19%, while the three other cities are tightly clustered in the middle with rates between 48% and 44%.

Figure A4.2 attempts to correct for the distortions introduced by aggravated assault trends by adding only the top six declines in the measure of long-range decline and averaging them.

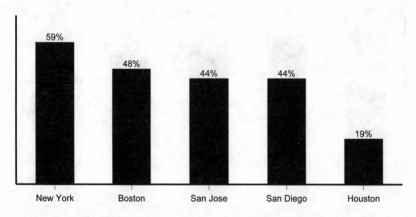

Figure A4.1. Mean decline in seven index crimes in five U.S. cities, 1980–89, 2000. Source: Tables A4.1 and A4.2.

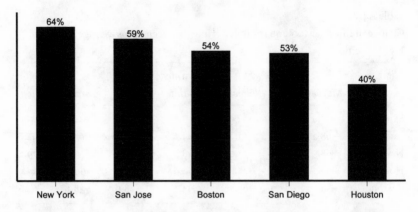

Figure A4.2. Mean decline for top six index crime declines from 1980s rates, in five U.S. cities. Source: Tables A4.1 and A4.2.

The use of a six-crime rather than a seven-crime standard doubles Houston's average decline from 19% to 40%, but does not change either the rank order of cities or the gap at the bottom between Houston and the other four.

Figure A4.3 uses a third approach to measurement of average long-term decline by reporting the decline of the middle offense of the seven index offenses in its drop since the 1980s.

The rank order in figure A4.3 matches the other two figures, but the cities are separated by smaller margins both at the top and at the bottom of the distribution.

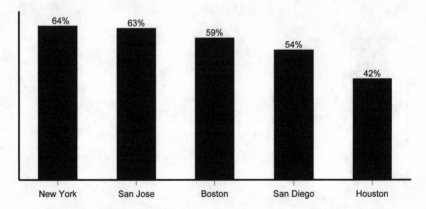

Figure A4.3. Long-term decline of the median declining index offense in five cities. Source: Tables A4.1 and A4.2.

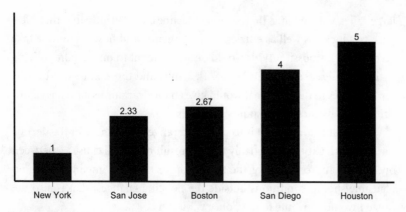

Figure A4.4. Average rank in three measures of decline among high-decline cities, 1990–2000. Source: Tables A4.1 and A4.2.

If only one of these three measures were to be used, the six-offense mean seems to me the best of the lot, given this data. But even better would be the use all three measures cumulatively. The rank orders of these five cities selected for extreme values in 1990s decline are provided in figure A4.4.

The two largest cities other than New York are at the bottom of this distribution. If the issue is New York's relative rank, as opposed to the magnitude of the difference between New York and other cities, the answer is clear.

Estimating the Amount of New York's Crime Decline That Might Be Attributed to Distinctive Causes

Since every large city in the United States experienced a crime decline during the 1990s, the city of New York would have probably experienced a decline in crime even if no special conditions had occurred. But by how much? One method of guessing the division between expected and experienced decline is to assume that New York would have performed close to the average of the other nine of the largest cities in the United States during the 1990s. Using this standard, about half the actual decline exceeds this expectation and is thus a candidate for attribution to the complex of policing changes discussed in chapter 6.

But some cities will experience greater than average declines even without discrete causes. San Diego and Houston are examples of very large cities with greater than average declines. Isn't it possible that New York was lucky as well as efficient in its policing, and how might one take account of this possibility? It would not be prudent to only credit policing with the difference between New York results and those in the next of the top five cities in decline. That would give chance variations a preferred position over distinctive substantive changes.

The best I can counsel is to provide a range of the share of the decline for New York City that probably was the result of special causes—between one-fourth and one-half of the total drop in the city. Since there are no plausible special conditions outside the policing changes, that is also the range I would attribute to the police variations.

References

Adler, Freda. 1975. Sisters in Crime. New York: McGraw Hill.

Allen, Francis. 1981. The Decline of the Rehabilitative Ideal. New Haven: Yale University Press.

Bayley, David H. 1994. Police for the Future. New York: Oxford University Press.

Berk, Richard A. 2005, August. "Knowing When to Fold 'Em: An Essay Evaluating the Impact of Ceasefire, COMPSTAT, and Exile." Criminology and Public Policy 4 (3): 451–465.

Berk, Richard, Susan B. Sorenson, Douglas J. Wiebe, and Dawn M. Upchurch. 2003. "The Legalization of Abortion and Subsequent Youth Homicide: A Time Series Analysis." Analyses of Social Issues and Public Policy 3 (1): 45–64.

Blumstein, Alfred, Jose A. Canela-Cacho, and Jacqueline Cohen. 1993. "Filtered Sampling from Populations with Heterogeneous Event Frequencies." Management Science 39 (7): 886–899.

Blumstein, Alfred, Jacqueline Cohen, and Daniel Nagin, eds. 1978. Deterrence and Incapacitation: Estimating the Effects of Criminal Sanctions on Crime Rates. Washington, D.C.: National Academy of Sciences.

Blumstein, Alfred, and Joel Wallman. 2000. "The Recent Rise and Fall of American Violence." In Alfred Blumstein and Joel Wallman (eds.), The Crime Drop in America (pp. 1–12). New York: Cambridge University Press.

Blumstein, Alfred, and Joel Wallman, eds. 2000. The Crime Drop in America. New York: Cambridge University Press.

Bratton, William, and Peter Knobler. 1998. Turnaround: How America's Top Cop Reversed the Crime Epidemic. New York: Random House.

Canada. Statistics Canada. Integrated Meta Data Base (IMDB). No. 3302. Uniform Crime Reporting Survey. Ottawa.

Canada. Statistics Canada. Integrated Meta Data Base (IMDB). No. 3315. Homicide Survey. Ottawa.

Chiricos, Ted. 1987. "Rates of Crime and Unemployment: An Analysis of Aggregate Research Evidence." Social Problems 34 (2): 187–212.

Coase, Ronald. 1978. "Economics and Contiguous Disciplines." Journal of Legal Studies 7 (2): 201–211.

Cohen, Jacqueline, and Jose A. Canela-Cacho. 1994. "Incapacitation and Violent Crime." In Albert J. Reis and Jeffrey Roth (eds.), Understanding and Preventing Violence (vol. 4, pp. 296–388). Washington, D.C.: National Academy of Sciences.

Conklin, John. 2003. Why Crime Rates Fell. New York: Allyn and Bacon.

Cook, Philip J., and Jens Ludwig. 2000, August 2. "Homicide and Suicide Rates Associated with Implementation of the Brady Handgun Violence Prevention Act." Journal of the American Medical Association 284(5): 585–591.

Council on Crime in America. 1996. The State of Violent Crime in America: A First Report of the Council on Crime in America. Washington, D.C.: New Citizenship Project.

DiIulio, John. 1996. How to Stop the Coming Crime Wave. New York: Manhattan Institute.

DiIulio, John. 1995. "The Coming of the Super-Predators." Weekly Standard, November 27, p. 23.

Donohue, John J. III, and Ian Ayers. 2003. "The Latest Misfires in Support of the 'More Guns Less Crime' Hypothesis." Stanford Law Review 55(4): 1371–1398.

Donohue, John J., III, and Steven D. Levitt. 2004. "Further Evidence That Legalized Abortion Lowered Crime: A Reply to Joyce." Journal of Human Resources 39 (1): 29–49.

Donohue, John J., III, and Steven D. Levitt. 2001. "The Impact of Legalized Abortion on Crime." Quarterly Journal of Economics 116 (2): 379–420.

Donohue, John J., III, and Peter Siegelman. 1998. "Allocating Resources Among Prisons and Social Programs in the Battle against Crime." Journal of Legal Studies 27(1):1–43.

Duncan, Greg J., and Willard Rogers. 1991. "Has Children's Poverty Become More Persistent?" American Sociology Review 56: 538.

Eck, John, and Richard Maguire. 2000. "Have Changes in Policing Reduced Violent Crime? An Assessment of the Evidence." In Alfred Blumstein and Joel Wallman (eds.), The Crime Drop in America (pp. 207–265). New York: Cambridge University Press.

Ehrlich, Isaac. 1976. "The Deterrent Effect of Capital Punishment." American Economic Review 65 (3): 397–417.

Fagan, Jeffrey, and Richard B. Freeman. 1999. "Crime and Work." In Michael Tonry (ed.), Crime and Justice: A Review of Research 25: 225–290. Chicago: University of Chicago Press.

Fagan, Jeffrey, Franklin E. Zimring, and June Kim. 1998. "Declining Homicide in New York City: A Tale of Two Trends." Journal of Criminal Law and Criminology 88: 1277–1323.

Foote, Christopher L., and Christopher F. Goetz. 2005. "Testing Economic Hypotheses with State-Level Data: A Comment on Donohue and Levitt (2001)." Federal Reserve Bank of Boston working paper no. 05-15. Available at the website of the Federal Reserve Bank of Boston: www.bos.frb.org/economic/wp/wp2005/wp0515.pdf.

Fox, James. 1996. Trends in Juvenile Violence. Boston: Northeastern University Press.

Grogger, Jeffrey. 1998. "Market Wages and Youth Crime." Journal of Labor Economics 16: 465–492.

Hagan, John. 1993. "The Social Embeddedness of Crime and Unemployment." Criminology 31: 465–492.

Harcourt, Bernard, and Jens Ludwig. 2005. "Broken Windows." University of Chicago Law Review 73: 271.

Imrohoroglu, Ayse, Antonio M. Merlo, and Peter Rupert. 2004, August. "What Accounts for the Decline in Crime?" International Economic Review 45(3): 707–729.

Joyce, Theodore J. 2004a. "Did Legalized Abortion Lower Crime?" Journal of Human Resources 39 (1): 1–28.

Joyce, Theodore J. 2004b. "Further Tests of Abortion and Crime." Working paper no. 10564. Washington, D.C.: National Bureau of Economic Research.

Karman, Andrew. New York Murder Mystery: The True Story behind the Crime Crash of the 1990s. New York: New York University Press, 2000.

Kelling, George L., and Catherine M. Coles. 1996. Fixing Broken Windows. New York: Simon and Schuster.

Kelling, George L., Tony Pate, Duane Dieckman, and Charles E. Brown. 1974. The Kansas City Preventive Control Experiment: A Summary Report. Washington, D.C.: Police Foundation. Available at: www.policefoundation.org.

Kelling, George L., Anthony Pate, Amy Ferrara, Mary Utne, and Charles E. Brown. 1981. The Newark Foot Patrol Experiment. Washington, D.C.: Police Foundation.

Kelling, George, and William H. Sousa, Jr. 2001. Do Police Matter? An Analysis of New York City's Police Reforms. Civic report 22. New York: Manhattan Institute.

LaFree, Gary. 2002. "Does Too Much Democracy Produce Punitive Punishment? The Case of California's Three Strikes Law." Review essay of Punishment and Democracy, by Franklin Zimring, Richard Hawkins, and Sam Kamin. Law and Social Inquiry 27: 875–902.

Laub, John. 2001, May. Review of The Crime Drop in America, edited by Alfred Blumstein and Joel Wallman. American Journal of Sociology 106 (6): 1821.

Levitt, Steven. 2004. "Understanding Why Crime Fell in the 1990s: Four Factors That Explain the Decline and Six That Do Not." Journal of Economic Perspectives 18 (1): 163–190.

Levitt, Steven. 2002. "Using Electoral Cycles in Police Hiring to Estimate the Effects of Police on Crime: A Reply." American Economic Review 92(4): 1244–1250.

Levitt, Steven. 1999. "The Limited Role of Changing Age Structure in Explaining Aggregate Crime Rates." Criminology 37: 581.

Levitt, Steven. 1997. "Using Electoral Cycles in Police Hiring to Estimate the Effect of Police on Crime." American Economic Review 87(3): 270–290.

Levitt, Steven D., and Stephen Dubner. 2005. Freakonomics: A Rogue Economist Explores the Hidden Side of Everything. New York: Morrow.

Lichter, Daniel T. 1997. "Poverty and Inequality among Children." Annual Review of Sociology 23: 121–145.

Lott, John R., Jr. 1998. More Guns, Less Crime: Understanding Crime and Gun-Control Laws. Chicago: University of Chicago Press.

Lott, John R., Jr., and John E. Whitley. 2001. "Abortion and Crime: Unwanted Children and Out-of-Wedlock Births." Yale Law and Economics research paper no. 254. New Haven, CT. Available at the website of Lott: http://ssrn.com/abstract'270126.

Lucas, Gregg. 1993. "Wilson Turns Up the Heat on Crime." San Francisco Chronicle, December 30, p. A14.

Marvel, Thomas P., and Carlysle E. Moody. 1991. "Age Structure and Crime Rates: The Conflicting Evidence." Journal of Quantitative Criminology 7: 237–273.

Martinson, Robert. 1974. "What Works? Questions and Answers about Prison Reform." The Public Interest Spring: 22–54.

McCrary, Justin. 2002. "Do Electoral Cycles in Police Hiring Really Help Us Estimate the Effect of Police on Crime? A Comment." American Economic Review 92(4): 1236–1243.

Messinger, Sheldon, and Phillip Johnson. 1977. "California's Determinate Sentencing Statute: History and Issues." In Determinate Sentencing: Reform or Regression? Washington, D.C.: U.S. Department of Justice, National Institute of Science.

Morrow, James. 1999. "The Incredible Shrinking Crime Rate." U.S. News and World Report, January 11, p. 25.

Mucchielli, Laurent. 2004. "L'évolution de la délinquance juvenile en France (1980–2000)." Sociétés Contemporaines 53 (1): 101–134.

Ouimet, Marc. 2004, January. "Oh, Canada! La baisse de la criminalité au Canada et aux États-Unis entre 1991 et 2002." Champ Pénal 1 (1). Available at <http://champpenal.revues.org/document11.html>.

Podger, Pamela. 1993. "Murder Victim's Father Launches Repeat-Felon Penalty Initiative." Fresno (Calif.) Bee, November 16, p. B1.

President's Commission on Crime. 1965. The Challenge of Crime in a Free Society. Washington, D.C.: Government Printing Office.

Raphael, Steven, and Rudolph Winter-Ebmer. 2001. "Identifying the Effects of Unemployment in Crime." Journal of Law and Economics 36: 259–283.

Reeves, Brian A., and Mathew J. Hickman. App. A of Police Departments in Large Cities, 1990–2000. Washington, D.C.: U.S. Department of Justice, Bureau of Justice Statistics.

Rosenfeld, Richard. 2004, February. "The Case of the Unsolved Crime Decline." Scientific American: 82–89.

Rosenfeld, Richard, Robert Fornango, and Eric Baumer. 2005. Did Ceasefire, COMPSTAT and Exile Reduce Homicide? Criminology and Public Policy 4(3): 419–450.

Seidman, David, and Michael Couzens. 1974. "Getting the Crime Rate Down: Political Pressure and Crime Reporting." Law and Society Review 8: 457–493.

Sen, Anindya. 2005. "Does Increased Abortion Lead to Reduced Crime? Evaluating the Relationship between Crime, Abortion, and Fertility." Unpublished working paper. Department of Economics, University of Waterloo, Canada.

Shepherd, Joanna M. 2002. "Fear of the First Strike: The Full Deterrent Effect of California's Two- and Three-Strikes Legislation." Journal of Legal Studies 31: 159.

Silberman, Charles E. 1978. Criminal Violence, Criminal Justice. New York: Random House.

Snyder, Howard, and Melissa Sickmund. 1995. Juvenile Offenders and Victims: A National Report. Washington, D.C.: Government Printing Office.

Sorenson, Susan B., Douglas J. Wiebe, and Richard A. Berk. 2002. "Legalized Abortion and the Homicide of Young Children: An Empirical Investigation." Analyses of Social Issues and Public Policy 2: 239–256.

Spelman, William. 2000. "The Limited Importance of Prison Expansion." In Alfred Blumstein and Joel Wallman (eds.), The Crime Drop in America (pp. 97–129). New York: Cambridge University Press.

Spelman, William. 1994. Criminal Incapacitation. New York: Plenum.

Sprott, Jane B., and Carla Cesaroni. 2002. "Similarities in Trends in Homicide in the United States and Canada: Guns, Crack or Simple Demographics?" Homicide Studies 6 (4): 348–359.

References

Steffensmeier, Darrell J., E. A. Allan, M. D. Harer, and C. Streifel. 1989. "Age and the Distribution of Crime." American Journal of Sociology 94 (4): 803–831.

Sykes, Bryan L., Dominik Hangartner, and Earl Hathaway. "Fertility and the Abortion-Crime Debate." Unpublished working paper, Department of Demography, University of California, Berkeley.

Tonry, Michael, and David Farrington, eds. 2005. Crime and Punishment in Western Countries 1980–1999. Vol. 33 of Crime and Justice. Chicago: University of Chicago Press.

United Nations Office on Drugs and Crime. 2000. The Seventh United Nations Survey on Crime Trends and the Operations of Criminal Justice Systems (1998–2000). Vienna: United Nations Office on Drugs and Crime.

United Nations Office on Drugs and Crime. 1990. The Fourth United Nations Survey on Crime Trends and the Operations of Criminal Justice Systems (1986–1990). Vienna: United Nations Office on Drugs and Crime.

U.S. Department of Commerce. Bureau of the Census. International Data Base (IDB). Available at the website of the Census Bureau: www.census.gov/ipc/www/idbnew.html.

U.S. Department of Commerce. Bureau of Economic Analysis. 2006.Quarterly Data on Real Gross Domestic Product in Year 2000 Dollars. Available at the website of the Bureau of Economic Analysis: www.bea.gov/bea/dn/nipaweb/TableView.asp?SelectedTable'253&FirstYear'1990&LastYear'2002&Freq'Qtr.

U.S. Department of Commerce. Bureau of Economic Analysis. 2006. Selected per Capita Product and Income Series in Current and Chained Dollars. Washington, D.C.: Government Printing Office.

U.S. Department of Justice. Bureau of Justice Statistics. 2006. Correctional Surveys (National Prisoner Statistics and Survey of Jails). Washington, D.C.: Government Printing Office.

U.S. Department of Justice. Bureau of Justice Statistics. 1990, 1996, 2000. National Crime Victimization Survey. Washington, D.C.: Government Printing Office.

U.S. Department of Justice. Federal Bureau of Investigation. Various years 1970–2003. Uniform Crime Report. Washington, D.C.: Government Printing Office.

U.S. Department of Labor. Bureau of Labor Statistics. 2006. Labor Force Statistics from the Current Population Survey. Available at the website of the Bureau of Labor Statistics: www.bls.gov/cps/cpsatabs.htm.

U.S. Department of Labor. Bureau of Labor Statistics. 2006. The State of Working America. 2004–2005. Available at the website of the Bureau of Labor Statistics: www.bls.gov/cps/cpsatabs.htm.

U.S. National Center for Health Statistics. 2005. Health, United States, 2005. Hyattsville, Md.: U.S. National Center for Health Statistics.

U.S. National Center for Health Statistics. 1990. Vital Statistics, 1990. Hyattsville, Md.: U.S. National Center for Health Statistics.

Wilson, James Q. 1995. "Concluding Essay in Crime." In James Q. Wilson and Joan Petersilia (eds.), Crime (pp. 488–507). San Francisco: Institute for Contemporary Studies Press.

Wilson, James Q. 1974. Thinking about Crime. New York: Basic Books.

Wilson, James Q., and George L. Kelling. 1982, March. "The Police and Neighborhood Safety: Broken Windows." Atlantic Monthly, pp. 29–38.

Wilson, William J. 1987. The Truly Disadvantaged. Chicago: University of Chicago Press.

Windesham, Lord. 1998. Politics, Punishment, and Populism. New York: Oxford University Press.

World Health Organization. 2002. World Report on Violence and Health. Geneva: World Health Organization.

World Health Organization Regional Office for Europe. 2005, June. European Health For All Database (HFA-DB). Available at the website of the World Health Organization Regional Office for Europe: http://data.euro.who.int/hfadb/.

Zeisel, Hans. 1985. Say It with Figures. 6th ed. New York: Harper and Row.

Zimring, Franklin E. 2004. "The Discrete Character of High-Lethality Youth Violence." Youth Violence: Scientific Approaches to Prevention. Annals of the New York Academy of Sciences 1036: 290.

Zimring, Franklin E. 1998. American Youth Violence. New York: Oxford University Press.

Zimring, Franklin E., and Gordon Hawkins. 1997. Crime Is Not the Problem: Lethal Violence in America. New York: Oxford University Press.

Zimring, Franklin E., and Gordon Hawkins. 1995. Incapacitation. New York: Oxford University Press.

Zimring, Franklin E., and Gordon Hawkins. 1973. Deterrence: The Legal Threat in Crime Control. Chicago: University of Chicago Press.

Zimring, Franklin E., Gordon Hawkins, and Sam Kamin. 2001. Punishment and Democracy: Three Strikes and You're Out in California. New York: Oxford University Press.

Zimring, Franklin E., and David T. Johnson. 2006, May. "Public Opinion and Governance of Punishment in Democratic Political Systems." Annals of the American Academy of Political and Social Sciences 605: 266–280.

Index

Index

Index

causal, post-decline, 73–103
gender role, 57
testing methodologies for, 125, 143
U.S. only, problem of, 103
Threatened punishment
general deterrence and, 48, 53–54
as untestable, 53–54
Three Strikes and You're Out law, 37–40, 192
Timing, of U.S./Canadian declines, 127
Total Fertility Rate (TFR), 94–96, 94f, 98–99, 99f
Trend(s). *See also specific crimes*
1990 v. 2003, 188–89, 189t
aggregate, 49f, 50f
birth, 93–96, 93f, 97
Blumstein on disaggregating, 82f
in Canada/U.S., aggregate, 16t, 117
Canadian, long-term, 227–28, 227f, 228f
child poverty, 96
economic, 51, 63, 64–65, 65f, 66f, 67–69, 96, 130
five-year, 49, 50f
historical, 180, 206
homicide, 49, 49f, 131–32, 132f, 180–81, 181f
level, 175
recent v. 1990s, 175–76
regional, 10–11, 11f, 19
in second half of 1980s, 81
three-year, 1997-2003, 172–73, 172f, 173t
twenty-first century, 187–89
two-nation, 19
Western European crime decline, 101–2
Triangulation of proof, 203
New York City and, 143–44
Turnaround: How America's Top Cop Reversed the Crime Epidemic (Bratton/Knobler), 37
Two-nation trend, 19
Two-step nation(s)
abortion legalization in, 100
Canada as, 124

Unemployment, 63, 65–67, 66f
New York City's, 147, 229–30, 230f
Uniform Crime Report (UCR), 6
household survey v., 8, 8f
Uninterrupted time series, 92–93
United States/Canada, 105–34, 108f, 110f,

112, 112f, 200–201. *See also* Australia; New South Wales; Western Europe
1961 homicide rate in, 131–32, 132f
abortion in, 124–25, 124f, 125f, 130
aggregate trends in, 16t, 117
assault/sexual assault in, 112–13, 112f
auto theft in, 128
burglary in, 117–18, 118f
cyclical variation in, 130–32, 133–34, 200
demographics of, 129–30, 133, 198, 200
differences between, 127–29
imprisonment in, 56, 120–21, 121f
Index offenses of, 16, 108, 108f, 126, 127, 128
property crime of, 115–19, 115f, 116f, 117f, 118f, 119f
punishment policy of, 120, 121
rape in, 112, 112f
robbery/robbery killings in, 113–14, 114f
similarity between, 126–30, 198
unemployment in, 121–23, 122f, 129

Victim reluctance, 4–5
Victimization, 159, 160–61, 160f
Vietnam, 30
Violence offenses, in France, theft and, 216–17, 217t
Visibility, 141–42, 141f
gun removal and, 158
Vital statistics, 4–5

Wages, 67, 67f, 69
Watergate, 30
West Coast and crime policy, 37–40
Western Europe
abortion legalization, 213–14, 213f
abortion policy in, 211–12
crime decline in, 101–2
homicide/other convictions, 212, 212t, 214–17, 214f, 215f, 217t, 218t
"What Works" (Martinson), 28–29
Whitley, John, on abortion legalization, 91
Wiebe, Douglas, 91–92
Wilson, James Q.
on 60s paradox, 57–58
Kelling and, impact of, 35–36
predictions of, 21, 62, 165
Wilson, Pete, 38

HV 6783 .Z56 2007
Zimring, Franklin E.
The great American crime
 decline